"Mr. Jackman has struck gold a̲ᶢ *Healing Your Wounded Relationship*, provides optimistic, realistic, and most importantly, practical guidance for the bewildered and chronically saddened codependent. Readers will be gifted with his one-of-a-kind knowledge, insight, and exquisitely personable yet erudite guidance. Like no other author I have read, Jackman explains and clarifies the problems, where they came from, and who is responsible, while providing an accurate and detailed road map toward healthy and enduring relational love. This book will surely strike a resonate chord for those who dream of the 'other side' of their seemingly insurmountable wall of chronic relational heartbreak but lack the information and tools to safely get to the other side."

—Ross Rosenberg, MEd, LCPC, CADC, CSAT, Psychotherapist, Self-Love Recovery Institute CEO, author *of The Human Magnet Syndrome*, and Codependency Cure™ Treatment Creator.

"Robert Jackman, LCPC, has written another superb and informative book, this one for guiding couples toward a healthy, loving relationship. *Healing Your Wounded Relationship* is a must-read for anyone looking to recognize unhealthy behavior patterns and move forward toward healing and repair. Jackman walks the reader through the healing process with self-help questions, healthy advice, and examples from his private practice. Read this book and learn from one of the best. It should be on everyone's bookshelf. It is a masterpiece."

— John Roth, MD, Medical Director, Kentucky Dermatology and Cosmetic Specialists

"Robert Jackman's latest book, *Healing Your Wounded Relationship*, picks up where he left off with his first book, which laid a compassionate road map to assist the reader in healing their inner child wounding. He now examines dysfunctional intimate relationships, giving the reader tools to create and expand the possibility of an intimate relationship. Jackman introduces and defines the concept of the synergistic wounding cycle as he walks the reader through identifying red flags and how unre-solved wounded parts play out with our partners. He presents the STARR Reset tool and additional avenues toward healing, revealing to the reader how to develop compassionate and inten-tional communication. I highly recommend this book to couples, singles, and anyone who are struggling in their relationships.

As with his first book, *Healing Your Lost Inner Child*, Robert Jackman talks directly to the reader, revealing that the path toward healing is not a straight road but one that is taken courageously, with lot of hidden twists and turns. He supports the reader from beginning to end and guides them toward an opportunity to discover and exercise an open heart, with the ultimate goal of healing their relationship."

— Joanne Kittel, MSW

"Robert Jackman's book *Healing Your Wounded Relationship* will open the reader's heart and mind to better understand how one's past trauma can have an impact on relationships with current or future partners. The reader will learn why patterns repeat themselves in unsuccessful pairings, and how to foster and encourage balance in the relationship. All aspects of this book—the exercises, checklists, couples' stories, and the STARR Reset—will help the reader understand and reflect on how their wounded inner child shows up in their relationship and how to work through this pain.

Jackman helps the reader focus on success, which is possible when couples are willing to to be there for each other, make certain sacrifices, and "courageously surrender." I was pleased that he addresses the particular woundings of adult children of alcoholics (ACOA).

This book is best for the reader who can read it with an open mind and heart, and who truly wants positive change in their relationships."

— Amy VanRoekel, MSW

"Wow, this book is amazing and so genuine. *Healing Your Wounded Relationship* by Robert Jackman is a wonderfully creative book that helps the reader work through the myriad of life's relationships and unfold into new beginnings. This powerful book does so by sharing stories of relationship journeys using archetypal examples. Exercises throughout challenge and propel the reader forward through self-awareness of their patterns and strengths to heal. This book is a magic wand for all to shape their future. Great book!"
— Dr. Sandra Kakacek, LCPC

"Robert Jackman artfully and compassionately brings together his years of experience in private practice and research on inner child wounding to provide couples with insight and strategies toward loving and openhearted partnerships. Through thoughtful and strategic therapy practices and guidance, he navigates individuals and couples through the STARR Reset (Stop, Think, Act, Reset and Repair) to better manage conflict and find solutions to unstick unhealthy patterns. *Healing Your Wounded Relationship* is an optimistic book that is easy to read and understand, full of wonderful examples of archetypal couple pairings to guide the reader. Jackman offers the reader simple-to-understand explanations and examples of inner child wounds and their involvement in couple bonding and wounded attractions. Jackman's books and workbooks are convenient tools for coaching individuals, couples, and clinicians alike. They have been and will be a resource I recommend to my clients and colleagues."
— Georgina Srinivas Rao, MD, Psychiatrist and Medical Director of In Step Behavioral Health

HEALING

Your Wounded Relationship

HEALING
Your Wounded Relationship

How to Break Free
of Codependent Patterns
and Restore Your Loving
Partnership

ROBERT JACKMAN
MS, LCPC, NCC

 PRACTICAL WISDOM PRESS

Published by Practical Wisdom Press
The author may be reached through his website at www.theartofpracticalwisdom.com.

ISBN (paperback) 978-1-7354445-4-3
ISBN (ebook): 978-1-7354445-5-0

Edited by Jessica Vineyard, Red Letter Editing, www.redletterediting.com.
Book design by Christy Collins, Constellation Book Services.

The image on the book cover is that of the Rakotzbrücke bridge in Kromlau Park, Gablenz, Saxony, Germany.

Printed in the United States of America

To my love, Drew Caldwell, thank you for your consistent, gentle strength, unlimited kindness, and your affirming and embracing love. I cannot imagine my life without you.

Now I know what others have told me: that I am a good person, that I am worthy of kindness and love. I have put down the illusions of the false narrative that I held so dear for way too long. In my new limitless landscape, with my love beaming with pride by my side, I now embrace the shiny healed parts of me and my hard-won medals of accomplishment, valor, surrender, and love.

—ROBERT JACKMAN

Contents

Preface

In my practice, people would ask me why they kept dating losers, why they had bad luck in who they married, or why they were so unhappy in their relationship when they used to love each other so much. In response, I wanted to write an approachable book with practical solutions to these questions. I wanted to provide some practical insight from my clinical work, stories from couples shared anonymously, their struggles and triumphs, and useful tools to healing that I find effective. With my more than two decades of experience as a psychotherapist, I wanted to share my theories and perspectives as to how and why some couples get stuck, and how to help them get out of their toxic spirals.

The inspiration for this book came quickly after my first book, *Healing Your Lost Inner Child,* was released. In that book I take the reader through understanding the origin story of their childhood wounding and the false narrative that perpetuates, causing all sorts of problems. In this book, I take this concept further and explore how the story plays out for the wounded inner child who then becomes an adult, and how most of us try to navigate difficult issues using outdated wounded tools from childhood, often with disastrous results.

I see two themes that consistently show up in relationships.

The first is when one partner tries hard to guard their vulnerability and is shut down in some way, and the other partner tries to get them to open up and participate in the relationship. The second theme is when the couple really wants the relationship to work but they keep stumbling over their own emotional baggage and getting in their own way.

To illustrate this wounded attraction, I created nine synergistically wounded archetypes. Many are pairings we are all familiar with, such as the wounded hero and the rescued victim, that I relate to inner child wounding origins. As far as I know, this concept has never been explored in the way that I present here. The synergistically wounded archetypal pairings I created were inspired by the seminal work of Joseph Campbell in his book *The Hero with a Thousand Faces*.

I believe that, at their core, everyone is a good person, but good people often make bad choices. Most of the time their wounded parts make the bad choices; this is when couples have big fights, make up to break up, or shut their partner out in passive-aggressive ways. Throw addictions, health issues, or problems with money or kids into the mix, and they have a disaster.

Early in my young adult life I chose people who were narcissistic and sometimes not very nice to me. My inner child wounding didn't see any of this and I kept chasing after them, using all of my codependent wounded tools to try to make the relationship work. I define codependency as having a higher regard, esteem, love, trust, and respect for someone else than one has for oneself. There is an overreliance on other people for a sense of self or validation of self. It wasn't until I started doing my own work to heal those hurting parts that I began to truly see the wounded drama that I was creating and enabling. Once this heavy curtain is pulled back, we can begin to know more about ourselves and others, and we can begin to make better choices. Even though we are each unique and special, these patterns and themes are repeated universally.

This book is built on the foundational work of many relationship experts and thought leaders, including John Gottman, Harville Hendrix, Brené Brown, Jackson MacKenzie, Rachel Hollis, and others who have paved the way in how we look at relationships today. The original material in this book may be similar to what other therapists and thought leaders use, but it is my take on how inner child wounding shows up and the theme of getting a person to stop, think, and use intentional communication for a better outcome.

Please note: Throughout the book I use the pronouns him/he, her/she, and they/them, but none of the wounded impulsive behaviors, relationship dynamics, or synergistically wounded archetypes I refer to are gender specific in any way. No matter the gender or relationship type, the inner child wounding usually finds a way to present itself to get those emotional wounds acknowledged and healed.

There are many relationship books in print, and this book is my take on how to heal and improve your relationship so that you can feel closer to the one you love. The information herein will hopefully give you a window of insight into parts of yourself you have never seen before, and may help you see your partner in a new light. You will be learning new ways to express yourself so that all of you can be seen and heard. No one book can answer all of your questions about how to heal your relationship, but my hope is that this book can illuminate some of the reasons as to why you chose to be in certain relationships and how to use more intentional communication. The material and exercises in this book will be equally useful to those who are dating or in a committed relationship.

Like the moon bridge image on the cover of this book, I want to help you open a bridge of healing within yourself, and between you and your partner, so you can join with each other openheartedly, unreservedly, and lovingly.

I want to thank Drew Caldwell, my partner of more than three decades, for hanging in there with me as I went through my own inner child healing, during which time our love deepened and matured and we both embraced a place of mutual love, trust, and respect. I would not be the man I am today without you.

I also want to thank all of the individuals and couples I have worked with over the years, as you all have contributed to the knowledge that I bring forth in this book.

I would like to thank all of those who have helped me produce this work, as you each played such an important role in what I call birthing of the book. Thank you to my editor, Jessica Vineyard, with Red Letter Editing; my book designer, Christy Collins, and Maggie McLaughlin, both with Constellation Book Services; and Martha Bullen, with Bullen Publishing Services.

For any partnership to thrive there needs to be humility, vulnerability and honesty within each partner and in the relationship. The act of courageous surrender from another is the signal that tells the heart that it is safe to become open and welcome a love inside. Be gentle with yourself as you do this work, and trust yourself. There is at least one message in here that you have been waiting for.

The book to read is not the one that thinks for
you but the one which makes you think.
—HARPER LEE

Introduction

How do some couples make their relationship look so easy and natural, while others are challenged to make theirs work? Why do some relationships seem to flow, while others have so many obstacles that basic communication is a struggle? Why are some people attracted to partners who don't treat them well? Many people are mystified as to why they can't have a fulfilling and loving relationship like others they know. They wonder how theirs got so off track when it didn't start out that way. But relationships don't have to be so hard; sometimes we just have to get out of our own way.

You have probably known couples who were perfect for each other and others you thought were doomed from the start. Maybe you know someone who has a bad "picker" and keeps choosing the wrong partner to date or marry. Why don't they see that they are going down the wrong path? How do they miss the red flags? How do they get lost in their wounded drama?

Most people don't realize that they were drawn to their partner because they instinctively knew how to be in synergy with their partner's healed and emotionally wounded parts. It was as if the heart had a homing beacon that pulled them toward someone whom they understood at a deep emotional level, and then they clicked. This wounded attraction is in all of us from childhood and is a unique combination of our healed and wounded parts that join together in a perfectly imperfect way.

You probably picked up this book because you are tired of the dysfunctional cycles you and your dating or relationship partner keep repeating. The practical information herein will help you to understand how and why you chose your partner based in part on your and their emotional pain, or what I call *synergistic wounding*. It will provide a window of insight into how your unhealed emotional wounds subconsciously guided you to specifically choose your partner, and offers a step-by-step process to work through this pain. All of this applies whether you are dating or already partnered.

Importantly, you will learn that when someone is upset and loud or withdrawn and sad, their behavior is often related to their unresolved wounding. You will begin to develop a deeper and wiser empathy for your partner's feelings instead of focusing on their behaviors. You will clearly begin to recognize that whatever unhealed, unresolved wounding you carry on the inside is also reflected on the outside.

Throughout each chapter I present my perspective, examples, and insights from my more than two decades as a psychotherapist. The stories, examples, and exercises will guide you toward accessing a wounded part of yourself that yearns to be more emotionally available. What you will learn about yourself won't shock you, but it will open your eyes to your reality.

Part I, Wounded Pairings, focuses on how and why we carry inner child woundings, how they manifest in adulthood, and how we join with another to create a synergically wounded pairing. You will learn through exploratory exercises how to identify the broken communication tools you and your partner use. You will learn how to transform the language between you by using the STARR Reset process (Stop, Think, Act, Reset and Repair), a simple but powerful communication tool designed to get you out of your repeating cycles. I will give you plenty of practical examples of how to use this process to develop more functional tools and make them easily accessible in your day-to-day life. You will learn the techniques of thoughtful, intentional communication so that you can create the emotional legacy you want to have for your relationship.

Part II, Wounded Archetypes, provides a catalog of information on common synergistically wounded pairings, from the oversharer and the scorekeeper to the mindreader and the blame-shame game pairing. You will see the STARR Reset put into action through stories of couples who represent each archetype and how they apply the STARR Reset to their relationship.

Part III, Restoring a Healthy Relationship, brings all of this information to fruition by showing how you can bring healing to yourself and your relationship. You will learn how to set strong boundaries and how to put the knowledge you have gained into practice by bringing a sense of openheartedness to your relationship as it heals.

As you work through the chapters, use a notebook to write down your responses to the exercises, as you will be referring to them many times throughout the book. It will also be useful to keep a marker or tabs handy so you can note certain sections to refer back to when you prepare to have discussions with your partner.

Ideally, a couple would read this book together and do the exercises in tandem, but your partner may not want anything to do with this process. We heal and expand in our awareness at different rates; this is normal. Perceptions of relationship dynamics are personal, so if your partner doesn't perceive that there are issues in your relationship, they may not be ready for this work. If you are doing this work on your own, please know that the knowledge you will gain and the healing that will occur within you will have an impact on your relationship. You will be able to see your interactions with your partner in a new light, and you will have greater access to being more openhearted and making clear-headed decisions. This alone will create a shift in your relationship that your partner may not consciously know but will probably feel.

Throughout the book I reference relationships, partnerships, marriages, and commitments. The stories and exercises focus on examples of two people in one relationship. It is assumed that the couple is consensually monogamous, each partner has an intention to be faithful to the other, and one or both want to work on their relationship. Please note that I respect every relationship structure no matter what it looks like. The concept of relationships as they are traditionally known is evolving, and what works for one person or couple may not work for another. Whatever term you and your partner use to describe your relationship, I am referencing you in these stories. I don't explore nontraditional relationship combos such as open, polyamorous, and consensually nonmongomous relationships in this book, but the communication tools I describe apply nonetheless.

I reference the words *wounding* and *trauma* broadly throughout the book, and while their origins are too numerous to name, the effects of trauma and the pain are relevant to each of us individually. One person's deep wounding may be another person's bad day. How we take in a trauma, whether small or large, is related to many factors, but a successful healing comes about when we are ready, willing, and able to face this hard truth, be gentle with ourselves, and work through the pain.

Finally, I recommend reading my book *Healing Your Lost Inner Child*, which addresses how to identify and heal the core wounding that drives much of the impulsive reactions that many people experience in relationships. It includes some key tools to help you to become an intentional and conscious creator in your relationship.

Its companion, *Healing Your Lost Inner Child Companion Workbook,* is an excellent expansion that takes you deeper into this work. You can use the workbook alongside the material in this book as an adjunct to understanding your relationship. Use the exercises in Part I of the workbook to prepare to understand your inner child wounding and how it plays out in your relationships. Part II of the workbook focuses on codependent relationships; doing these exercises will provide great support as you work through the healing process with your partner. I refer to sections of *Healing Your Lost Inner Child* throughout this book. It is not necessary that you have that book or the workbook, but it would certainly help to deepen your experience. You can learn more about my other works on my website: www.theartofpracticalwisdom.com.

As you read through this book, stay open-minded. Observe yourself, and do not condemn yourself. Be receptive to hope and open to the potential, as relationships are dynamic and meant to flex, stretch, and grow.

We are all doing our best, and we only know our own experience each moment in time. In those moments, that is who we think we are. Only when we grow and heal do we see how far we have come, how wounded and lost we once were. Today this is our wisdom speaking. Be kind to the shadow of your former self.

There is always light. If only we're brave enough to see it.
If only we're brave enough to be it.
—AMANDA GORDON

A Word of Caution

The STARR Reset, the communication techniques, and the exercises I describe in this book are designed to help couples work through issues in their relationship and deepen their connection with each other. It is designed for couples who are experiencing difficulties and who have, at their core, a foundation of respect, love, and trust. One or both want to better the relationship to fully realize a heart-centered love and commitment.

This process and the techniques described herein will not work and *are not recommended* for couples who are experiencing domestic violence (physical and sexual violence, economic control, psychological and emotional abuse), a highly manipulative relationship, a toxic environment, or extremely traumatic events.

You can gain knowledge from the information in the book, but please do not attempt to use the techniques outlined if you are in such a highly dysregulated environment. Doing so will often lead to more violence, control, and abuse, and may put you or your children in mortal danger. The recommended conversations will be seen by the abuser as a challenge or that you are trying to take over control; this will only embolden them to become more rageful and resentful. If you have tried different techniques to talk to your abusive spouse on your own and they haven't worked, please seek outside assistance. You will not be able to navigate or fix this situation on your own.

If you are in an environment like this, there are ways and methods for you to seek help safely and discreetly. Take care of yourself, and get yourself and your children to safety.

I want you to know that you deserve to be safe and loved.

The following are domestic violence resources:

For female and male victims of domestic violence in the US:

National Domestic Violence Hotline: 800-799-7233 or www.thehotline.org.

National Coalition Against Domestic Violence: www.ncadv.org.

PART I

Wounded Pairings

CHAPTER 1

Beginnings Are Fun

Love doesn't come in a minute, sometimes it doesn't come at all.
I only know that when I'm in it, it isn't silly.
Love isn't silly. Love isn't silly at all.
—PAUL MCCARTNEY AND WINGS, "SILLY LOVE SONGS"

Being in a relationship and having a deeply loving, intimate connection with another is a great joy. Beginnings of relationships are usually fun-filled, free-flowing adventures. Our endorphins swirl with delight as we get to know the person to whom we are attracted. Our biology kicks in, and we are magnetically drawn to another. We can't get them out of our head. We daydream about them, and our heart swells as everything reminds us about them: their smile, their touch, their scent. We instinctively start to think about being with them, and fantasize about the adventures and events we could experience together. We are head over heels in what feels like love, and we rush into their arms every moment we can.

HEAD OVER HEELS

This euphoric beginning, this feeling of being head-over-heels in love, is one of the greatest joys in life, and it is priceless. We are drawn to the other based on any number of factors, such as appearance, personality, humor, intelligence, abilities, and sometimes just because. But one of the lesser-known aspects of this attraction is how we are subconsciously attracted to another because their emotional wounding and healed parts are synergistic with our emotional wounding and healed parts, like a puzzle piece fitting into place.

Being attracted to someone because their emotional wounding matches ours may sound counterintuitive, but this experience is at the root of the saying, hurt people find hurt people. We do not consciously attract another wounded person to us, and we certainly don't want the euphoric fantasy sequence to end. But the reality is that part of the reason we are drawn to another person has to do with our unresolved wounding and their unresolved wounding, our healed parts and their healed parts, plus mutual attraction, shared interests, and other qualities. This synergistic pairing feels right when we first get to know another. At a deep level and in an unspoken way, we understand them and they understand us.

This is one of nature's little secrets: our partner has the blueprint for our growth. The trick is for the partner to present it to us in a way that we can hear.
—WADE LUQUET, *SHORT-TERM COUPLES THERAPY*

As relationships mature, most couples are able to hang in there through good times and bad, using their familiar relationship tools to make their partnership work. They are able to balance their healed and wounded parts. Sometimes, however, the emotional wounding goes so deep that they can't see beyond it, and they get stuck in destructive cycles. Life becomes a juggle of priorities, with relationships taking a back seat to more pressing matters, such as family, kids, and work.

The hard part is continually moving the partnership in a positive direction, where both partners grow and expand at similar rates, and where they reach out to support and encourage each other to keep moving forward. We have a built-in desire to move ahead together, to be in union, and to make it work. Inevitably, life has a way of getting in the way of our best-laid plans, and that is when most couples struggle. Unforeseen events challenge even the best of relationships, so we have to rely on the integrity and foundation of the relationship that we established from the very beginning. The relationship bedrock of continual validation, humility, love, trust, mutual respect, and reciprocity reinforce a strong pairing. Without a good measure of each of these, any relationship will struggle to some degree, especially when times are hard.

Early in my adult life, before I met my partner, the wounded, codependent part of me was attracted to narcissistically wounded people. I would cater to them and make myself smaller to fit into their world. I didn't realize that my inner child wounding, my adult-child-of-an-alcoholic wounding, was playing itself out; I just thought I was attracted to this type of person, and it felt right—at least, at the beginning. It wasn't until I started therapy in my twenties that I realized my inner child wounding was coming forward in these synergistic wounded connections. I was trying to make the relationship work using my codependent tools, but the relationship wasn't right for me. My wounded parts were louder than my healed parts at this point. My wounded parts didn't recognize my dating partner's narcissistic wounding.

THE SYNERGISTICALLY WOUNDED PAIRING

When we meet and then fall in love with our partner, we don't realize that we are choosing a synergistically wounded partner with whom to play out our unresolved childhood emotional wounding in an attempt to heal that part. But that is what emotionally wounded people do. We search for someone who can uniquely help us process complicated emotional wounding from our childhood, which happens without any conscious knowledge on the part of either person. The cycle perpetuates, and we will subconsciously call other wounded people into our lives over and over to play out the wounded drama until this underlying wounding is healed.

The unresolved emotional wounding between the partners is usually complementary and synergistic.

We are often attracted to our partner based on their healed parts as well, because this is the part we ourselves are missing. Someone who is looking to be rescued finds a rescuer because a part of them deeply wants to heal, wants to learn, in fact, how to rescue or be a champion for themselves. This hidden agenda is carried down the aisle during commitment and marriage ceremonies. Each partner brings into the committed relationship the unhealed emotional baggage of their childhood, subconsciously hoping their partner can help them work through it.

*The wounded part in each of us is yearning
to be seen, held, and heard so it can heal.*

Consider a partner who has an unhealed childhood emotional wound that shows up as anger outbursts, while their partner grew up with a parent who had similar anger outbursts. The partner who grew up with this anger expression in their family is familiar with the dance they need to have with the partner who has the outbursts. Neither person set out to find a partner who could handle this situation, but once they are together, they subconsciously fall into the wounded inner child roles they learned in their childhood families. This is especially true with adults who grew up in alcoholic or addicted households. They developed a complicated set of codependent skills to help them navigate their early childhood experiences, and as adults, they often choose partners who grew up in similar circumstances.

Another example is someone who keeps dating or marrying the same type of person over and over, even when they are not good for them. You may see a friend get involved with someone who is not good for them, but they don't see that this new person has the same emotional qualities as their ex. Your friend's unresolved emotional inner child wounding is subconsciously trying to heal that wounding by drawing in this type of person, a watered down version of the relationship they just left.

You may know the expression "what at first attracted you now repulses you," and maybe even see it in your own relationship, but why is that? A man, for example, who initially stated that he liked how "she speaks her mind" may later say that this trait is the one most irritating to him. Equally, she initially liked that "he is laid back and funny" but later doesn't think he is that funny and wants him to show more motivation.

The other has a quality that they are trying to learn and promote in themselves—the energetic meaning of the expression "opposites attract." The euphoric part of the early relationship is long gone, and they are now in the meat and potatoes of their relationship dynamic. Now it takes real effort to make it functional and to work through the harder issues, especially if one of the two has healed and moved on emotionally. Over time, one gets triggered by the other and is more irritated than impressed. The wounded relationship limps along.

At this stage, there is often one partner who doesn't want to do the work, who just wants to coast in the relationship, not make waves, and stay in resentment and denial. They are fearful of getting into discussions that could lead to upset feelings. They don't feel they have the skills to expand their relationship and operate in a new type of communication dynamic, so it is easier to avoid this all together. They are in a dysfunctional dance that often becomes an uneasy emotional equilibrium.

Such a dysfunctional relationship may look like a train wreck to outsiders, but it feels right to the couple in some way. This is why people who are in the middle of their dysfunctional relationship can't always see that it is not healthy; they don't know (or maybe don't want to know) what a healthy relationship looks like. Their wounding obstructs their view of what a healthy relationship can look like. This wounded attraction is what I call having a "bad picker."

Hurt people find other hurt people.

These wobbly pairings are examples of a wounded archetype. Archetypes are useful for succinctly defining common wounded pairings; I use them here to describe attractions between two people that are easy to recognize.

THE IDEAL RELATIONSHIP

Intimate and loving relationships are unique to each of us. They can be partnerships, marriages, commitments, or unions. There is no one standard for what a relationship should look or feel like. How you go about creating your relationship feels right to you, has meaning for you, and fulfills or answers something within you.

Whether you are dating or in a partnership, the hope is that as you grow and change, you will find a way to celebrate the changes in yourself and the person you are in relationship with; to face in the same direction, as it were, so that you will be able to grow together instead of apart as time and life events unfold. In the end, it's all about living a full and loving life in a way that works for you and those you love.

We each define ideal relationships in our own way based on our family of origin models and cultural influences. Some may say that an ideal relationship is one in which both partners cherish each other and feel cherished; smile when they hear their partner's voice; know the warmth of love, contentment, and companionship during the quiet times; and are there for each other during times of challenge.

What does your ideal relationship feel like? The specifics are less important than giving some thought to what you are looking for, the feeling of connection, and the mix that works in the ebb and flow of life events that you and your partner experience together over time. Life throws us curve balls, so perfection isn't a thing in this context; a loving, dynamic, responsive balance between the two of you and your life situation is fundamentally more important over the lifespan.

Move from having cloudy judgment to wise clarity.

Once you know what you are looking for in a relationship, you can make conscious decisions about the choices you make as you share your life. You can do the work within to make sure your inner child is in balance and not skewing your relationship choices, and to learn to thoughtfully approach communication and nurture this important aspect of your life.

SYNERGISTIC WOUNDED ATTRACTION
(OR, HI, HONEY! MY INNER CHILD AND I ARE HOME!)

We all have unhealed, unresolved emotional wounds carried over from childhood years. We also have the healed parts, the functional or responsible adult parts, that know the right things to do to keep the relationship afloat.

Most successful pairings have disagreements. For the most part, couples learn to surf these issues and come to mutually agreed-on resolutions. They can work through these issues because their synergistic wounding is more functional and co-ordinates well with the other's wounding. When two people are not well matched and their individual wounding is severe and toxic, they may have a desire to make it work but their individual struggles and conflict keep them lost in the pain.

It is not impossible for a couple who has serious emotional wounding to work through their issues; it just takes more effort and specific tools that few couples naturally possess. Sometimes the emotional wounding is so toxic that each partner may need intensive therapy before they can begin to work on their issues as a couple. One partner may be so reactive and dysregulated that they cannot even sit still in a therapist's office, much less talk to their partner calmly at home.

The hidden reality during times of great conflict is that the wounded inner child is getting triggered and stepping in front of the responsible adult self, making decisions that the adult self has to clean up later. They may be so lost in their own wounding that they don't see this agitated inner child; they just say that's how they are. They have emotional blinders on.

Our wounding sits in the frozen vacuum of what we needed as children but didn't get.

When we are lost in our emotional wounding, we don't know the difference between our healed self and our pain. The healed parts and the wounded parts are intermingled, and we feel like ourselves but lost in a fog. We don't know any better and can't have a larger perspective about ourselves because we are doing our best with the emotional intelligence we have. Without any kind of therapeutic intervention or self-help review, few of us have a sense of what our inner child wounding is, much less where it came from. All we know is we feel hurt, sad, and confused in our relationship and want the pain to stop.

It is usually only after we experience some sort of crisis in our relationship that we seek out counsel and begin to look at life differently. Once we gain perspective on our own or things are pointed out to us, we begin to see the work we still have to do with our wounded parts.

A small percentage of couples consciously know of their inner child pain and how this wounded attraction process happens behind the scenes at the start of their relationship. Everyone else thinks they chose their partner based on all of their wonderful attributes, and that may be true, but there are some attributes they are synergistically attracted to that would never appear on a card.

Here are some of the unhealed inner child woundings that people subconsciously use to choose their partner:

- My partner yells at me, just like my mom did. I chose them so I can try to find my authentic voice, because I didn't feel like I had a voice as a child.
- My partner is emotionally shut down, like my dad. I can use my mindreading skills to try to get my "dad's" attention.
- My partner abuses me and reinforces that I'm a bad person, just like I learned as a child from my sister. I put myself down, feel rejected, and act like a victim so I never have to face my truth and feel my own power.
- My partner is always upset about something. I'm going to rescue them over and over to try to make life better for them, sacrificing myself in the process.
- My partner grew up in an alcoholic household, just like I did. We both feel pretty bad about ourselves, know how to avoid difficult situations, and become quiet when the other is angry. It feels natural to ignore what we both actually need.
- My partner is too good for me, just like I thought everyone in my childhood was better than me. I feel like an imposter and a fake, even though my partner loves me. I test them and make them prove that they love me over and over, even though I never bring their love into my heart.

All of these are examples of hurt people subconsciously finding other hurt people to play out and potentially heal their inner child wounding. They have a *synergistic wounded attraction.* Each one is an example of a wounded archetype. Neither person in these pairings is consciously aware of the underlying dynamic. They may see some of these behaviors, but they don't realize that they are seeing the wounded inner child, not the functional adult self, coming forth. Their wounding is in synergy with the other's wounding. It is a wonder that most relationships even survive, given the tremendous tasks that our wounded inner child wants us to achieve in our adult relationships.

> *When we name something, even if it stings a little bit, we feel a sense of relief inside from this validation and endorsement.*

You may relate to some of these scenarios or are thinking about your own synergistic wounding cycles right now. The fact that you now know this synergy occurs will help you start to heal this part of yourself and your relationship. These examples and your own self-examination will reveal where you are today and how your wounding and your partner's wounding show up. The real opportunity is in choosing where you want to go with your newfound knowledge. How do you want to heal yourself and your relationship with your newly expanded emotional intelligence?

> *Joining with your partner is an unspoken invitation offering to help heal the other.*

Know that you aren't doomed to have your wounded inner child run your life. There is something you can do about it, but first you need to discover how you got to this point with your partner.

EXERCISE: EXPLORE YOUR SYNERGISTIC WOUNDED ATTRACTION

Based on what you have learned so far, write in your notebook your first impressions of what you feel your synergistic wounded attraction is with your partner. Just take some guesses; this is just for you. Using the bullet list on page 20 as a guide, look at what you do that you know does not help the relationship, and try to determine why you make those choices. Why do you think you joined with your partner? What were you trying to answer within yourself? What were the qualities they had that you were attracted to? Save these notes for later exercises.

EXERCISE: DREAM BIG—YOUR IDEAL RELATIONSHIP

Before you move on, take a moment to dream big for that part of yourself that is yearning for a deeper connection and a more openhearted relationship. Save your answers to refer to for the self-reflection in chapter 20, where you will compare the two sets of answers.

Answer the following questions as best you can with the perspective on yourself in the present moment. You may not know how to respond to some of the questions or what they even mean. Set aside any objections you think your partner would have, and avoid self-limiting thoughts, such as how your answer would be possible only if you had a different life circumstance. Imagine a grander version of yourself, one who can step forward and unfold with intention as you do this work.

Sit in a quiet, comfortable spot. Close your eyes and imagine your relationship as it is right now. Then think about how you want to experience your relationship in the future, apart from anything physical, situational, or dependent on a bank account. Take your time, as your answers will help you go deeper with this work.

Now open your eyes and answer the following questions in your notebook.

- Do you experience your relationship today as a bystander or an active participant? How do you know?
- What are some examples of how you show up in your relationship?
- What are some examples of how you do not show up?
- If you live your life on autopilot, what one specific thing can you change to live, speak, and create with intention?
- How do you bring your own dream forward?
- How do you express your needs?
- If you give power to your partner's relationship dream instead of your own, how do you do this?
- How would you like to be more emotionally present in your relationship?
- How would you like your partner to be more emotionally present?
- How would you like love, trust, and respect to be demonstrated?
- If this were to happen, how would it impact your sense of self and the relationship?
- What needs to heal so an openhearted love can unfold and manifest in your life?

- How would you like you and your partner to interact, communicate about issues, and create a deeper connection?
- What expressions of deeper connection (verbal and nonverbal) can you imagine each of you using?

Now go a little deeper and think about which parts of your relationship dream you feel deserving to manifest and receive. Make a wish list of everything you can visualize in your dream relationship (basically, the key elements that are missing in your current relationship). Examples are how you feel in the relationship and what it is like day to day. Circle the items you think are achievable in your current relationship. Choose three of these circled items, then look inward to answer the following questions. Write them down.

What steps will you need to take to begin realizing each of these three items?

What relationship tools will you and your partner need to make this happen?

You can probably make more changes in the relationship than you think; at the very least, you can be the change you want to see.

We make conscious and unconscious choices every day in how we show up in our relationships. The degree to which we can see our wounded and healed parts is dependent on the work we have put into ourselves.

COURAGEOUS SURRENDER

Through recognizing your healed and wounded parts, you can open your heart to yourself and your partner with a courageous surrender. Give yourself permission to set aside the squabbles and the fears and to see your partner for who they are, with clear expression of feelings. Have love for yourself and your partner by holding your partner in high regard and seeing their true nature underneath all of the pain that is present.

If you are able to suspend this judgment of your partner, see if you can do the same for yourself. See how hard you have worked to do the right thing in the relationship, even if it didn't work out as you had hoped. Forgive yourself for this expectation gap. Hold yourself in high esteem, and if you can show your vulnerabilities, your pain, and your truth to your partner, then reveal these things to them. If you feel you cannot do this because there is a lack of trust or respect in the relationship, then reveal them to yourself. You will be learning many ways to courageously surrender to yourself and your partner throughout this book.

Love is patient, love is kind, and love is messy.

The action of being honest with yourself will open doors to healing within. A heart that is more healed can sit with itself and another who is healing. You can learn how to hold space for your partner, to hold the energy of someone who is in pain and not get overwhelmed or sucked into it while they work through their pain. It's like holding the hand of someone getting a splinter taken out; you have empathy for the other but do not get lost in their journey.

Once we have been honest and surrendered within, we can open up our hearts to another more fully.

CHAPTER 2

Bright Future, Red Flags

When all you know is fight or flight, red flags
and butterflies all feel the same.
—CINDY CHERIE

Many people naturally want to be in a relationship to connect on a deeper emotional level. One of life's great gifts is sharing experiences with someone else, enjoying the simple pleasures of just being together, embarking on new adventures, celebrating with passion, and creating shared memories. Most of us enter into a relationship imagining what our life will be like with our partner and dreaming of how things could manifest over time. We project a future for ourselves that has everything in it that we dream about.

We begin dating someone with whom we have an interest, connection, or attraction, wanting to see if there is potential with this person. If we are lucky, we enter into a committed relationship with an intention that it will work out. This new beginning is enveloped in hope, promise, brightness, and sparkles. We hope (or expect) that this person will fulfill our projected future dream.

As we put our best foot forward, we simultaneously hide, push down, and ignore the emotionally wounded parts of ourselves that we don't want our potential partner to see. However, despite our best intentions, our unhealed inner child wounding comes forward in our adult relationships. Guarding our fragilities and woundings is easier in the beginning, but in time they tumble forth, creating havoc in our relationships.

> *Loving relationships take work to succeed,*
> *but they shouldn't be a struggle.*

Our emotional wounding supplies the wishful narrative for our fairy tale. Take, for example, Justin and Claire. Justin has an emotional wound of always seeing himself as a victim and less-than. He has feelings of being abandoned. He knows he doesn't have a high opinion of himself. He subconsciously looks to be taken care of or rescued. In a dating context, Justin subconsciously looked for someone who has the synergistic wounding of being the caretaker, controller, abuser, or manipulator, which would match his wounding.

Justin started dating Claire, who seemed on the surface to be his love match, as she was nurturing and accommodating of his feelings. But she was also controlling, telling him what to do and how to behave. An attraction was there, but their synergistic woundings were matching up, not their grounded, healed selves. This newly in love young couple didn't know it yet, but their relationship was challenged from the start. They had rose-colored glasses on, so neither could clearly see how they were plugging into the other's wounded parts.

Justin and Claire's inauspicious beginning loaded up their future relationship with huge expectations. Justin wanted to feel validated, nurtured, and cared for, and Claire wanted to be the caretaker, fixer, and the one in charge. Their wounded parts were louder than their healed parts. As long as neither works on healing and growing within themselves and with each other, their wounded relationship will struggle along.

We can only see what we are ready to see.

At the beginning, two people in a new relationship seem tailor made for each other, but often, one or the other eventually emotionally heals and grows out of their paradigm while the other stays stuck. When one or both breaks free of their wounded attraction in some way, the spell is broken, and it is hard for them to recapture the original illusion of synergy. They can't stay in the wounded dance because they have healed enough to see beyond it.

When couples don't achieve happily ever after, they are often incredibly disappointed in themselves and their partners, and feel like a failure. They may never consciously know that their relationship house was built on unstable ground based on unresolved issues (and, often, unrealistic expectations) that they each subconsciously hoped the other would fix.

SYNERGISTIC WOUNDED PAIRINGS

Few of us are equipped with the necessary tools to have a healthy, productive, and fulfilling relationship. As you have just learned, we subconsciously choose our partners based on our unresolved wounding, or synergistic wounded pairings. It's not as if we are all doomed from the start, but the more emotionally unaware we are, the more likely we are to fall into the traps of our own dysfunction.

No matter our age, when we are in a new relationship, we rely on the incredible euphoria and excitement of young love, where everything is possible and nothing is insurmountable. These feelings of invincibility and limitless potential are especially true and necessary when we are younger, because that is when we are best equipped to take risks. This is also why getting into a relationship is easier when we are younger. We tend to look past imperfections and red flags, and we don't even know what red flags we should be looking for. We only know what we have learned growing up, who we are attracted to, and what has worked for us so far. We look for a mate based on instinct, attraction, impulse, and drive rather than wise discernment or judgment.

Wisdom comes from paying attention to our wounded choices rather than pretending they didn't happen.

Oftentimes we look to our partner to heal the relationship. My theory is that we subconsciously believe that our partner has a synergistic wound that matches ours, so we project that they have the answer to heal this wound. Of course, they don't have the answer because they are probably just as lost and are, in turn, reacting and responding to our wounding, looking for their answer. I believe both partners can find the answer with all the wisdom each carries, but that takes time, patience, introspection, and a lot of good communication.

Red Flag Warnings

A red flag is a behavior or action that stands out as a warning. The term signifies an aberration or danger that needs to be addressed. In relationship terms, red flags are warning signs that another person's emotional wounding is coming to the surface and will potentially impact the relationship. It is very easy to overlook these red flags when the flush of early romance obscures our ability to see the other person clearly.

> *A wounded heart cannot clearly see, hear, or feel red flags because the pain coming from the other person isn't recognized as a major problem. A wounded lens distorts the view.*

The red flags aren't always noticeable when we are excited and beginning a new relationship, but if we are honest with ourselves, we sense or intuit that something is not right. When red flags are not addressed, they become systemic wounded patterns that often show up throughout the lifespan of the relationship. A wounded heart cannot recognize a red flag as clearly as a healed heart can. Emotional wounding comes disguised as personality quirks, which are too often dismissed as aberrations or a one-off event until we are ready to see the pattern. Red flags are often dismissed because if we were to be honest about why the red flag is a problem, then we would have to look at a deeper wound that needs to be healed within ourselves.

You may have noticed some red flags in your relationship. Take an inventory of the following red flags, and mark the ones that have meaning to you:

- I think I can change the things I don't like about them.
- They always tell me that something is my fault and that I can't do anything right. They are angry a lot.
- They never tell me that I am loved, but they will say this to the dog.
- I work so hard to get them to talk, but I can't read minds.
- I can't laugh or express my feelings, and when I do, they tell me that's not how I feel.
- I make myself smaller and ignore my needs so theirs are fulfilled.
- I think their addiction isn't that bad; everybody has something, and nobody's perfect.
- They don't like to have sex. I guess that's fine, because we get along most of the time.
- I always make excuses for them and have to explain their behavior to others.
- I say I'm sorry, but it doesn't make the relationship better.

These and other red flags represent the unresolved inner child wounding within ourselves and the other person. They are explanations people say to themselves to make red flags fit into their narrative. But as you are learning, the wounding we carry distorts our impression of others, like looking through a dirty window. We can see part of the view but not all of it. Maybe you have made up some stories that the person in your life matches your desires instead of facing the realities.

Our ability to see and identify red flag warnings is tied to the degree that we are emotionally healed. If we ourselves are as wounded as our partners, then we don't see the red flag warnings at all; we just see them as personality traits. When others point out the red flags, we make excuses. This is how we are synergistically wounded with our partners and lost in the drama.

Some people say they always find the ones who look normal on the outside, but the red flags they overlooked would have revealed that this person was emotionally damaged or addicted to something.

One rule that I teach regarding recognizing red flags is to say no to something you don't want and see how your partner responds. For example, your partner asks if you want to go to a certain restaurant for dinner, and you say no. How does your partner respond to your no? Is your answer respected, or does your partner try to talk you out of your no? If they try to change your mind, then discern if this is a bigger pattern. Are there more instances where you are not respected and are overlooking your feelings and giving your power away? This is a red flag pattern that needs to be addressed before you go any further.

Don't be paralyzed by red flags. They are simply wounding, yours or the other's, coming forward looking to be healed. Take this as a recognition of something that you both need to actively work through. You will later learn how to express your feelings regarding the red flags in a way that your partner can hear.

Love Bombing

One of the most hard-to-recognize red flags is love bombing. Love bombing involves a cycle of intense affection and adoration followed by devaluation and denigration. Typically, one partner goes overboard with love and affection, sometimes showering their partner with gifts and treats. This is followed by a period during which they put their partner down. It can sometimes be the reverse, with poor treatment coming first, followed by a showering of attention. The love bomber feels in control with this push-pull cycle, but it creates a roller coaster of confusing mixed messages for the recipient.

Check in and trust yourself.
Your internal gut reaction is very wise.

Something that feels like intense love at the beginning may not be love at all. The key is to look at your partner's overall pattern. Your being loaded up with affection, gifts, and adoration initially feels amazing, but it is important to discern whether your partner's actions match their words. Healthy relationships are not an emotional roller coaster. An emotionally healthy love is consistent.

A love bomber is all about maintaining control by building up their partner and then tearing them down (or vice versa), manipulating the other for their own satisfaction. A love bomber's inner child wounding and unhealthy attachment styles, along with possible narcissistic traits and the need for control, come through full force. The insecure recipient who needs to be filled up and adored soaks up all of this affection like a sponge. Their woundings are in synergy.

Psychologist Dale Archer explains, "The key to understanding how love bombing differs from romantic courtship is to look at what happens next, after two people are officially a couple. If extravagant displays of affection continue indefinitely, if actions match words, and there is no devaluation phase, then it's probably not love bombing. That much attention might get annoying after a while, but it's not unhealthy in and of itself."[1]

If you are concerned that you are being love bombed, step back and evaluate how your partner shows you love and affection. Then go within to check your gut reaction. Does the love feel genuine and sincere, or are there some strings attached? Love bombing feels confusing, especially if you feel like the most important person in the world one minute and less-than the next. If your partner is critical or controlling after having just said all these beautiful words and given you gifts, then they are manipulating you.

Sadly, once the love bomber feels they have "got" the person they were after, they often switch to being in full-on narcissistic mode. The charm and love bombs are gone, and now it is on to a new roller coaster of gaslighting and abuse.

If you recognize that you are being love bombed by a partner, please seek professional help, as this is an abusive relationship. Your love-bombing mate will not be interested in learning to heal and help to repair this relationship; they will want the game to go on forever. In short, start running now.

I wish the pain of betrayal was as easy to ignore
as the red flags that forewarned of it.
—STEVE MARABOLI

---

1. Dale Archer, "The manipulative partner's most devious tactic," *Psychology Today*, March 6, 2017.

RELATIONSHIP CHECKLIST

When we are dating, we hope to connect with another person and for a relationship to develop. Most people get intensely focused on impressing the other person and neglect to check in with themselves to see how they feel when they are with this person. The following is a useful checklist to use as a gut check. It applies to long-term partners, as well.

- When you state your boundaries, are you treated with respect or disrespect?
- Are you a priority, or does your partner spend more time with friends than with you?
- When you say how you feel, does your partner try to talk you out of what you know you feel?
- Are you changing yourself to accommodate your partner so they won't be upset?
- If you point out some red flags and want to work on them, does your partner get upset, or are they willing to listen to you?
- Is the relationship reciprocal, or do you feel you do all of the work?
- Do you avoid certain topics because the conversation won't go well?
- Can you trust your partner, or do you have doubts?
- Is the relationship free-flowing, or does it feel like work?
- Do you need to hide your authentic self because you know your partner won't like this side of you?

These red-flag questions apply whether you are dating or in a long-term relationship. If you notice some of them in your relationship, just make a note of them for now. As you go through this work, you will learn how to express your feelings productively so that you can address these concerns.

OVERVIEW: THE STARR RESET

After reading about all those red flags, you may already feel like there is no hope for your relationship. But hold on! There is a way to heal your relationship through better communication. That is exactly what this book is about. You will be learning about the STARR Reset, or how to Stop, Think, Act, and Reset and Repair the relationship after an emotional wounding has shown up and starts to spiral out of control. This process is designed to help you feel closer to your partner and to work through red flags and other issues that you have tried to avoid. Once you realize the conversation is not going to a good place, the process follows this pattern:

- **Stop**—Recognize what was just said, what just happened, or what is about to happen.
- **Think**—Assess the situation and discern how you feel about it. Then think about how you want to move forward.
- **Act**—Put your thoughts into action.
- **Reset and Repair**—State that you need a reset, then work on repairing the relationship by using better communication.

It is important to remember that our emotional wounding doesn't magically go away when we become adults, nor does it go away whether we are in a traditional or nontraditional relationship. If relationships were that easy, couples wouldn't break up and the divorce rate wouldn't be so high.

The following story of Rachel and Jason illustrates a common theme in wounded relationships and details how this couple learned to reset their relationship.

The Story of Rachel and Jason

Jason and Rachel have been married for fifteen years and have no children. They described their relationship as somewhat happy, with unforeseen life events that they navigated fairly well, some minor health issues, and a few job changes. Problems came up, of course, which they eventually started to ignore completely.

Their inner child woundings showed up in the following ways: Jason would have depressive episodes, during which he would isolate, withdraw, and sometimes drink alcohol. Like most depressive people, Jason wanted to isolate and go within, playing his video games and not talking with Rachel or anyone else. Rachel, who had periods of anxiety, would get upset and impatient with Jason's depressive symptoms, especially how he shut down and stopped communicating with her.

Jason's isolation was his way of finding peace and protecting Rachel from his depressive episodes, anger outbursts, and his wounding (his depression masked by anger). As a depressed teenager, he did the same thing to get away from his mom, who would try to get him to talk. He would hide out in the basement, shutting out the world by playing video games and being alone. Jason didn't see his current alcohol use as a problem, but Rachel knew that when he drank, he became more depressed and moody.

Rachel took his behaviors personally. She perceived his

behavior as shutting her out; she didn't know that Jason had behaved the same way as a teenager. She would get anxious and start yelling out of frustration. She worried and began to imagine the worst: that he would harm himself. She felt alone in their marriage.

Rachel would make up stories of what Jason was thinking and feeling, trying to figure out what was going on inside of him. She didn't know what to do with the fears she felt. She reverted back to the wounded tools she knew as a child, which was crying out in pain (yelling) so that someone would hear her distress, and her attempts at mindreading were her insecurities and wounding coming forth.

The more Rachel yelled and prodded Jason to talk, the more he shut down, just like he had with his mom. The more he shut down, the more she made up stories to fill in the blanks. This cycle repeated over and over until both felt frustrated and nothing was working. Jason retreated, going deeper into a depressive state. Rachel got louder, and he retreated even more. Eventually, all they could think about was divorcing because they hated this cycle and how they felt.

When Rachel and Jason came to see me, they didn't know anything about inner child emotional woundings; they just thought this was how they were. One of the first exercises we did was to identify how their emotional woundings were showing up. Once I explained how their woundings were showing up within their patterns of behavior, they began to understand how their behaviors were subconsciously driven. They worked on learning new ways of communicating, but a big part of their work was to understand how and when their wounded inner child was showing up, and what this looked and sounded like. Jason's wounded need to isolate into his depression synergistically matched with the wounding of

Rachel's broken trust issues and anxiety. They each needed to be seen and heard, but they were going about it in wounded ways.

Once they both understood their synergistic wounding attraction and completed their Wounding Profile Sheet (which you will do later), then they could begin to apply the STARR Reset so they could stop the cycle of avoiding their problems. When they started to go down the wrong path, one or the other would say "we need a reset." Then they would practice Stop, Think, Act, and Reset and Repair. Rachel agreed to stop demanding that Jason tell her what was going on, and Jason agreed to stop shutting down altogether. Once they each understood how their own wounding was coming out, they were able to respect the other's healing journey.

Jason and Rachel determined to honor each other's feelings. Jason needed to respect Rachel's concerns by telling her some of what was happening inside of him. He agreed that he would use the Feelings Chart (see appendix A) to give her a "weather report" of his feelings, even when he feels low and wants to isolate. He also agreed to cut back on his alcohol consumption to see if that helped his mood, as he hadn't realized that alcohol was a depressant.

Rachel agreed that she would accept Jason's answers and not try to get more information. In other words, she would learn to trust his answer, calm herself, and stop imagining what he wasn't telling her. They each learned how to pause and speak intentionally the first time, using words and phrases that were thoughtful and meaningful. By speaking clearly the first time, they won't need to go back to a conversation to clean it up.

From this new understanding, Jason and Rachel began to repair their relationship and restore normal communication.

They are learning how to speak to themselves and to each other.

I asked this couple to stretch to meet each other halfway. Initially, neither particularly wanted to do what I was asking of them because it was outside of their comfort zone. But they also knew that if they didn't try to connect to each other in a different way, then they would continue their ultimately destructive pattern. Rachel had to learn how to self-soothe and know that Jason was trying with the tools he was learning. Jason had to trust that Rachel could hold and respect his words and not use them against him.

I took this couple through an amended version of the HEAL process—healing and embracing an authentic life—that I describe in my book *Healing Your Lost Inner Child*.[2] They each needed to do their own work with their inner child wounding so that their wounded parts would stop coming up. Through this process, Rachel and Jason learned that being openhearted with each other was not tied to an outcome but to a possibility.

This couple went on to have deeper, more fulfilling conversations, and they are no longer in their wounded cycles. Jason is still tempted to isolate, but now he and Rachel talk about this. He says, "I'm feeling good today. I just need some alone time, so if you need me, I will be playing video games for a couple hours." He owns his feelings instead of slinking downstairs, acting out, and giving in to his wounded part. This helps Rachel know that he is being responsible with his feelings and his time, and she feels safer knowing he is not isolating from her.

For her part, Rachel wants to know what Jason isn't saying to her at times. When this wounding gets activated, she will

---

2. Healing Your Lost Inner Child (Practical Wisdom Press, 2020), available on Amazon and Audible.

say things like, "I want to make up a story about what you are thinking about, but instead I'm going to just ask you how you are feeling." Both are more responsible and more connected to what they feel, and they let each other know.

Jason and Rachel apologized to each other for how they had been behaving and what they had been doing that wasn't helping the relationship. A heartfelt apology is taking ownership of one's part in the co-creation of the relationship dynamic. By owning their truth, they are saying to each other, *I love you, I respect you, and I trust you with my feelings more than anyone else.* The apology is a big part of rejoining and repairing. It allows each to see the humility, vulnerability, and surrender in the other, and it reaffirms the commitment of the relationship. They reveal their humanity and kindness toward each other. This is what being openhearted is about.

We can't see our partner's wounded parts until we heal our own.

To help you understand how to apply this work to your own life, let's look more closely at how Rachel and Jason's woundings showed up in their relationship.

- Rachel's triggers: Jason would shut down or get very quiet, leading her to feel nervous or anxious.
- Rachel's wounding: She was subconsciously reminded of scary times as a child when her father would get angry and sulk. She wanted to control things so she could feel safe. There were parallels between her dad and Jason.

- Rachel's response: She would plead with Jason to tell her what was wrong, but she did not take his silence or his pleas to leave him alone as his answer. She also made up stories about what Jason was thinking and feeling. Her wounded inner child wanted Jason to reassure her and calm her down. Her amygdala would hijack the rational part of her mind (more on this later), causing her to lose the ability to think calmly and rationally.
- Jason's triggers: His depression would kick in, causing him to want to isolate, play video games, and drink alcohol.
- Jason's wounding: He felt that no one understood him. He felt that his mom wanted him to talk so she would feel better, not him. He feared that his mom (and then Rachel) would use his feelings against him. There were parallels between his mom and Rachel.
- Jason's response: He would isolate and withdraw by playing video games with headphones on, and refuse to help Rachel understand where he was emotionally. He would drink alcohol alone in the basement. He would shut down more as Rachel got louder. These were his wounded teenage boy responses.

You can see how Jason's and Rachel's woundings were synergistic and dovetailed with each other. This felt right to both of them, so it was hard at first for them to recognize how their woundings were showing up. Now, dedicated to each other and their relationship, they are working through their woundings using the STARR Reset and are in a much better place.

EXERCISE: YOUR SYNERGISTIC
WOUNDED ATTRACTION

This exercise will help you to gain perspective on the synergistic wounding that may be in your relationship. Write your thoughts in your notebook.

Think back to some of your bigger disagreements with your partner. What could you have done differently at the time? How could you have stopped yourself enough so that you could truly see and hear what was going on and determine what you were feeling?

What could you do in the future so you could think about what to do with the feelings you have? Based on this, how could you have repaired the relationship in a past disagreement?

Look at how your emotional wounding coordinates with your partner's wounding. Where and when do your wounded parts soothe and comfort, or join with, your partner's wounded parts? When do your wounded parts stir up and activate or annoy your partner's wounded parts?

EXERCISE: YOUR TRIGGERS,
YOUR WOUNDING, YOUR RESPONSE

In your notebook, write out a brief description of a synergistic wounding cycle that you get into with your partner based on what you know right now. You can use Rachel and Jason's story as a prompt for your own cycle.

On the first page, write out the following as best you can:

My triggers
My wounding
How I respond

On the next page, write what you know about your partner.

Through my observation and what they have told me, these are my partner's triggers:

Based on what my partner has told me, this is their wounding:

This is how I see my partner usually respond:

As you work through this exercise, notice how your partner's wounding is complementary to yours, even though it may be the opposite. Alternatively, notice how you and your partner may have exactly the same triggers and wounded responses.

Write out what your and your partner's wounded responses usually achieve.

Write out why you think your inner child wounding chose your partner. What were you trying to satisfy emotionally?

Use the knowledge you are gaining about your inner child wounding and the wounding you think your partner has. How are they synergistic, meaning how do they work together?

What insights do you have from your work so far?

Do you see some of the wounded reasons why you chose your partner?

If feelings of anger, resentment, or frustration at yourself or your partner are coming up, know that this is normal. You are looking at yourself through a new lens. You are learning to see more clearly how your wounding impacts you today. You are doing great work and beginning to understand why you do what you do.

We begin our relationships believing they will be bright and shiny for a long time, and that is true for some. However, red flags are raised in all relationships at some point, which, when acknowledged, can help us avoid going deeper into troubled waters. By learning how to recognize red flags in others and understanding your own, you can lay a foundation for a relationship that is built on honesty, trust, and the understanding that you each will always need to work at it to co-create a successful outcome.

CHAPTER 3

Synergistic Pairings

Entering a family system requires tact, humor, a generous spirit
and the ability to survive an occasional argument.
—AMY DICKINSON, FROM "ASK AMY"

Being in a relationship is one of the hardest things we do in life but also one of the most rewarding. Relationships require us to not only pay attention to ourselves and our needs but to go outside of ourselves and attend to someone else's needs and feelings. Relationships ask us to stretch and grow into better versions of ourselves. We show up for others, give more, and, hopefully, the relationship is reciprocal.

Are you growing and expanding or contracting in your relationship? Is your partner sharing their wisdom with you or just their wounding? Our adult relationships invite us to come out of any ego-centered child self we may still have inside and to mature. This is incredibly hard for people who are not emotionally ready and who have a lot of unresolved childhood wounding. They want to go back to the safety of the nest and the familiar instead of facing the immensity of the world and an adult relationship. However, the urge to get into a relationship is hard coded within most of us. The emotional range we experience in our adult relationships is huge, and we feel that at a deep level.

In our relationships we live, laugh, and love,
and most of us also experience the contrast
of pain, sadness, and despair.

For example, when your partner overreacts to something that you perceive as small by acting like a child—yelling, slamming doors, or isolating—their inner child wounding is coming out in the adult relationship. This wounding gets triggered and explodes with real-life consequences. Maybe you had never seen your partner do this before and it scared you. You wondered who this person was you thought you knew. They are still the same person you met when things were going great, but they feel more comfortable with you now, so they are showing you their pain.

In those moments of intense feeling, few people see that they are acting out emotionally, because at that moment they feel scared, unloved, hurt, sad, exposed, and vulnerable. All they know is they are hurting; they don't see that their inner child is raging, they just want their pain acknowledged.

At this point, one of two things happens in the relationship: the witnessing partner either shuts down or mirrors back to their partner with the same intensity they are receiving. Sometimes the witnessing partner will have the presence of mind to see that this is emotional pain coming out, and they remain grounded and calm. But most of the time, both partners' emotional wounding becomes activated, turning the situation chaotic. Their woundings are synergistic; one partner's wounding coordinates and aligns with the other, like a puzzle piece. Neither person has any idea what their wounding is or that it is in synergy with the other; they are simply feeling their emotions in a big way and playing out their emotionally wounded drama.

We all need to be a cheerleader at one time or another for our partner, which is how we support each other in times of challenge. But sometimes one becomes dependent on this encouragement and does not work to find the motivation within themselves. The cheerleading behavior becomes codependent and enabling and is not healthy for the relationship. There is a self-serving codependent payout for the person who overdoes being the cheerleader, as in, *I'm able to do this for them. They need me. I am important in their life. I feel better about myself because I'm helping.* The wounded partners fill up the subconscious void, so if some is good, more is better; their partner's wounding says *give me more of that!*

THE BALANCE OF HEALED AND WOUNDED PARTS

When we begin to date a new person, our healed self and our wounded parts collide with the healed and wounded parts of the other person. This commingling is often synergistic and opportunistic; it is what feels so right about being with the other person. The pairing is opportunistic in that there is great potential for tremendous growth within each person if the synergistic pairing can be capitalized on and used as a springboard for healing at a deeper level. When in balance, our healed and wounded parts create a stable point that is emotionally healthy, providing an open landscape of opportunity for the relationship to flourish.

We are a combination of our synergistically healed and wounded parts, which exist on a continuum inside of us. Sometimes we operate with our more healed issues, and we feel more whole. And sometimes we carry a heavier burden of working through some tough emotional issues. We don't have to resign ourselves to be lost in the weight of our wounding.

Where you are on the healed-wounded continuum is a subjective measure. You can rate yourself based on the level of dysfunctional wounded dramas in your life and the emotionally healthy relationships you have. You can also measure where you are by the language you use to express yourself, the volume you use, and the actions you take. All of these are your wounded or healed responses. A wounded response is yelling at the top of your lungs, for example, while a healed response is respectfully expressing to your partner using "I feel" language.[1] Your reaction to a person or situation depends on which part is louder inside of you at the time.

How do you feel inside right now, more healed (soft and light) or more wounded (loud and heavy)? Chances are you are working with more healed parts at the moment, but the wounded parts come out spontaneously, often loudly, and take a lot of energy to hold, so they are harder to ignore.

The healed-wounded continuum can help you to see that you have the ability to work toward a more healed self. Take a moment to do an inventory of your healed and wounded parts. Draw the Healed-Wounded Continuum (shown in figure 1) in your notebook. Use the initials for each relationship sphere to indicate how you show up for each sphere, and where each one lands on the continuum (trending more toward the healed or

---

1. "I feel" language is when we express our emotions to another before we state a logical explanation or description.

wounded side). Be honest with yourself, and think about how you feel when you interact in each sphere.

Relationship Spheres
R—in my relationship
S—with myself
F—in my family
FG—in my friend group
W—at work

Figure 1. Healed-Wounded Continuum

HEALED----|----|----|----|----|----|----|----|----|----WOUNDED

What do you notice? Are you more toward the healed side or the wounded side in each sphere? This is how you show up in these areas. Many people are more healed in their work sphere than in their relationship sphere, for example, and this is directly related to their boundary setting (which you will learn more about in chapter 19). Keep this continuum in your notebook, as this snapshot will tie in with other exercises throughout the book.

Wholeness is achieved through forward progress and momentum, not perfection.

Each day we bring forth our healed and wounded parts, trying to make our relationships work. For some, this flows pretty easily, with a few bumps here and there. Those who have healed bigger parts of themselves have more of the tools they need to help them navigate through difficult times.

Others may struggle to make their relationship work, as their wounding is loud and they keep bumping into obstacles and road blocks. When our wounding is loud, it is harder to access the right tools to navigate the course, and our relationships feel anything but smooth sailing. However, when we are brave during times of struggle or challenge, our healed parts can often come forward, illuminating courage, passion, and drive to help our wounded parts feel strong, and to trust that we can overcome adversity. Even though most of us have more healed parts than wounded, a shadow of our wounding is always there as a reminder of pain, old behaviors, and ideas of self, all of which can spring to life if we give them power.

The wounding we carry is an invitation for us to heal. If we don't, we will just stay in the fog, recycling old pain.

Not every relationship pairing is fraught with inner child wounding that will tear apart a secure bonding. Within each of us is a combination of unresolved emotional inner child wounds, healed and authentic parts of ourselves, and parts of ourselves that we have yet to explore. I believe most people make what they feel are the best choices in their relationships based on their consciously available emotional intelligence. We only know what we know, as no one goes out and says, what is the worst choice I can make today? Most people do not have a conscious recognition of their emotional wounding, much less how this wounding attracts them to similarly wounded people. We start each day trying to make the best choices—given what we know and what we have healed—even if we later realize that a particular choice wasn't the best one.

ELEMENTS OF SECURE RELATIONSHIP BONDING

Many couples get together with their synergistically healed and wounded parts and develop healthy communication patterns and a secure bonding. They can weather the storms that naturally come up within relationships with some degree of success. Even though they each have unhealed emotional wounds, they are able to find tools to make their relationship work. It may not always be perfect, but such partners are able to have good communication and a strong relationship bond because of a number of factors. These include:

- having a temperament of humility, respect, compassion, and forgiveness for the other;
- holding respectful boundaries for each other and reciprocating needs and feelings;
- being able to compromise and accept what is important to each partner;
- relying on each other but having autonomy in making sure one's own needs are met;
- knowing one partner will be patient, supportive, and fill in the gaps while the other heals;
- feeling one's words are respected, heard, and valued, and knowing one can lean into the other in times of need;
- discussing one's needs for physical and sexual intimacy as the relationship matures;
- sharing responsibilities equally, and doing one's fair share so the burdens are not greater for either partner;
- feeling a sense of safety and equanimity when bringing up tough topics to discuss and work through; and
- being able to repair the relationship after a

disagreement and recommit to their relationship in a way that is restorative and loving to each other.

This list is certainly not comprehensive, but it represents the qualities that a healthy and securely bonded relationship embodies. These relational aspects are ones that most couples aspire to, but often their woundings and unresolved issues put a detour in their path.

As a securely attached relationship matures, a couple may or may not be able to add to and refine their relationship bonding in one of two ways: 1) they can find healthy ways to process and work through difficult topics, resulting in a better chance of having a thriving and deeply committed relationship, or 2) they cannot find a way to deal with their emotional woundings and create stronger attachments with each other, thus finding it difficult to cultivate a long-lasting and committed relationship.

Successful couples are able to be there for the other and sacrifice or put aside what they want for the benefit of their partner. They have seen how their partner reciprocates and honors what they want, as well. This reciprocity is part of what is termed an interdependent relationship; the most successful pairings have mastered this respectful and reciprocal dynamic. What one gives doesn't have to be equal in monetary value, size, or scale, but each partner needs to feel they are getting their needs met and being nurtured.

An interdependent bonding is one in which partners feel connected and autonomous, with a sense of agency within themselves. This is especially likely if the person has a secure attachment from childhood. Even if their partner disagrees with them, they don't feel crushed and defeated; they have a sense of boundary and separation.

Even if you lacked secure attachments as a child,
you can create secure attachments in adulthood.

My partner and I have used some version of the exercises and tools that you are learning about at one time or another throughout our more than three decades together. I can see how my wounding came forward, especially early in our relationship. I am an adult child of an alcoholic, so my need to be the hero—the overly responsible one, the controlling one, the peacemaker—used to come out from me all of the time. It wasn't until I began to heal these wounded behaviors in my late twenties that they started to go away. My sense of freedom and respect for myself and my partner expanded as I worked on healing those wounded parts of myself. We always had a deep love for each other, which helped us reach through the painful times and hold the other, reassuring and reminding ourselves that we would get through the hard times together. We are each a work in progress no matter our age or how long we have been in our relationships.

Please note that when we are lost in our wounding and working toward healing, we are still experiencing life as what I call "in the movie." That is, our wounded parts are louder, and we know ourselves only up to that moment in time. After we heal big parts of ourselves and come out the other side, we are no longer in the movie, we are watching the movie. We can then see how our wounding got triggered and how we struggled in our relationships because we didn't have all the healed tools we needed. As you do this work and read stories and examples of how other couples moved out of their dysfunctional dance, you will gain more tools and perspectives so you will no longer be lost in the movie.

You may have a strong reaction to some of the stories and examples herein. If this is the case, hold this feeling and try to connect with the activated emotional wounding. This is your internal response system telling you where the opportunity for healing lives within you.

Levels of Relationship Bonding

This section will help you begin to evaluate your relationship bonding with your partner.

The following are four levels of relationship bonding that are most common in synergistic pairings.

Strongly bonded partners—This is a relationship in which there is a deep love, trust, and respect for each other. This couple has a good foundation, although they may need some additional skills to help their relationship continue to thrive and deepen. They would not call their relationship perfect, but their good times far outweigh the times of struggle. Their inner child woundings do not affect them much, and they have a strong resilience that helps them to navigate and heal those issues or traumas from childhood that do arise so they don't dramatically impact their adult relationship.

This couple would like to have more communication skills to help them navigate the troubling times of life. They do not shy away from the hard work within their relationship. They are aware of what they have but also know what they need help with. They are clearly seen by others as committed, caring, intimate partners. Others can feel their bonding and love.

Struggling yet loving and committed partners—This is a couple who has a somewhat strong foundation of love, trust, and respect, but their love has been tested by relationship traumas, such as infidelities, addictions, health issues, issues related to their children, financial, and work issues. This couple has been through a lot in their relationship. They want to make it work, but they need more skills, especially when times are bad. Their relationship is a bit battle-scarred, and their inner child woundings show up when they are not at their best. Sometimes there is a lot of emotional clean-up to do afterward.

They may or may not be aware of how their inner child wounding impacts their relationship. They may have a sibling or best-friends energy between them. Their unhealed wounding patterns show up frequently in the form of arguing, shutting down, and avoiding. This relationship goes hot and cold and needs an infusion of additional tools to help them clean up their hurts.

Indifferent and disconnected partners—This is a couple who are staying together, but it is very tough; they are just holding on by a thread. It is hard for them to see why they are together anymore, because their foundations of love, trust, and respect have been shaken to the core. Either they have tried remedies or just don't bother. Their inner child woundings are present in the relationship practically every day, primarily demonstrated through avoidance, isolation, and withdrawal, and this unhealed emotion is a clear detriment to any functioning within the pairing.

This couple is in denial and works to actively avoid each other and any confrontations. They are on parallel tracks and act like roommates or co-managers rather than intimate partners. Often these couples remain together for the kids, out of a sense of obligation to family, or for religious reasons. It is not impossible for this couple to accomplish a healthy and secure relationship bonding, but it will take more work.

Trauma-bonded partners—This couple has deep emotional wounding that comes out in highly destructive ways, characterized by ongoing cycles of abuse. They stay together not to resolve any wounding or to improve the relationship but to play out their unresolved and unrecognized deep trauma wounding. Their inner child woundings often come out as rage, hurt, feeling traumatized, and being deeply confused. These are the couples that have big fights, dramatic breakups, and reconnections with no explanations or apologies. The abuser and the victim can't quit each other, and all of this is enabled through a punishment-and-reward cycle that keeps them engaged. The victim often emotionally aligns with and has sympathy for the abuser, locking them further into this lost landscape.[2]

That may have been a lot for you to take in, so take a deep breath.

As you read over the levels of relationship bonding, what category would you put your relationship in at present? Does your relationship fit in between two categories? Did your relationship used to be like one described, or are you concerned that it is headed toward one? In your notebook, write out a description of where your relationship is at the present, using some of the words and phrasing above. Read this out loud. Does this startle you or motivate you to action?

---

2. If you are in an abusive relationship, please see the Resources section in appendix B for guidance. You can get help or get out of this relationship, but you will need assistance.

Growing pains are natural in a relationship. This is how we flex our relationship muscle to see the extent that we can heal and grow within the construct of the relationship. The pain you feel is your stretch to open yourself up and become more openhearted. This is the larger call of your higher self to reach for the type of relationship bonding you want to create. It is your call for self-excellence. Look within as you go through this process, and ask how you can be the bigger version of yourself, rising to the occasion and healing the wounding that holds you back.

THE RELATIONSHIP TIMELINE

Creating a relationship timeline can help you identify the inner child wounding patterns that show up in your relationship. When we look at our history from this perspective, experiences and reactions stand out that we otherwise take for granted. From your personal timeline you may be able to see where you overlooked and made allowances for red flag warnings that later became problems.

EXERCISE: YOUR RELATIONSHIP TIMELINE

Step back and look at your relationship with a soft gaze: where you were, where you are today, and all the time in between. Take out your notebook and draw a line top to bottom down the center of the page. At the top left of the line, enter the year you were married or partnered. Move down the line and enter, year by year, events that stand out for you. To the right of the line and next to each entry, write out your feelings about each event or this time in your life. As you write out your timeline, you will notice different choices you or your partner could have made. That is normal. Most of us can be harsh critics of ourselves and others. Remember to simply observe, not condemn, yourself and your partner.

Once you have completed your relationship timeline, look it over. What stands out as you review these events and feelings? See if you can discern some of the red flags you identified earlier and where, how, and when they show up on your timeline. If you notice that the same kinds of events or feelings come up on your timeline, you are seeing a theme or pattern that is probably related to your wounding.

You are learning new ways of looking at familiar parts of your relationship life. When we can step back and observe our own and our partner's wounding, we can have more respect and perspective for the journey. Being able to objectively look at yourself in your relationship will help you better determine how to interact with your partner. It helps us to step out of the movie. If you are thinking of working with a therapist, the timeline is a great starting point for you to show the cycles and patterns that you or your partner keep repeating.

We all try our best with the tools we have. The more you understand your own wounding and begin to heal, the better the outcome for your relationship.

CHAPTER 4

Childhood Emotional Wounding

Thirty-four-year-old Rachel can see all of this so clearly in hindsight.
Nineteen-year-old me was in love and insecure, so I justified
everything he said or did that was hurtful.
—RACHEL HOLLIS, *GIRL, WASH YOUR FACE*

Many wounded reactions we have as adults have their origins between birth and twenty. When we are loud or have a reaction that is out of proportion to a situation, it is often our inner child wounding coming forward to protect us, just like when we were young. Many of our inner child woundings originate in the attachments that we formed or didn't form in our childhood families. We keep using the tools we have until we learn more functional tools and get better outcomes. How we believe and behave as adults has a great deal to do with the connections we had to our caregivers growing up.

ATTACHMENT STYLES

Secure attachment styles with our caregivers that we experienced in childhood help us to see ourselves as separate from our caregivers. They regulate our emotional reactions and help us to become our own person, feeling strong, self-reliant, and free. Simply put, secure attachments form when a child who is in distress receives comfort, love, reassurance, and a sense of resilience within from a caregiver. The caregiver is available and responsive, and the child receives in kind.

Attachment traumas are unique and relative to each of us. We are not in a competition with another for who had it worse off.

Insecure attachment styles develop when needs are not met, creating distress within the child. The caregiver is unresponsive even when the child is trying hard to get them to respond. This creates great internal turmoil in that the child learns how to adapt, overcompensate, hide, and deny as a way to navigate this uneven caregiver-child relationship. The child has to find a solution, change themselves, or shut down and avoid. These distortions and adaptations for needs not met become the wounded tools that the child, then the adult, uses to navigate life's ups and downs, ultimately leading to how we (subconsciously) choose a partner. The level of secure attachment that you developed in childhood will impact how you see and experience your adult relationships.[1]

---

1. To read more on the effects of secure and insecure attachment bonding and how they affect us as children and adults, please see *Attachment* by John Bowlby (New York: Basic Books, 2nd Ed., 1982).

UNRESOLVED EMOTIONAL WOUNDING

Unresolved wounding from childhood does not automatically go away when we become adults. This unhealed part of us, our wounded inner child, is always there, waiting for something to happen, looking for a threat or a hurt similar to what happened to us as a child. Once triggered, the wounded inner child springs into action, pushes the adult self out of the way, and tries to protect all parts of us from people or situations that look, sound, or feel like what happened to us as a child.

A friend of mine once described children as being very emotionally tough and resilient but also soft as peaches that bruise easily.

This emotional wounding can come about because of a single event from childhood or a pattern of events that was pervasive in the childhood home. This can range from being put down or neglected to more serious forms of abuse. As a result of these experiences, the child experiences a deep emotional wounding that leads to the forming of false ideas of self, such as feeling rejection, confusion, frustration, and not being good enough. These distorted ideas of self then manifest into a false narrative that the adult carries, such as feeling like a victim or an imposter.

If this false narrative persists and is never healed, then the adult develops a set of skills that I call *wounded emotional response tools*. Wounded tools are behaviors and thoughts— such as lashing out, throwing temper tantrums, withdrawing, isolating, being the victim, or being passive-aggressive—that are not functional in relationships.

*Wounded tools protected the inner child well,
but they only cause further confusion
and pain in adult relationships.*

We grab these tools impulsively, without thinking, and use them as responses to situations, but they are not the best or healthiest choices. This is why I call them wounded tools—they are stored in a wounded place within that is waiting to be healed. These tools are essentially codependent patterns. They are all the ways we learned to adapt ourselves to someone else, making them greater and ourselves smaller, for example. We may have learned to do things so that others are not uncomfortable and their needs are met while we sacrifice ourselves, or we may become bigger and louder to feel a sense of power and control. Both of these behaviors are exaggerated wounded responses. We carry these codependent patterns and tools into our adult life, subconsciously thinking that the same skills that worked for us as children will work for us in adulthood.

*Our inner child grabs a wounded tool to
use when we come from a place of fear.*

We also learn in childhood what I call *functional emotional response tools*—such as pride, responsibility, humility, generosity, empathy, and a sense of ownership—that grow out of feelings of love and trust, which we then carry into adulthood. We use functional tools more often when we feel whole, authentic, and grounded. The functional tools are learned over time, either on our own or by watching how others handle a situation. We can more easily grab a functional tool when we feel grounded, safe, authentic, and sure of ourselves.

*When our hurts are too loud inside, we need
to do more internal work so we don't
project this hurt onto our partner.*

The challenge in our relationships is to recognize when our wounding shows up and whether to grab a wounded tool or a functional tool. We also need to determine whether we are in a place of love and trust or in a place of fear, whether the inner child or the responsible adult self is in charge. All of these responses are normal, and most people use a combination of them to navigate their relationships.

Adult Children of Alcoholics (ACOA)

I want to specifically address adult children of alcoholics for a moment. Adults who grew up in an alcoholic or addicted household learned many codependent tools in childhood to cope with their chaotic emotional environment. The attachment styles developed from living in an addicted household are often insecure, disorganized, and unpredictable. This results in the child developing unique coping strategies to deal with the swings between feeling safe and unsafe. Some of the emotionally wounded response tools that an ACOA person brings into their adult relationships include being overly responsible, isolating then wanting closeness, being impulsive, avoiding conflict, taking things personally, and blaming others, to name a few. The wounded inner child doesn't always know the war is over, so this part keeps coming forward to protect the adult, fighting with the same wounded tools, hoping to get a different result.

Later you will read more about the effects of ACOA adults and how this shows up in their relationships. If you recognize yourself in these descriptions, know that you don't have to keep using those same tools over and over just because you grew up in that environment. You can heal these patterns. Discover more about ACOA traits in my book *Healing Your Lost Inner Child*.[2]

This work is about honoring and accepting all of your parts, not just the ones you consider to be the better ones.

Explore: Your Wounded Emotional Response Tools

The following list will give you a broader idea of the wounded emotional response tools that you may use when you are in a place of fear. Look over the list, then circle the ones that you use in your adult relationships. Checkmark the ones you have seen or heard your partner use.[3]

- Acting passive-aggressive so as not to show your anger directly
- Shutting down or withdrawing emotionally; checking out
- Projecting or mindreading what others think or feel about you
- Using drugs, alcohol, food, pills, weed, or other substances to escape or cope
- Pushing emotions down until they manifest as anxiety or depression

---

2. See also *Recovery: A Guide for Adult Children of Alcoholics* by Herbert L. Gravitz and Julie D. Bowden (New York: Simon & Schuster, Inc., 1987), and *Adult Children of Alcoholics* by Janet Woititz (Florida: Health Communications, Inc., 1990).

3. This partial list is from the author's book *Healing Your Lost Inner Child* (Illinois: Practical Wisdom Press, 2020).

- Overcompensating
- Playing the victim for attention
- Attacking others out of anger because of the shame you feel
- Rebelling at authority or those who you think are trying to control you
- Feeling responsible for everything bad that happens
- Avoiding conflict
- Saying "I'm sorry" a lot
- Giving away your power
- Enabling others' destructive habits and avoiding real discussions
- Trying to be a peacemaker
- Getting really loud or demonstrative so that others hear and see you
- Giving too much or too little
- Being clingy, then pushing away
- Changing yourself for someone else's comfort
- Manipulating others

What do you notice about the wounded tools you identified within yourself? You may be overwhelmed by the number of wounded tools you use. Most of us have a combination of tools that make up how we express ourselves and the reactions we have to various situations. These wounded tools helped protect you in times of stress, especially when you were growing up. The same is true for what you see in your partner; they also have a combination of wounded tools they use that were formed early on in their development. You simply brought these tools into your adult life and are now using them in your relationship because it feels normal.

Explore: Your Functional Emotional Response Tools

The following is a partial list of functional emotional response tools. Circle the ones that you use in your adult relationships, and checkmark the ones you have seen or heard your partner use.[4]

- Feeling proud of yourself even when you aren't acknowledged by someone else
- Recognizing the healthy and positive actions and choices you need to help you through your day
- Acknowledging the friends who are good for you and encourage you
- Honoring yourself when you have accomplished something that was really challenging to do
- Respecting yourself and your decisions
- Recognizing when relationships are reciprocal and when they are not
- Knowing that you make the best choices possible each day, even if they are not perfect
- Encouraging yourself to move forward, and finding the motivation to do things that you know are the right for you
- Loving those parts of yourself that still need care so they will heal
- Asking for help from others
- Practicing good self-care by getting extra rest when you need to, or participating in hobbies or sports as a way to relax

---

4. This partial list is from the author's book *Healing Your Lost Inner Child* (Illinois: Practical Wisdom Press, 2020).

- Being emotionally vulnerable with others whom you trust
- Connecting with family and friends who help you feel whole
- Discerning who or what is working for you and who or what is working against you

As you look over the functional tools that you circled or marked, what do you notice about yourself and your partner? You and your partner probably have more functional tools than what is listed; write them down, as well. It is easy to take them for granted because you use them when things are going well, so they don't stand out as a problem.

Making a list of your wounded and functional tools will help you discover your synergistic wounding. It will also help you see that behaviors you learned to think of as normal may not be healthy. This will help you understand the deeper emotional attraction you had with your partner and they with you.

How Wounding Shows Up

Each partner brings into the relationship a tool kit of wounded and functional emotional response tools that they grab when they want to express a feeling. When things are good and they are coming from a place of love, they can easily grab a functional tool. But when they are in fear, it is harder to grab a functional tool, so they use a familiar wounded emotional response tool instead.

As the relationship progresses, each partner begins to relax into its rhythm and becomes more comfortable with each other. They begin to use more emotionally wounded tools in the relationship to express feelings directly or indirectly, such as the following:

- shutting down or isolating
- using controlling or directive statements and behaviors
- being loud and shaming
- apologizing for things out of one's control to make things better
- throwing temper tantrums to get one's way
- blaming or criticizing
- being passive-aggressive or sarcastic
- avoiding conflict
- manipulating or being the victim
- giving ultimatums

This is a partial list of how emotional inner child wounding can present itself within a relationship when we let our guard down. When you read these behaviors with the concept of the wounded inner child in mind, you can see how childish they are. They contribute to the convenient narrative of the wounded inner child, as they feel natural and familiar. They are the attributes of a wounding profile.

We guard our emotional wounding like a fragile bird, not wanting to reveal any vulnerabilities until we think the other person won't hurt us.

Wounding may also show up as projection. This is like having a movie projector in the center of your chest that projects onto someone else something you don't like to look at within yourself, causing you to put them down and make yourself feel better. For example, someone who is self-critical and self-judgmental will project this harsh lens onto someone else and point out in the other person the same things they think or say about themselves. This is that person's way of saying,

I don't like this about myself, so I'm going to find that wounding in others, even if it's not really there.

Discern whether your reactions come from a grounded, loving place or a place of fear.

Why do people keep making the same emotionally toxic choices in their lives? Most people come about this honestly, in that they only know what they know at that moment in time. This lack of awareness of their emotional wounding, or lack of interest in healing in general, is mainly because they feel that if things are going fine, then leave well enough alone. They know the relationship isn't perfect, but they feel they are doing their best, and they just want to go along and hope things get better. With this comfortable denial, they create an illusion of a dysfunctional functionality within the relationship. What I often say is that they get used to sitting in the dirty bathtub together; it's not great, but it's what they know. Once one or both can't stand it anymore and feel a great urgency for things to change, they will begin to shake up the status quo.

Your Wounding Profile

The fact that you are reading this book indicates that you are ready at some level to heal your wounding. Determining how and how often your emotional wounding shows up will help you to create a healing plan and help you both to work on restoring the relationship to a healthy and secure bonding.

Wounding is a strong wind that redirects your internal compass, pushing you off course and into a storm with your partner.

To create a healing plan for yourself, you need to have a clear idea of your wounding and the wounding you have seen your partner demonstrate. In the following exercise, you will create a wounding profile for yourself, and your partner will create their own. Your wounding profile will give you a snapshot of how you respond to situations in your relationship. It will help you to observe yourself so that you can better determine the steps you want to take to heal this pattern going forward. If your partner is not reading this book with you, you can create one for them based on what you know about them.

As a reminder, if your partner is not doing this work, create a wounding profile for them based only on the emotional wounding you have heard or seen them demonstrate. For example, if you have seen them throw temper tantrums or shut down and withdraw, then you could put this on their wounding profile. You need to have seen it or know it for sure before putting it on their profile. Be diligent and avoid thinking you know how they feel. You are not diagnosing your partner, you are creating a reference point to examine their wounding and how it is synergistic with your own.

EXERCISE: CREATE YOUR WOUNDING PROFILE

Look over the wounded emotional response tools on page 65, and refer back to your answers in the Synergistic Wounded

Attraction exercise on page 22 to help you complete your wounding profile.

Take out your notebook and write out the wounded tools you circled earlier and others you use. To the right of each, write out when, why, and how you use these wounded tool in your relationship.

Let's say you have a wounded emotional response tool of making yourself smaller. To the right of this wounded tool you might write the following:

I make myself smaller . . .

When: when my partner yells at me or is upset.

Why: because I don't want my partner to get louder, and I'm scared and want to control the situation.

How: by becoming really quiet, avoiding my partner, and hiding in the house until the storm passes.

Do this for each of your wounded tools. If you are unsure as to when, why, or how, just write unsure or I don't know. When you are done, look over your list. When do you use these wounded tools? What are the themes related to why, when, and how you use them?

On a separate page write out the wounded tools your partner uses. Skip the why part (chances are you don't know why), and just write out the when and how.

You may notice that it is easier to identify the when and how of your partner's wounding than your own. Seeing someone else's pain is easier to recognize than our own. Don't focus too much on your partner throughout this process, because that encourages the desire most people have of finding fault in their partner. This work is about owning your own reality, not finding out how bad your partner is.

Once you have your and your partner's profiles written out, step back and look at the connections of your synergistic wounding. How does your wounding intersect with theirs? Do you notice the cause and effect, for example, when they behave in a certain way, you respond in a certain way? Can you see how they respond when you act out in a specific way? That cause-and-effect is how your wounding dovetails with theirs.

Once you recognize something consciously, it is hard to unsee, and an *aha!* epiphany occurs. These are moments of healing. In doing this exercise, you are getting important clues to your own and your partner's woundings.

Take a deep breath, as this is a lot to examine. Know that you and your partner are a work in progress and that none of this can be healed in a day. Allow yourself to feel your feelings. Sit with them and realize they are not going to consume you.

Childhood wounding shows up in many facets of our lives, and none more dramatically than in our close relationships. Each of us has healed and wounded parts that come forth that are directly connected to the attachment styles of our childhood families. Through this work you are revealing to yourself those healed and wounded parts that have always been hiding in plain sight. Once you understand your own personal woundings, you will begin to see how they impact your relationships. Fortunately, you are laying the groundwork for healing these wounds and thus healing your relationship.

CHAPTER 5

Wounded Tools of the Wounded Dance

You were the sweetest thing that I ever knew, but I don't care for sugar, honey, if I can't have you. Since you've abandoned me, my whole life has crashed.
—ANNIE LENOX, "WALKING ON BROKEN GLASS"

I see a lot of couples who yearn for a deeper connection with their partners, but they don't know how to get past the noise of the hurts and unresolved issues to a place of openhearted healing. Most couples just learn to navigate the tough times with their own shorthand and their wounded tools, creating their own dance. Their wounding normalizes the abnormal, giving them a distorted view of how things really are.

If there is discord in the relationship, the partners tend to focus on what they don't have and what isn't working well. As a result, anything good or functional is taken for granted. The focus is on the gaps: what is not working, what they don't have, and what they are missing out on.

For the most part, people don't like to shine a bright light on their relationship and will do so only when things are going badly, when problems are persistent, or when a trauma has occurred in the relationship. This is why so many couples come in to see a psychotherapist only once things are really bad—and they often want to get in right away. They want the quick fix, the "tell us what we have to do to get better." The reality is that most issues aren't a quick fix, but it isn't hard to begin to develop self-awareness.

BROKEN COMMUNICATION TOOLS

You may wonder why couples don't do this work up front in order to determine their synergistic woundings and how to heal them. Most couples will not proactively work on themselves in a holistic way to prepare themselves for a relationship because they think, if it ain't broke, don't fix it, or, we will figure it out as we go. They stay in the same cycles using the same broken communication tools to just get to the next day. They are in a state of reaction, not creation.

As a result of their broken communication tools, couples can get to a point where they establish what I call an *uneasy emotional equilibrium*. They have learned a way to weave their wounding with their partner's wounding, and they adapt, adjust, and react (in a wounded way) to make the relationship as functional as they can. This wounded integration has all kinds of red flags around it, and it is not often functional or sustainable. This is all these couples know, and they live out their married lives in this dance.

An uneasy equilibrium happens because each partner gives up or gives in to enabling the other's emotional wounding. It feels easier to adapt than to do the hard work to make the relationship functional. They learn to dance around difficult topics, and default to using wounded emotional response tools because that is easier and what they know. This is different from compromising; this is each partner's denial that there are real problems in the relationship as evidenced by all the emotional wounding acting out.

Your words and behaviors are the big clues to your and your partner's emotional wounding.

The following sections describe examples of broken communication tools that most couples have used at one point or another.

Shorthand Communication

Couples often go on autopilot and develop what I call *emotional shorthand communication,* in which one partner says something and the other partner knows immediately what it means and how to respond in kind. The wounded inner child can hide behind the shorthand, speaking in incomplete sentences and often with sarcasm, thereby not having to reveal too much.

The downside to this is that couples basically stop communicating complete thoughts. They get used to hearing and speaking to each other in their shorthand language. They stop discussing things in depth and instead rely on the shorthand messaging as a way to express themselves. Shorthand communication isn't always bad, but many couples rely exclusively on shorthand, even for topics that demand more care.

Wounded pain often comes out in these shorthand ways, which can be hurtful and tear at the fabric of the relationship. Name calling, cursing, labeling, shutting down, or leaving the house in a fury are some of the ways that partners tell the other the amount of pain they are in. They use their wounded tools and shorthand to communicate volumes of emotional information. The wounded inner child comes out, and they are no longer talking with each other but using the language of their hurting child self. The shorthand is how their wounded inner child communicates within the synergistically wounded relationship.

Another type of couples shorthand is not as toxic but can still be unhealthy. For example, *I don't want to go to dinner with the Smiths* means to the other partner, *I don't like them very much because they drink a lot.* This shorthand develops over time and is unique to each couple. One partner says a word or raises an eyebrow, and the other partner knows what this signal means. In many ways it is an intimacy within the relationship, a unique language for the couple, but when overused, it has drawbacks and can be limiting.

Shorthand communication becomes part of a convenient wounded narrative couples hide behind.

Many relationships start to falter at this point. They rely heavily on the shorthand, important issues are not discussed, and their emotional wounding goes on autopilot. Words are said impulsively, actions are taken dramatically (using wounded tools), and both partners know what it is all about. The relationship languishes as important words are left unsaid.

Don't Use That Tone with Me

If you haven't heard the phrase "don't use that tone with me" at least once in your life, you haven't lived. It is natural to occasionally speak with a voice inflection that is not helpful to the conversation. Usually people who regularly have a particular tone in their voice don't realize it, so when it is pointed out, they get defensive. *I do not have a tone!* They do not hear themselves talk, but the receiving partner hears their tone as dismissive, condescending, patronizing, or shaming. This shorthand reveals a lot to the receiver. The receiver not only hears the message but also hears and feels the unresolved emotional wounding that the speaker carries, either about this issue or something else. The speaker is trying to communicate complicated feelings in a short punch.

Neutral questions can be turned into something else whenever a certain tone is used. *Did YOU leave this OUT?!* A simple question gets loaded up with the speaker's frustrations, irritations, sarcasm, impulsivity, and projected displaced anger. The receiver, taken off guard, immediately hears the tone and gets defensive, points it out, and then the speaker gets defensive. The question turns into a defensive battle in which there are no winners. The question itself gets buried underneath the noise of all of these emotions trying to come out.

Even though couples use dysfunctional shorthand and feel unhappy or unfulfilled, they avoid delving into emotional landmines. It is easier for them to keep up the elaborate dysfunctional dance of the wounded inner child to maintain an uneasy equilibrium than it is to go into the landmines and bring up sensitive topics.

Hot Buttons

Couples who use shorthand and a tone all of the time have more unsaid than said. They make value judgments about what they want to bring up to talk about. One partner may say to themselves, *I don't want to bring this up because if I do, they will go off on a tangent, and I don't want to hear it (again)*.

Partners learn each other's hot buttons and use them to create elaborate ways of distracting or avoiding topics that need to be discussed. Each partner develops an intricate matrix of what the other likes, dislikes, loves, fears, hates, despises, yearns for, or is addicted to. All of this data is considered when a topic to discuss comes up. When there are a lot of unhealed emotions, each partner operates more and more from a place of wounding (being shut down or in fear) rather than a place of love, trust, and healing. Their wounded inner child is in full swing and uses their wounded tools more frequently; the couple's shorthand becomes the preferred form of communication and hot buttons are pushed.

Making Big Statements

Couples sometimes use big statements or dramatic gestures as shortcuts or conversation enders. These loud "mic drop" moments come in the form of ultimatums, such as threatening to divorce or stating "I'm leaving," "I don't want to talk about this anymore," or "You're crazy," and sometimes even threatening to kill themselves. These dramatic statements are designed to get attention, shut the discussion down, and let their partner know of their emotional distress. They are usually said for shock value. Partners who get loud and storm out of the room are trying to end the conversation just as much as the partner who completely shuts down, withdraws, and doesn't say anything. (These are both controlling moves, which you will learn more about in chapter 17, "The Tug-of-War Controller Archetype.")

Threatening divorce is a dramatic and traumatic statement to make, one that slices through the heart of a relationship.

Think very carefully before you say you want a divorce. Saying this to your partner cuts deep into the fabric of the relationship. Hearing it repeatedly is extremely damaging and leads to a sense of hopelessness for the couple. If you are frustrated in your relationship, want things to change, and want your partner to hear you, there are many other ways to get their attention instead of threatening divorce or making other big statements.

Threatening Suicide

Any time a partner threatens to kill themselves, take it seriously. It is the loudest message one can give to another, letting them know how much emotional pain they are in. If this is a repeated behavior in your relationship, please say something similar to this, and follow through:

> Sometimes you tell me you are going to kill yourself, and this frightens me beyond belief. I love you, and I don't want anything bad to happen to you. I want you to know that the next time you say that you are going to kill yourself, I'm going to take you seriously and call 911. I want you to get the help you need, and I don't want to lose you.

There are two reasons why you need to say this boundary statement to your partner. One is to let them know you are concerned about their safety and want to get them the help they need. The second is for you to acknowledge how much this statement scares you. The person making such a statement is the one in control. They know if they are going to do this or not. You, their loving partner, only hear that they are going to kill themselves, so of course you get freaked out. Most people experience a shock wave of panic when they hear this, and tremendous fear goes through them.

The emotional experience of the person saying they are going to kill themselves and that of the person hearing it are very different. This is true even if the first person says dramatic and outrageous things all of the time. No matter how many times you have heard this, it is still traumatic at some level.

Making the statement that you will be calling 911 or emergency services next time signals to your partner that you love them and that you are serious. You are also setting a boundary within yourself and with your partner that you are looking out for yourself and them. You are not making a threat to call 911, you are drawing a line and saying that this repeated threat and expression of self-harm is too much for you, and you *will* make the call.

Betrayals of Trust

A common issue that shows up in various forms is the loss or betrayal of trust. This complex relationship trauma affects partners in different ways based on their own wounding history. If someone has a history of broken trust issues as a child, when a similar event happens in adulthood, it is incredibly hard to move past; it is hurt on top of hurt. Traumas of trust happen because of infidelities, sharing secrets, sneaking into a partner's phone, and having sexual or emotional affairs, among others. One commonality with those who betray a trust is that, at some level, their wounding convinces them that doing this behavior is fine. This rationalization fuels the betrayal and encourages the wounded pattern to continue.

Once the betrayal is revealed, the one who is betrayed has the longer road to walk, as they experience emotions ranging from shock, sadness, and anger to hurt, rejection, and a deep heart wounding. The one who was wayward and betrayed the trust has their own hard road to walk if they wish reconciliation with their partner. Working to restore trust is effortful and incredibly difficult, more than any pleasure a momentary affair can give. I can't begin to tell you how many times I have heard from a wayward spouse, *I don't know why I did that. It wasn't even worth it.*

Some people who experience betrayals of trust say they cannot move beyond it. I find this to be especially true in cases of repeated sexual or emotional infidelities. Couples can survive this kind of relationship trauma, but they often need assistance. There is so much that needs to be said about betrayals of trust that I cannot devote enough space in this book to do this trauma wounding justice. For more information on this topic, I recommend reading the work of Esther Perel.

If you are struggling with betrayal of trust on either side of this issue, know you can get help from professionals who work with this all of the time. They can create a road map for you so you don't have to spin in the heaviness of confusion, hurt, betrayal, and resentment.

See if you can love your partner for where they are instead of where you want them to be.

You have now learned much about how a relationship can get off course. I want you to know that these negative forms of communication, these wounded tools, can be healed. In chapter 6 you will learn ways to deepen your relationship using the STARR Reset, and in chapter 7 you will learn how to begin to heal these dysfunctional forms of communication.

Texting Your Feelings

I am seeing an increase in couples using texting as their main form of communication. Going beyond the use of texting for arranging schedules and giving quick reminders, more couples are texting as the main way to express feelings or discuss major events. Many say texting feels safer because their partner can't talk back or interrupt. They are effectively curating their communication so that their partner sees or experiences them one way, justifying this behavior as making communication easier.

Overreliance on texting as communication creates a disconnect in the energy of the relationship. It moves the couple one step back from closeness and puts a safety net between them. They get comfortable hiding behind their screens, saying things they can't say in person. They lose context, depth, and tone when they don't hear the spoken word.

Ask yourself why you need a screen or barrier between you and your partner's feelings.

Texting as the primary form of communication speaks volumes about the state of a relationship. Each partner needs, at some level, a safety barrier between them. They don't trust themselves or the other with in-person discussions, and sometimes they want a record of a conversation because they feel their words are often misinterpreted or used against them.

If you use texting as your primary form of communication with your partner, consider the following:

- If you use texting as a way to avoid your partner, why is that?

- Do you use this electronic barrier because you do not feel physically, emotionally, or mentally safe with your partner?
- Have you tried to talk with your partner outside of texts but find that they just won't listen?
- If you were to talk with your partner face to face, how would it go? What problems are there with this form of communication?
- If you were to ask your partner not to use texting so much, how do you think they would respond?

If you don't feel safe talking with your partner outside of texts, there may be deeper issues that need to be looked into, such as domestic abuse, manipulation, and control. Speak with a trained professional about what you need to do to keep yourself safe, as these are complicated relationships. I don't recommend trying to navigate an abusive relationship on your own, as your wounding is what got you into this hurting relationship, and your wounding alone won't be able to get you out of this.

LEVELS OF FUNCTIONALITY

Understanding levels of a relationship's functionality will help you to identify how you and your partner function on a day-to-day basis within your relationship. These levels correlate with the levels of relationship bonding you learned about in chapter 3. Within each level of functionality you may see how a couple's wounding contributes to their situation. Notice that there is no category for a great relationship. Even couples in a "great" relationship have some bumps now and then.

Level 1. The relationship is mostly good, with a few bumps now and then. This couple has good back-and-forth exchanges and is able to work through issues when they come up. They are a good team, pragmatic and heart-centered. There is a lot of love, which is expressed freely and openly. Other couples look to them and want to model their relationship on theirs. Upsets happen, but they get resolved. They each have worked through big parts of their own wounding, and when wounding does show up, it is acknowledged and dealt with right away. The terms loving, steady, and consistent describe this relationship. This couple will usually stay together for a lifetime.

Level 2. The relationship is surviving more than thriving. This couple is just getting by. They have good times when things are going well and when no major trauma events are happening. They have done some work on themselves and may have been to therapy but are not consistent. They are good co-managers of the household and parent well, but they place more emphasis on the kids or outside activities instead of on themselves. As the kids leave the house, they become nervous about what life will look like. This couple will reach a decision point in their relationship when they become empty nesters; they will choose to either come together and reconnect or split up.

Complacency is easy in a relationship that is steady, but even a stable relationship needs to be fed and watered regularly.

Level 3. The relationship has more bad times than good. This couple has a pot of lingering resentment that is ready to boil over, but they pretend it doesn't exist. They live in denial. They aren't happy, and have frequent arguments. There may be times when each partner lives in their own part of the house, separate from the other. They function by avoiding each other. When they do have to come together, they keep it short so they can go back to living independently under one roof. One or both know that therapy would help, but they are scared to look at themselves; it is easier to compensate for their problems than it is to fix the underlying issues. They would rather take antidepressants or antianxiety medications than see a therapist. It will not take much for this couple to slide into quiet complacency or decide that being in the relationship is too much work and split up.

Level 4. Toxic. This couple cannot coexist well. They hardly tolerate each other, and when they do have to interact, the conversation usually erupts into a shouting match, or worse, acts of violence. They yell over each other and don't take the time to recognize or respect the other's pain. Most of the people they know have said they need to divorce, but they stay together because of circumstance, their wounding and misplaced sense of loyalty, or commitment. Unfortunately, something dramatic, like an affair, illness, or death, has to happen to break the cycle. This couple is trauma bonded; they can't live without the other but can't live with them, either. They don't want anything to do with therapy and completely reject the idea altogether. One believes that they can outlast the other, so this couple is often very competitive and carries spite and contempt toward the other. The last one standing wins.

Maybe you recognized yourself in one of these levels. Each one requires work, and if things are not done to heal the wounding within the relationship, the couple has a greater chance to decompensate, unravel, and become worse off. Too many couples rely on what they have always done to make their relationship work, but relationships are living entities that need to be nurtured, encouraged, and given attention.

If you feel despair after recognizing your relationship in one of the more challenged categories, know that there is hope. The path to healing involves first acknowledging where you are so you can develop a plan to get to where you want to be.

Hold a place for the relationship you desire with intention so that you can bring this reality to you.

Take a deep breath and acknowledge the state of your re-lationship. This list of levels is not comprehensive, and the reality is that most relationships are a combination of levels based on the events that are going on in one's life. All is not lost. You will soon receive clear instructions on how to help heal the parts of your relationship that you are concerned about through better communication techniques.

Refer back to your relationship bonding on page 55 and your relationship's level of functionality you just completed. Consider the combination and hold it gently as you do the next exercise.

EXERCISE: HOW YOU FEEL RIGHT NOW

Take a moment now to write a sympathetic and understanding letter to yourself in your notebook. Write something like, *Now I understand that when I feel a certain way and my partner does or says something that triggers me, I am reacting to their words. My reaction is a reflection of our level of bonding and functionality.* Expand on your new insights into yourself and your relationship. This awareness will help you to be consciously aware in the moment when you are interacting with your partner. You will begin to make better choices with this broader view. Keep this letter handy for future reference.

A Way Out of the Maze

How a couple deals with the gaps (disappointments, loss, pain of any kind) in their relationship are make-it-or-break-it decisions. Those who see the gaps as a loving opportunity to become closer and figure it out together are going to make it. Those who see the gaps as a fault of the other, take them personally, and feel resentful will usually struggle.

Feelings need to be addressed before
a problem can be resolved.

There are many ways couples misuse connection opportunities by using their broken tools of communication. In general, the success of a relationship greatly depends on each partner's self-awareness. When we lack self-awareness or introspection, we impulsively run on autopilot, use our couples shorthand, and are reactionary with our partner. We just react to life, going from one thing to the next with no conscious intention about our choices or interactions. This impulsivity is because of a lack of awareness of unresolved emotional wounding. You will read many examples in Part II of how this lack of awareness of emotional wounding plays out over and over in relationships.

What have the exercises revealed to you so far? You probably have some idea of the strong, healthy parts in your relationship and the areas of opportunity for healing. It can be difficult to look at your relationship with a bright light, but this kind of evaluation is necessary if you want to figure out the steps you both need to take to make the relationship more functional. No matter how bad things are now, there are things you both can do to create a better outcome. Making a commitment to open up to yourself and your partner takes great courage and surrender, yet with that courage and surrender comes the chance that the two of you will begin to feel emotionally safer and more openhearted toward one another.

I give myself permission to set down my wounded tools so I can learn and embrace new, functional ways of relating.

In the following chapter you will learn about the powerful STARR Reset process and how to better express your emotional needs. Once you start practicing intentional communication (chapter 7), everything can start to change. Things can get better.

CHAPTER 6

The STARR Reset—Stop, Think, Act, Reset and Repair

When you get into a tight place, and everything goes against you till it seems as if you couldn't hold on a minute longer, never give up then, for that's just the place and time that the tide'll turn.
—HARRIET BEECHER STOWE

Over the years I have noticed, both in my own relationship and with couples coming into my practice, that too often we are in a hurry and say things we don't mean, causing a conversation to go off track. We use our shorthand and our wounded tools, thinking that they completely express how we feel. When this happens, conversations with those we love can derail quickly. I developed the STARR Reset process (Stop, Think, Act, Reset and Repair) as a way to head off or interrupt these wounded tools, thereby allowing space to reset and repair the relationship.

You can begin to use this simple process right away to reset the communication in your relationship and create a path toward reconciliation and repair. In this chapter you will learn about the amygdala hijack and how to override this trauma response in order to calm yourself so you can gain control over your automatic reactions. You will learn techniques for improving your communication to get a better outcome, and how and when to implement the STARR Reset.

The STARR Reset will help to train your body-mind reaction so that your amygdala, a primitive part of the brain and the source of your fight-flight-freeze reactions, does not "hijack" your rational decision-making functions in ordinary situations. The first step is to *stop*, to consciously interrupt the beginning of this amygdala hijack cycle and tell your activated inner child that the responsible part of you will in control. Once you calm this wounded reaction, you then *think* clearly about how you want to respond in a concise, thoughtful way. Next, you decide how to *act* based on your thoughts and assessment of the situation. Finally, you are fully present to *reset* and *repair* the relationship using intentional communication.

When done consistently, this process will help you and your partner to become more emotionally aware, grounded, and able to move away from the impulsive knee-jerk reaction cycle. Using the STARR Reset teaches you how to directly intervene your wounded communication style. Over time it can transform your relationship dynamic.

THE AMYGDALA HIJACK

The amygdala is part of the limbic system, the most primitive part of the brain. Its function is to make the body automatically react to a perceived threat without giving us time to think about it. The amygdala is where the fight-flight-freeze reaction originates, and it comes in handy when we need it. However, the amygdala can also be triggered when it is unneeded and unwanted. Understanding the amygdala hijack will give you a biological reference point behind the dramatic reactions you or your partner have at times.

In contrast to the amygdala, the frontal lobes, located behind the forehead, help us to ascertain what is actually a threat and what is not. This is where executive functions occur, including critical thinking, attention, reasoning, judgment, problem solving, creativity, emotional regulation, and impulse control. The frontal lobes help us to choose patient, thoughtful responses by taking many things into consideration. It is the last part of brain to fully mature, in the mid-twenties. When young adults make irrational and illogical decisions, a contributing factor is that their frontal lobes are still developing.

Daniel Goleman coined the term "amygdala hijack" in his book *Emotional Intelligence*.[1] He describes how the amygdala takes over, or hijacks, the thoughtful, rational frontal lobes and triggers a fight-flight-freeze response, even when it is not warranted. I see this play out in my work when a person's inner child wounding or attachment trauma is triggered and they start screaming at the top of their lungs in reaction to a tame situation. They probably reacted to stressful events this way as a child. Whatever triggered the alarm in the present, the threat feels relative, imminent, and intense, so the amygdala overrides any rational frontal lobe decision-making. The inner child doesn't have any guardrails for emotional behavioral displays, so this attachment trauma wounding spills out with abandon, resulting in outsized reactions. At other times, when the person is not activated, they react in a calm, thoughtful manner.

---

1. Daniel Goleman, *Emotional Intelligence: Why It Can Matter More Than IQ* (Bantam, 2005).

The amygdala of a child who grows up in a chaotic situation or disruptive household is frequently activated. The amygdala partners with the learned responses of the wounded inner child to keep them safe by always being on alert and ready to override the frontal lobes. As this process repeats, the brain learns and adapts, creating outsized reactions around the associated triggers when the child becomes an adult. In my experience, highly anxious or traumatized people have overdeveloped, hypervigilant, generalized anxiety and are defensively guarded, even when sitting in my office, out of harm's way.

Once the person has calmed down after an amygdala hijack, they often feel a sense of shame or regret for reacting in such a way. The rational part of their brain is once again in control, and they don't understand their own reaction. None of it seems logical. Their responsible adult self comes back on line and assesses the situation: *What did I just do?* Without practiced intervention, the amygdala will continue to hijack the rational frontal lobes, activating their inner child and leaving emotional land mines for the individual and their partner to work through.

Over time, you will begin to notice when your amygdala gets hijacked. Once you are able to identify these moments, you can begin to use the STARR Reset. You can learn how to have a more thoughtful response instead of an impulsive reactionary response. You will learn to interrupt the hijack and engage your frontal lobes, helping you to slow down and calm your thoughts. This, in turn, will help you to stop the pattern, breathe, and reassure your inner child that you're safe right now. Once your frontal lobes are engaged, you can think and assess, act on what you want to do next, and then reset the conversation and repair any damage done.

(If you want to do deeper work on these impulsive reactions and heal your inner child, work through the exercises in *Healing Your Lost Inner Child*.)

The STARR Reset

The STARR Reset is a process that interrupts the amygdala hijack and allows you take charge of how you communicate. It is simple to learn but challenging to apply when emotions are running high. It is the first step in working toward healing your wounded relationship and the foundation for restoring and reconnecting in your relationship.

Most people reach a point at which they want negative patterns in the relationship to stop. They reach their *personal threshold*; they are tired of the back and forth, tired of feeling less-than, and they want the toxic cycle to end. When one or both of you reach this point, you have reached your limit. You have healed enough to see the dysfunction, and a curtain has been pulled back, illuminating the wounded dance. You want to stop the cycle and learn another way.

The STARR Reset involves four steps that you repeat as needed to get to a clearer connection with your partner: Stop, Think, Act, Reset and Repair. The goal is to end up with what I call a *clean transaction* between the two of you, with no leftover loose ends or hard feelings. It is designed to get you out of your familiar dysfunctional spiral and into a heart-centered communication flow. Once you begin to use this process regularly and repeatedly, you will be able to catch yourself before you start to impulsively react, allowing you to make better choices the first time and to consciously and intentionally create your couples communication.

The following describes how to use the STARR Reset

process to interrupt a predictable negative chain of events, and how to adapt it to your own relationship.

Stop—This step is to interrupt the amygdala hijack and stop the argument cycle, not to shut down the conversation. You recognize the familiar feeling of the amygdala hijacking your rational brain as you start to have a big reaction. You know the discussion is headed in a disrespectful dead end; you or your partner are saying the wrong things, and that is not where you want to go. As soon as you recognize this, you immediately stop what you are saying or doing. This is your opportunity to change the tone and direction of the discussion, even when the topic is difficult.

Think—This step is when you engage your frontal lobes— the calm, rational part of your brain—so you can think clearly. Take slow, deep, calming breaths in through your nose, out through your mouth, as if you are blowing out a candle. Once your frontal lobes are back in charge, you decide, based on the best of yourself, what action you want to take as you move through this moment, this challenge, and build what you want in the relationship. This is your real-time moment of choice, when you ask yourself: *What is the action I want to take now? What do I want to say?*

Act—Once you have regained control of your impulses and had time to think clearly and calmly, it is time to act. Put into action the behavior, words, or deeds that you thought about. Whether you need to walk away for the moment, ask for forgiveness, or give forgiveness, this is the time to act.

Reset and Repair—You stopped the amygdala hijack from causing an impulsive reaction, you thought calmly and rationally about what you want in the relationship, and you acted in a manner according to that desire. You then call for a reset, asking, *Can we try this again?* Acknowledge that you avoided repeating a familiar, dysfunctional cycle and that calling for a reset is the best way forward. You can now repair: *We've got this. We are getting better at this. We are headed to a good place, facing difficult challenges side by side, communicating better. We are stronger for our differences and are building the relationship we both want, together.*

The STARR Reset requires you both to slow down and contain your feelings enough so that you can put into adult language your feelings about a situation and what you would like to do to resolve the issue and repair the relationship. You both must slow down and treat each conversation as important. You will begin to more clearly see how your wounding and your partner's wounding show up. A reset helps to cut down the noise.

You can use the STARR Reset even when you are in the middle of a conversation and your inner child starts raging, when your amygdala hijacks your rational brain, and when voices raise and accusations start to fly. This is the moment when you say: *We are going to a bad place here, and we need a reset,* or, *We need a time out so we can restart this conversation.* Either way, you need to stay with that conversation, not just put it off and never come back to it.

As you begin to imagine yourself using this process, here are some things to remember.

- You and your partner are trying to work through issues together and are using this process to make the communication better. It will be rough at first because you have never used this process before, so be patient.

- Remember the good and loving qualities your partner has. You may feel high emotion around a topic, but take a deep breath and know that you will get through this. Your partner has chosen to be with you, and at some level they want to work through the issues just as you do.

- Know that you are going to feel many feelings throughout the course of the resumed discussion; that is normal. See if you can reach through your pain to express yourself in the best way you know how so you can be heard. Stay calm and focused on the topic.

Softening the Hard Edges

Many couples have a backlog of unexpressed feelings, resentments, and hard edges that prevent them from having a civil conversation. Hard edges are when couples are emotionally guarded and defensive, or when things are said in spite or with an emotional punch. Their feelings are so loud inside that it is hard for them to express themselves in a grounded way so they can be heard. A lot of couples will say they need to reset the conversation, but it is important to also check in and reset their own emotions first.

It is hard to take back words that are said in anger. Be intentional with your words around sensitive topics.

It is important for you to be grounded and emotionally available when you want to initiate the STARR Reset. Check in with yourself to see if you are feeling:

- scared
- hurt

- emotionally shut down
- agitated
- abused
- resentful
- rageful
- hateful

If you have any of these feelings, see if you can work through them by naming and claiming them in order to identify and soften the hard edges before you try to have a significant conversation. You can write about your feelings, talk with a therapist, exercise, or do some other form of body movement so you are in the right head and heart space. By relieving this pressure inside, you can go into the conversation and express yourself in the way you want to be heard.

> *It's hard to be openhearted when*
> *you are in a place of fear or pain.*

Consciously acknowledging your feelings and putting them to words will help you in your discussions. Your feelings are still there, but you have softened some of the sharp, hard edges. Know that it is hard to debate a feeling, but many people will try to talk you out of yours. Trust that your feelings are your feelings.

Being Open to the Reset

When you soften the hard edges, you are not necessarily taking your feelings out of it, you are helping yourself put your best foot forward in the conversation. As you decide what you want to say, resist the urge to map out your conversation.

When you are in a negotiating, strategic mindset, you may miss the nuances and connection that would be available if you were in an openhearted mindset.

Once you are clear in how you feel, put this into "I feel" language by starting your sentences with "I feel." If you get into *if I say this, they will say that* thinking, this strategy will prevent you from being emotionally available and keep you in a thinking/logical place rather than a softer, openhearted place. This strategic positioning in a conversation usually drives the conversation to where you want it to go instead of hearing your partner and being open to an outcome that you both co-create. Begin by simply saying to yourself, *This is how I really feel. How can I put this into the best possible language for them to hear?* This will get you off to a good start.

Someone once told me that it took him two weeks to find the courage to bring up an issue with his wife, and when he finally did, she was fine with what he wanted to talk about. Don't build the conversations up too much by planning it in your head; this will stop you in your tracks.

After one or both of you has reached your personal threshold and said *we need a reset*, you will begin to use new language to repair and restore the relationship. You can begin your reset by saying, *We need a reset. This is what I'm trying to say,* or, *This is what I meant to say, but it was coming out wrong the first time.* Or, *I know we are learning to talk with each other in a new way, but I think this is important.* Or simply, *Let's start over.*

When the amygdala hijacks the rational brain, you can't run away from it, and you think you are doing something wrong. You are in a reactionary survival state. Just calm down, center yourself, and know you will get through this.

As couples begin to see the need for and use the STARR Reset in their communication, most realize there is a backlog of issues that they haven't discussed in their relationship for years, or ever. They have a lot of containers inside of them that are about to burst from the backlog of unexpressed, unresolved emotional baggage. This is when the responsible adult self steps forward to take control, set boundaries, and become responsible for an outcome while telling the activated wounded inner child everything will be fine. You can discuss these issues with your partner in a thoughtful way one by one, when the time is right.

Setting the Stage for Repair

Repairing the situation is about having empathy for your partner's feelings and acknowledging their struggle. When you have empathy for your partner, you connect to their feelings and express your concern and care for how they feel in a deeper, more heartfelt way. This aligns you with your partner. Instead of saying something like, *This situation must be hard for you*, you express something more heartfelt: *I hear how hard it is for you to be juggling two jobs and doing all of the yardwork, and I'm really sorry. I love you, and we are going to get through this together. It's going to be OK. How can I support you best right now?* This deeper level of reconciliation will do wonders for each of you on a fundamental level. It will be a great gift for you both.

Once you have interrupted the cycle and done a reset, you are both more present in the moment, so now it is time to talk together and begin to repair the relationship. Try these steps to have a successful conversation. Have them in place before you start.

- Slow down and be intentional.
- Limit distractions (put screens away, no TV, no kids around).
- Don't have any alcohol to "loosen you up."
- Think before you speak the first time. Be intentional.
- Be openhearted and willing to join with your partner.
- Stay in a reflective listening mode, not in a problem-solving mode (*I hear you say that you feel this way*).
- Resist the urge to tell your partner what they are thinking or feeling.
- Avoid negative projections (*You always do this to hurt me*).
- Be kind with your words.
- Surrender to the process; connect with your power, speak your truth, stay connected, and trust the process.
- Use "I feel" language, and stay in a feeling place rather than a logical place.
- Avoid personal attacks.
- Paraphrase back what you hear.
- Break down the issue into smaller chunks.
- Stay focused on what you each feel, address the feelings, then go into problem solving.
- Avoid shaming an idea.
- Approach the discussion as a team, not adversaries (*We will figure this out together*).
- Use heartfelt apologies when needed; if you are in the wrong, own that you are wrong.

After you have had a good talk with your partner and expressed your feelings openly, then say to the other, *I love you, and each day I choose to be with you. Even though we are still working through things, we are going to figure this out together.* You can also check in with each other: *Are we good? Is there more we need to talk about? Are there any emotional blocks between us?*

Work toward getting to a place of vulnerability and surrender, where you join with your partner to come up with a solution instead of defending your side of the story.

EXERCISE: AN INTERNAL RESET

As you are learning, we often bring our emotional baggage into the conversation. When we do that, it confuses the conversation and quickly gets it off topic. When you are able to take a step back, try these tools to help you evaluate how you can bring in the STARR Reset to your conversations.

Answer the following questions in your notebook to help you better determine how you feel before talking about the issues in your relationship.

What are the top three issues that you often get into arguments about?

Why do you think these same issues keep showing up?

What are you doing or not doing, saying or not saying, that perpetuates these arguments?

What unresolved emotional issues flare up within you, where you either get really big or shut down, when these issues come up?

How can you explore your feelings about these issues before the conversation so you can use your words more effectively?

How would you say to your partner that you need a reset if you get into your dysfunctional cycles again? Write out how you would say this.

When you check in with yourself and complete this internal reset, you prepare yourself to show up in the best way possible. You are in control of yourself and how you create the experience on your end. Your partner is responsible for how they respond.

Slow down and use your words with care.
This is not a race.

Please note that being hesitant to ask for a reset often points to a much deeper relationship issue. If you are in a manipulative or domestic violence relationship, please seek professional help. The STARR Reset is not meant for these types of highly toxic and volatile relationships. It will not work and is not advised.

Problems are not rare in relationships, but effectively talking through problems is rare because people are scared to do so and don't feel they have the tools. What you are doing with this work is changing how you go into these conversations. From your heart, tell your partner this work is important to you and ask if they will try to join you in this process. Create a safe place for you and your partner to talk about difficult things by saying, *I know in the past it's been hard for us to talk about this, but I want you to know I'm going to try to be patient and listen to you. I'm asking for you to listen to what I have to say, as well.* This is all new for you both, so be prepared for an answer like, *Why are you talking to me this way? What's gotten into you?* Sometimes it may feel like you are taking two steps forward and one back. Resist the urge to back out or say, *This isn't a good time.* Kindness, compassion, and humility are not always at our fingertips. Slow down and find the words that will have meaning. Cleaning up can be messy, but it feels good afterward.

Long-Term Healing

The goal of learning and using the STARR Reset is to help you and your partner learn how to be civil in your conversations and respect each other's feelings. It is meant to get you out of your dysfunctional ways of relating to each other so that you can hear each other and come to a resolution for which you both feel honored and valued.

I think we retain specific parts of any self-help book or process that we resonate with and feel has value. The main message with this process I want you to remember is just to say you need a reset. Couples have come back and said to me, "We had to do a reset last week." Doing this work consistently will give you insights into yourself and your relationship. Hopefully you and your partner can apply the STARR Reset long enough to bring real healing to your relationship. Hang in there, as you are learning new ways to introduce more functional language into your relationship.

Be careful with your words.
They can only be forgiven,
not forgotten.

Now that you understand how to integrate the STARR Reset into your relationship, you can start to put it into practice by using *intentional communication.* Chapter 7 takes a deep dive into changing old patterns of communication so that you can begin to heal your relationship from the inside out by being intentional with your words.

Intentional Communication

*Look out how you use proud words. When you let proud words go,
it is not easy to call them back. They wear long boots, hard boots;
they walk off proud; they can't hear you calling.*
—CARL SANDBURG, "PRIMER LESSON"

As you are learning, your unresolved synergistic wounding is revealed by your word choice with your partner. Doing your healing work and being intentional with your communication will make the difference between a productive conversation, during which you feel aligned with each other, and one that quickly derails. Couples often keep recycling the pain in the relationship because they continue to use the same wounded communication tools and shorthand they have used for years. Putting into place the practical knowledge you are gaining will go a long way toward becoming openhearted, and move you away from being guarded, careless, or defensive in your conversations.

Intentional communication is about being authentic with your words and your truth while being thoughtful with your delivery. All of the communication approaches discussed in this chapter can be used with your family and friends as well as your partner. You are filling up your toolbox with functional tools that will transform the energy and patterns in your relationships.

COMMUNICATION STYLES

We all communicate in our own style that uniquely expresses our personality. The work I am teaching you is not about changing your personality; it is about how to express yourself in the best way to get the best possible outcomes. You will be learning how to speak your truth while you also listen to your partner and begin to really hear what they are saying. As you learn about your communication styles, you will begin to see opportunities where you can quickly change the quality and the depth of your conversation by being intentional with your words the first time. The following section provides a window of insight into how men and women think and feel about communication in general.

How Men and Women Communicate

Women and men process complex emotional information differently. Women need to talk about difficult topics, and men want to think in silence. These examples sound stereotypical, but stereotypes exist for a reason: they play out all over the world. There is a natural dance between the two that complements both. While these differences can be frustrating and confounding, they also deserve respect and even celebration.

Women are as old as they feel,
and men are old when they lose their feelings.
—MAE WEST

The following are some generalizations to keep in mind when talking with another. They may not apply to how you process things, but they might apply to how someone else in your life interacts in the relationship. Having these differences doesn't mean they will break you apart; rather, this is an invitation to become closer.

Men and people with masculine energy:

- want to feel prepared before talking, which is why they retreat to their "cave"; if they talk about something before they are ready, they often lash out because they feel vulnerable, off balance, and exposed. They don't want to appear as though they don't know what they are talking about.
- prefer to be direct and to the point; they want to talk once and be done.
- can process only one, maybe two, issues at a time; they literally get overwhelmed when presented with a long list of things that need to be addressed.
- shut down or freeze up rather than cause further harm; they see this behavior as a safe alternative and not a personal attack.
- see sex as reassurance that they are loved.
- feel that they have screwed up or failed when presented with things that are wrong in the relationship, which results in their shutting down and avoiding any further discussions. They just go to the garage and grumble.

- are not interested in changing or growing; they feel complete as they know themselves in the present. Or, they may know they need to improve themselves, but they don't know how and are not interested in sharing what they perceive as faults with anyone else.
- are sometimes able to receive feelings when they are written down, as this gives them more room to consider and formulate a response (but this approach cannot be the default).
- say I love you and mean it; they don't feel the need to say it over and over.
- have a hard time accessing their words and feelings, so they often perform acts of service (fixing or doing chores) as a way to express apology or love.
- have a "fifty-page manual" for what to do or say that is good (or bad) for the relationship.

Women and people with feminine energy:

- want to talk things through and then revisit the same issue again at a later time. If they don't get to do this, they feel blunted, invalidated, and the conversation feels incomplete.
- can talk about issues at a moment's notice because they often play these conversations over and over in their heads.
- prefer to be indirect and address issues from many different angles; this helps them to feel like they have examined their feelings and not left anything unsaid.
- avoid conflict so as not to upset a friend; they talk with others about an issue but not the person directly involved. If they talk about others behind their backs,

they are perceived as being insecure, gossipy, jealous, or passive-aggressive.

- are great multitaskers and can juggle multiple issues and topics at once with great skill.
- already know of an issue when they are presented with things that are wrong in the relationship; they often see it as an opportunity for growth and healing. They want to talk about the things that are wrong; they aren't afraid to get into a meaty conversation.
- desire intimacy more than sex, and usually only after they feel emotionally safe and nurtured.
- want to stay in the moment and emotionally connected until an issue is worked through.
- need to hear frequently and spontaneously that they are loved.
- talk over men and do not let them think; they are high-level communicators.
- want their partner to read their mind; when the partner fails to do so, they will sulk in silence, perceiving their partner as uncaring, unloving, and not understanding.
- think that when their partner doesn't communicate, he does so on purpose; in other words, they think he has the skills but doesn't use them.
- are interested in personal growth and change; they want to improve relationships to their highest potential.
- are direct in freely expressing feelings with their partner, which is often the opposite of how they talk with friends.
- have a "five-hundred-page manual" on what to do or say that is good (or bad) for the relationship.

Notice the traits that you connect with and those you have a strong reaction to. These reactions may indicate areas where you hold some of your emotional wounding. How you identify and express yourself represents the unique, beautiful, and wonderful person you are.

Learning to talk with the opposite sex is about learning the best way to express yourself so that your emotional expression can be heard and dealt productively. The same can be said for talking with people in general. The goal is to learn functional language to get your message across and to be authentically present with anyone.

Historically, men have been socialized to have bigger expressions of feelings that are meant to be seen and heard. They want to yell and be impulsive. Women are socialized not to make waves and are encouraged to be quiet and undemonstrative. It is important to recognize the baseline for men and women so as to know what most people are starting with and the tools they may need to learn. With all of these contrasts, it is no wonder why women and men are so often mystified by each other.

In his book *Men, Women and Relationships*, John Gray writes that masculine awareness tends to relate one thing to another sequentially, gradually building a complete picture. This perspective relates one part to another part to produce a whole. Feminine awareness is expanded; it intuitively takes in the whole picture and gradually discovers the parts within, then explores how the parts are related to the whole. There is more emphasis on context than content.[1]

---

1. John Gray, *Men, Women and Relationships: Making Peace with the Opposite Sex*, (New York: Harper Torch, 1996).

Thinking versus Feeling Partners

A common pairing in couples is where one partner is more logical or thinking oriented and the other is more feeling or emotionally oriented. *This is not gender specific.* Conflicts often arise within this sort of pairing. For example, if the feeling partner wants to talk about an issue, such as *I feel that you think I'm stupid because you always reload the dishwasher after I have it all set,* the logical partner says, *Well, you don't load it right, so nothing will get clean.* This classic example creates hard feelings (often shame), especially for the feeling partner. Both partners feel justified in their thoughts and feelings. But until the feelings are acknowledged by the logical partner, the "logical" argument about loading the dishwasher will go on far longer than it needs to. The logical partner doesn't hear the shame in their language because they feel justified in their statement.

We all like to think that we are reasonably logical human beings. In reality, the more logical partner is often working off of incomplete information, context that can help enhance a successful, loving relationship. For example, a feeling man might say to his logical wife, *My mother constantly gaslighted my father. One of the ways she did that was to get this look in her eye, purse her lips, then reload the dishwasher "correctly." When you do that to me, it stirs up negative emotional context for me, even though I know it's unintentional. The reality is that loading the dishwasher is small potatoes. Since I am telling you why this bothers me, could you please pick your battles more wisely?* The feeling partner expressing things in this way gives a deeper meaning to the exchange and informs the logical person about why this bothers them.

The classic defense mechanism of a logical person defending themselves via scorekeeping grinds away at what could otherwise be a loving relationship. You will learn more about this scorekeeping in chapter 11, The Scorekeeper Archetype.

How Best to Support Your Partner

To best support your partner, ask what they need. Asking your partner what they need in the moment shows respect and honor. If they are in distress, ask them whether they need comfort, a solution, or a conversation. *Comfort* is giving a hug or words of reassurance; this is good for feeling partners. A *solution* is coming up with alternatives that will fix or remedy the situation; this is good for logical partners. A *conversation* helps them to process the situation, which may lead to their needing comfort or a solution; this is good for both partners.

Asking your partner what they need creates a moment of connection and validation, and allows your partner to be seen. It demonstrates a reciprocation, where you both step up and are present in the relationship, one asking and the other responding with what they need. A good rule is to focus on the feelings first, then join together to create a solution.

Insights to Inner Child Wounding

People who are logical thinkers were often bright children who had to learn very quickly in their family of origin how to survive a complicated or addicted dysfunctional environment. They learned that they couldn't rely on their feelings to help them out if Mom or Dad was raging or spinning out of control. The logical child's (and then adult's) heart was often lonely and missed a closeness and a sense of belonging.

People who are feelings focused were often allowed and encouraged to have a broad expression of their emotional range as children. They learned that it was normal to access their feelings, express themselves, and expect their feelings to be heard. The feelings child's heart naturally looked for others who could hear and see their pain. As adults, they don't understand why others struggle to access feelings naturally as they do.

Children learn at a young age whether their parents can hold their emotion for them or not, and whether they can lean into the adult caregiver. They also quickly learn whether or not the adult is emotionally unstable or unavailable. In the case where the parent or guardian is not emotionally available, the child often becomes overreliant on their mind to help them navigate family dramas. They feel their emotions are not going to help them out, which makes them more confused and possibly hurt. They learn to pack away their feeling self and go into survival mode. This attachment wounding is often the origin of why some adults stay very logically focused and will not want to consider feelings; they are afraid of this unpredictability.

Find one person in your life to show your feelings to; your feelings need to be validated.

One way to look at your relationship is that you probably brought into your life a person who is a master at what you didn't experience as a child; they are often your opposite. If you are a feeling person and chose a logical partner, you may have done so because you didn't have a stable, thoughtful, rational experience as a child. You can honor and appreciate your logical mate by considering their thoughtfulness: *I understand how you have thought this through carefully. I appreciate how you handle these complicated issues.*

Conversely, if you are a logical person and chose a feeling partner, they may need to hear from you something like, *I hear that you feel hurt and neglected when I don't acknowledge what you do around the house*, or, *I hear you when you say you feel frustrated*. This will go a long way toward helping your connection, and your feeling partner will feel heard and seen.

> *Logic isn't warm and cuddly,*
> *but feelings certainly can be.*

Long after fights are over, most people forget what they were arguing about (the logic), but they usually don't forget how they felt. The sting of unacknowledged, ridiculed, or dismissed feelings stays stuck inside and is usually ringed with a degree of hurt and resentment. Feelings hurt the most when they are ignored and when we don't give ourselves permission to, or feel we cannot, express them. Logic and reasoning will always have a place in discussions, but most logical thinkers over-rely on their minds because it is often safer than dealing with feelings.

If you stay focused only on the logic, you are going to get into a logic battle, and it will be hard to join together and come to a resolution. If you focus on the feelings first, each of you are going to feel heard and validated. Then, once you feel heard, you can move on to logic and a solution.

Defensively Guarded Partners

Your partner may get defensive, deflect, start to blame you, or go into a victim mode when you are having a discussion. Just observe this, and don't get distracted by the deflections. You can acknowledge the points they bring up by saying, *I know what you are saying is important, but can we first talk about the issue that I brought up, and then talk about what you want to?* Remember that your partner's inner child wounding may be activated during a discussion. When this happens, you are no longer talking with your adult partner but their younger wounded part. Be clear within yourself and know that you probably won't come to a resolution in the first discussion.

Your defensive partner may bring in their wounded responses by walking away, finding a distraction, using sarcasm or exaggeration, or turning up the volume in a number of ways: yelling, stomping around, throwing things, and so on. These diversion tactics, all of which are inner child wounded responses, are designed to avoid and deflect. Your partner may use their wounded tools to express their feelings, which is a normal reaction for someone who is not familiar with using functional tools. The more they avoid, deflect, and distract, the more unsure or insecure they are, or don't know what to do or say. When you start to see how your partner uses their wounded defenses as protection, have compassion for them, as they are in a state of fear at that moment.

Defensiveness may also be present when one partner wants the other to read their mind, as in the statement, *If you loved me, you would know how I feel.* There are many reasons why someone would behave this way, but it is an unfair test and one in which the partner almost always fails. I often see this in adults who were emotionally neglected as children, usually by emotionally unavailable parents. Expressions of feelings were not encouraged or celebrated, and they never heard *I love you* or *I'm proud of you.* If you feel you are doing this, be gentle with yourself and say, *I see that I expect you to read my mind, and I'm sorry.* If you are on the receiving end, say, *I feel at times that you want me to read your mind, and I can't. I really need you to clearly express what you need from me.*

Shaming Language Self-Check

Words have meanings, even words that we use all of the time and that sound natural to us. When you communicate with your partner, see that you do not use shaming language. This type of communication makes absolute (*you always*) statements about who they are a person. An example of shaming language is, *You are such a loser*, or, *Why do you always do this?!*

A common shaming expression is *You made me feel this way.* In reality, no one else can make another feel a certain way; no one has that kind of power. When you feel upset and triggered, instead of saying, *You make me so frustrated because you always leave your shoes in the hallway*, you can say, *I feel really frustrated because of your shoes being left in the hallway.* You still communicate your feelings, but you own them and your reaction to the situation.

To avoid shaming language, focus on how you feel and what your partner has said they will do going forward. Clearly and respectfully express what you need. Be direct. Avoid making a statement about someone's character, which is a clear example of shaming language. (*Why do you load the dishwasher that way? It doesn't make sense.*) Make a statement about their behavior, not them, such as, *I am frustrated that I have to keep putting these things away when you told me you would do it. I really need your help with this. Is this something you can do?* Slow down, and say your words with thought and heartfelt intention.

CONVERSATION OPENERS

Couples often have trouble starting a conversation when high emotion is involved. People will say they don't know how to even begin. The following are some conversation openers you can use to begin those difficult conversations.

- This is hard for me to talk about.
- I don't know how to say it, but I just want you to know how I've been feeling.
- This might be out of the blue, but something has been on my mind that I want to talk with you about.
- I know we've talked about this before, but it still stays with me, and I can't let it go.
- When would be a good time to talk? I have some things that are on my mind.
- I have put a lot of careful thought into something I want to talk with you about.

Some additional conversation reminders:

- Bring up only one issue at a time, even if there is a backlog of things to discuss.
- Slow down. It's not a race to get through the discussion.
- Use "I" statements and use "I feel" language.[2]
- Don't accuse or use absolute statements, such as "you never" and "you always."
- Know that you and your partner are a team, not adversaries.
- Respect your partner's feelings even if those feelings don't make any sense to you.

Sometimes the road to freedom lies in deciding
you'd rather be happy than right.
—JEN SINCERO, *YOU ARE A BADASS*

---

2. See my workbook, *Healing Your Lost Inner Child Companion Workbook*, for an excellent section on using "I" statements.

Symbolic Letters

Writing stream-of-consciousness symbolic letters is a way to safely get your feelings out, free up space inside of you, and get a sense of where you are emotionally. It is a great way for you to purge pent-up information that you feel you can't say to your partner for whatever reason, and to let go of this heavy energy. Writing these letters, which you *will not* give or send, is not going to solve the issue for you, but you will have a clearer idea of how you feel about the topic.

Don't just *think* about what you would write in the letter; actually write it. You will be surprised how easy it is to let this flow. For an in-depth look at how symbolic letter writing can help you heal your own inner woundings and your relationship, see *Healing Your Lost Inner Child*.

Bringing Up Difficult Topics

Now that you understand how writing symbolic letters can help you to get clear on your feelings and the issue at hand, take a moment to write down some issues that you have been avoiding but know you need to talk about, such as issues you know would upset your partner. Think of it as your wish list of everything you want to talk about. Then look over the topics one by one and ask yourself if individual issues are tearing apart the relationship or if there are personality quirks your partner has that annoy you. (There is real meaning behind the phrase "pick your battles.") Put a star next to those items that you need to talk about. Choose just one to focus on, and write a symbolic letter about it. When you are done, burn it or tear it up. Notice if you feel better.

When you yell at me, I shut down; when you talk with me, we get a lot accomplished.

Sometimes the feeling partner wants to talk about something and the other partner shuts down the conversation by saying things like, *You're being so emotional. I can't talk to you when you are emotional.* If you hear this from your partner, look at how you deliver your messages. Your feelings are not the problem, but how you express them may be. Also consider that all of this may be overwhelming to your partner. If this is the case, then say, *I am working on expressing my feelings in a way that I can be heard. I'm asking you to be patient with me through this process.* Or, *I'm trying to say this the best way I know how, but it's not going to come out perfectly. Can you hang in there with me?* Hopefully your partner will be respectful. If they are not, that is an entirely different issue. Ask them to clarify what they are angry about: *Are you upset with me, or is this about someone else or another situation?*

Once you have talked about an issue, you may have some new feelings rise to the surface. This is normal; you are giving yourself permission to dig for buried treasure. Let the new feelings come forward, examine them, and ask yourself how you want to share this with your partner using your new tools. People will say that they intellectually know all about the situation and the patterns they get into, but they feel emotionally frustrated. This is normal, too, as feelings take longer to process and work through. Hearts take longer to work through pain even though the mind understands the situation completely.

You can fool yourself for a while and ignore a feeling, but that nagging issue isn't going anywhere until you look at it and determine the message it holds.

Talk to me like lovers do, walk with me like lovers do.
—ANNIE LENNOX, EURYTHMICS

Not all conversations can be neatly tied up with a bow, as most of the situations that come up for adults are complicated, involve other people, and have greater impact. When the two of you don't know how it will work out, or you are in a place of fear, you can hold each other's hands or sit close together and say something like, *I love you, and we will work through this together. I don't know what the answer is, but we will figure this out. It's going to be OK. We make a good team.* Or, *I don't need an answer now, but I need to know we are working on this together and that we both have the same goals.*

These types of statements reaffirm your love and connection. You are going to figure it out together; you are committed to each other. This reaffirms the commitment you made to each other long ago, and is one of the fringe benefits of being in a relationship: we can do things together. It also brings a sense of closure to the discussion and gives it a level of importance.

HEARTFELT APOLOGIES

Heartfelt apologies are much more than "I'm sorry." For a heartfelt apology to be effective, both partners need to know what the apology is for. The offended person needs to express how they are hurt using "I feel" language. The remorseful one needs to be careful with the words of apology to avoid offending the other a second time. Most people have heard the *I'm sorry, but* . . . apology. There is no place for this exchange in a heartfelt apology.

It is important to center yourself as you prepare to apologize, and to know that your apology has meaning for the other person. Your partner needs to hear a level of culpability and humility. If the remorseful person robotically says *I'm sorry*, the partner will not take it into their heart center. The half-hearted apology will fall flat, and another level of disappointment will fall over the relationship.

A half-hearted apology doesn't help; it only makes the original transgression sting that much more.

You may have heard an insincere apology before. These apologies are not heartfelt; they are just someone saying words they think the other wants hear. They go through the motions so they can check a box. A disregard for feelings perpetuates the unhealed wounds in a relationship. The same goes for an apology that is used as an excuse to attack. For example, *OK, I'm sorry, but you do the same thing to me, too.* For a heartfelt apology to work, the apologizing partner needs to own what they are sorry for, and then at a later time they can bring up that which they are feeling hurt or offended by, using "I feel" language.

Where there is hatred, let me sow love; where there is injury, pardon; where there is doubt, faith.
—ST. FRANCIS OF ASSISI

Many people feel so embarrassed, insecure, and awkward when they apologize that they want to do so as quickly as they can and then run out of the room. They want to get it over with because they feel the shame of a choice they made that hurt their partner, and they want to drop it quickly.

What I want you to learn here is how to slow down and honor yourself, your feelings, your partner, and their feelings.

As much as you want to get an apology over with because your insides are all torn up, just take a deep breath, compose yourself, and ask yourself, *What do I want my partner to hear right now? What will help them to feel better? What can I do to know that I have repaired this relationship the best I know how, and in such a way that I will feel good about myself afterward?* You are learning to contain your feelings so that you can be emotionally present with your partner. Your partner will remember the care you took in saying a heartfelt apology, and you will feel pride in yourself for stepping up and owning your truth.

Receiving a heartfelt apology tells you that your partner knows they hurt you. You may still be hurting, but you will know and feel that they have a sense of humility and are remorseful.

To give a heartfelt apology, take a deep breath, center yourself, and say to your partner:

I now know that my actions hurt you in these ways. I now know how you have felt and how you feel today. I want you to know it was never my intention to hurt you. I'm sorry for the words that I said to you, and I'm sorry for those things that I neglected to do that I now know I should have done. Going forward, I commit to honoring and respecting your feelings and not shut you out or disrespect you.

If you were on the receiving end of a heartfelt apology like this, you would probably feel incredibly validated, seen, and heard. The partner giving the heartfelt apology must put in intentional thought and practice, because this isn't how most of us normally talk in our relationships. This heartfelt statement uses way more words than we usually use, and it takes longer to say. But when you practice, get used to the words, and understand the purpose of the heartfelt apology, your partner will be grateful for this sentiment. A heartfelt apology shifts the energy between the two of you. You will both literally feel your heart's energy center open up.

If you have received and accepted an apology but still feel hurt or resentful, write some symbolic letters to better understand your feelings. Asking for an apology again once you have accepted one will not help you understand your feelings any better.

FORGIVENESS

Forgiveness is not an absence of consequence.

When we forgive another, we are not letting them off the hook for their transgressions. Rather, we are saying to ourselves, *I don't want to punish this person anymore. I don't like feeling separate, and I don't like this feeling inside. I'm still hurting, and I need them to make amends and show that they are truly sorry.* This is what I call *internal forgiveness.* It is a message to yourself. You can decide if you want to share it with your partner. You can ask for an apology, but you can first begin to transform that heavy feeling inside of you. Writing some symbolic letters may help you work through the feelings so you can get to a place of internal forgiveness.

In the end, hate and fear are healed by love and hope.

Words have power and meaning, and when we use words with care and intention, we shape and define the quality of relationship we want to experience. Most of the disagreements we have in our relationships are not over big things but over everyday annoyances that can tear away at the fabric of the relationship. When you slow down, are thoughtful and respectful, and use intentional language, you leave little room for misinterpretation. You are bringing in new norms for your relationship communication, so be patient with the process. With consistency, your relationship will embody and embrace a much deeper and more heart-centered place through your careful word choice.

Begin to have a greater sense of place and purpose as you craft your communication. This will reflect a new, healed part of you that is coming forth.

PART II

Wounded Archetypes

CHAPTER 8

Synergistic Wounded Archetypes

The meeting of two personalities is like the contact of two chemical substances: if there is any reaction, both are transformed.
—CARL JUNG, *MODERN MAN IN SEARCH OF A SOUL*

When we peer into someone else's life story, we can gain a window of insight into our own struggles. We recognize the human condition, the triumphs and the tragedies, which helps us to recognize the healing work we have accomplished and the woundings we still carry. Through stories and examples, Part II examines the *synergistic wounded archetype*, the personification of overly exaggerated wounded pairings, that are universal the world over. The wounded and healed elements merge within each archetype, manifesting a synergy specific to that archetype.

An archetype is a personification or an embodiment of a collection of traits or qualities that speak to a particular topic or identity. *Healthy synergy* is one in which partners demonstrate more functional and healed expressions; this is usually found in the early relationship stage or after a couple has done some healing work. It results in nicer, kinder, more patient, and more loving behaviors. *Wounded synergy* happens when partners have more drama, dysfunction, and wounded projections; this is usually seen when couples consistently ignore red flags and problems. It results in fearful, anxious, impatient, and untrusting behaviors. The archetypes in Part II are examples of how the wounded synergy can uniquely manifest.

Partners are in synergy when their wounded and healed parts mesh together, completing a circuit. When their wounded parts are louder, they are in wounded synergy. Only when one or both begin to heal do they grow out of this wounded synergistic connection.

There are three elements that show up in the archetypal examples:

- the wounding of the inner child as demonstrated by each partner;
- the synergistically wounded drama that uniquely unfolds for the archetype; and
- the responsible adult self, who uses the STARR Reset to repair and heal the wounded cycle.

When we meet a potential mate, our wounded and healed parts instantly magnetize an attraction to the other, and usually, most of our parts are in a healthy synergy. This deep and primal attraction is hard to explain; it just feels right. However, while it may feel right initially, sometimes the wounded parts of one or both partners becomes bigger and louder than their healed parts, especially when they become more comfortable in the relationship. This is what kicks off their *synergistic wounding cycles*, or what becomes their *wounded synergy*.

In Part II, you will read many origin stories of how the inner child wounding of one person attracted them to the emotional wounding of another. Of course, it is both their wounded and healed parts that inspire two people to come together. Through it all, each partner is living the best life they know how and using the relationship and communication tools they have available. Within each archetype, the synergistically wounded partnership plays out the emotional pain with one partner who is more expressive and one who is more responsive to the expression. The expressive and responsive partners both carry wounded and healed parts; their roles depend on which parts are louder inside and how much power they give to them.

The Expressive Partner—One partner is usually more expressive by what I call *overt wounded behavior*, or adult tantrums. Their wounding is activated and loud (inside and out), they act out their unhealed emotions all over the place, and they are usually unconscious of what they are reenacting from childhood. They see others as the problem or a barrier they are up against. They often take on the victim role.

The Responsive Partner—The responding partner's wounding recognizes this emotional acting-out behavior, these tantrums. They are usually defensively guarded and reactive toward the expressive partner, often through a wounded response of shutting down or yelling back. This relationship dynamic is familiar to both partners. Their wounding is in synergy, subconsciously coordinating with the other's wounded parts to hopefully work toward healing.

This classic stimulus-response cycle is one that synergistically wounded partnerships reenact in their relationships until one, the partner who has more healed parts, reaches their personal threshold and asks for a reset to either begin to repair the connection or come to a new understanding of their next action in the relationship. A personal threshold is reached when one or both partners have had their fill of the wounded dance, and know they can create a relationship that functions better. It is an invitation to heal, not an ultimatum to quit.

Sometimes, all it takes to heal codependent patterns is for one of the partners to realize this wounding, use the STARR Reset to begin to heal the cycle, and set boundaries. This process is about interrupting a destructive and dysfunctional communication cycle that, if left unacknowledged and unaddressed, will eventually lead to a breakdown in the relationship, undermining its fidelity.

As you learned in chapter 6, the process comprises four elements: Stop, Think, Act, Reset and Repair. Each part supports the main mechanism of stopping the spiraling cycle of disappointments, resentments, and bad words. The reset is initiated when one or both partners reach a personal threshold and declare, *We need a reset; let's start over.* How the partners say it is not as important as acknowledging that they are repeating a familiar cycle and perseverating in the toxicity that has developed in their relationship. Once they stop the toxic spiral, they can begin the process of restarting the conversation using intentional communication, thereby leading them to repair their relationship.

The Archetypes

In the next several chapters I illustrate many ways that woundings play out within the archetypes. All of the archetypes and situations are generalized and exaggerated in a black-and-white kind of way. This not a comprehensive list of pairings, and people and partnerships rarely fall into just one of the wounded pairing archetypes. The archetypes will help you to get an idea of how these types of woundings tend to show up in a relationship and how each couple uses the STARR Reset to get their relationship refocused toward a healthy synergistic connection.

You will notice that some qualities of one wounded pair sound similar to another. While there may be some overlap, I give specific descriptions of how certain woundings often play out so that you can see how they may be coming forth in your relationship. In some examples I offer both sides of the coin, or the synergistic wounding of each person. In all cases, one person's wounding is joined with the other's in some way. The couples wouldn't be together if they didn't know, at some level, how to mesh with their partner's personality quirks, addictions, mental illness, or emotional wounding from childhood. As you read each story, see if you can spot the point at which a partner experiences an amygdala hijack and responds inappropriately.

Within each archetype I focus more on the wounded aspects of the pairings to make a point, but they have many healed parts as well, which you will later see come forth when they use the STARR Reset.

We all use the tools we have. They may not be the best or the right tools, but they are what we know in the present. We are all works in progress.

Each synergistically wounded pairing story includes possible original inner child wounds or insecure attachment styles for each partner archetype. In all of the stories, when at least one of the partners acknowledges their wounded pattern, it is very hard for them to continue in the same way because they now know more about how the synergistic wounding shows up in the relationship. As you read over the archetypes, notice the similar wounded traits that keep showing up and how each couple uses their unique strengths and personalities to navigate their struggles.

As you read, you will see the inner child wounding of each partner and how this shows up in their wounded tools. Write down the wounded tools you connect to and use yourself, and compare them to the ones listed for each archetype. This will help you to determine which archetype you most closely align with. You may also want to refer back to your list of triggers and use your wounding profile sheet as a reference. You may see how you use the wounded tools found in many of the archetypes; this is normal, as we all use a combination of wounded and healed responses to navigate our relationships.

How you see your own synergistic wounding will not be exactly how it is described in each archetype. If you see yourself in an archetype, you may connect to how that archetype's wounding played out in their life. For other archetypes, you may connect to part of their origin story, but your life journey shows up differently. You don't have to connect to all of the qualities within an archetype; they are simply guides to give you an idea of how your wounding may reveal itself in your relationship. The point is to help you foster a sense of cause and effect so that you can begin to figure out your situation, discover the wounding that you and your partner have, and find a remedy.

Reality shows are popular for a reason: we get to
see how someone else is worse off than we are.
What is normal for one is abnormal for another.
In the end, we are each our own reality show,
playing out our dramas with those around us.

As you read the archetypal stories, you may be tempted to project who you think is the "good" partner and who is the "bad" one. We are trained to put people into these binary categories, but I want you to understand that even though some of the *behaviors* are good or bad, each partner is trying their best with what they know; determining whether they themselves are good or bad is not productive. Most people do not purposefully set out to screw up their relationship or date or marry the "wrong" type of person.

You will probably recognize in these archetypes stories your own children, extended family, friends, and others you know. The stories can provide a window into how the personalities of people you know interconnect with their partners, and it will be eye opening. However, as fascinating as it is to diagnose and figure out your friends and family, I encourage you not to be distracted by this and to bring your work back to your relationship and the wounding that the two of you carry. This work is about helping you achieve the type of emotional closeness that you desire.

You can reach a place of healthy synergy with your partner; it just takes time, patience, and intentional communication with each other.

To get more out of this experience, I highly recommend that you complete the exercises from Part II of my *Healing Your Lost Inner Child Companion Workbook*.

Please note: All of the archetypes are amalgamations of various couplings. Any resemblance to anyone living or dead is purely coincidental.

CHAPTER 9

The Wounded Hero and the Rescued Victim Archetypes

Hard times don't create heroes. It is during the hard
times when the "hero" within us is revealed.
—BOB RILEY

From classic fairy tales to adventure films, the relationship dynamic of the hero and the rescued plays out in our collective subconscious. The wounded hero and rescued victim archetypes exemplify this common wounded pairing.

More so than any of the other archetypes, the hero and the rescued need each other to complete their synergistic wounding. Their wounding synergistically calls out to the other to complete a wounded cycle. The hero looks for someone who needs help and rescue, and the victim seeks out a hero. The roles are not gender specific. We all have a bit of this synergistically wounded archetype pairing in us.

Seeing someone in distress, the wounded hero steps in and takes control to make sure the person they perceive as needing rescue is safe and protected. The rescued victim, unaware of their own wounded cycle, doesn't have self-agency and is unsure of how to get themselves out of their situation. The rescued victim feels overwhelmed and victimized by life situations, such as money problems, health issues, a poor living situation, and child care. The wounded hero sees these as problems that they can help fix. Being smart and creative, the wounded hero starts to come up with ways to solve them, and the rescued victim welcomes any help to make their situation better.

This sounds like a perfect match, as the wounded hero gets their need to be a hero met and the rescued victim has their need to be saved fulfilled. If it were as simple and straightforward as this, it would seem like the world would be a better place if there were more heroes. The problem comes in when the wounded hero and the rescued victim play out this drama in a wounded, subconscious way. Neither one is aware that they subconsciously reenact their hurts and perpetuate their internal dramas. They are not moving forward in their healing, they are spinning in their inner child wounds.

There is a third element to this dynamic, which is the persecutor. The persecutor is a person or situation that completes what is termed the *drama triangle*. All of the people in the drama triangle are wounded folks, and their wounding is fed by the others. Each plays out their wounding with a lack of conscious thought or boundaries. They are usually all good people who make bad, self-limiting choices that keep them in their wounded cycle.

(Please note: If the rescued victim has a persecutor who is a domestic violence abuser, it is crucial that they consult a trained professional before engaging with anyone who is prone to violence. An abuser is rarely interested in repair or reconciliation.)

This synergistically wounded pairing often has a very rocky relationship. A lot of this is due to the fact that the wounded hero wants to be in control, but when things are stable, the rescued victim, not liking stability, will often create chaos by re-engaging with the persecutor or creating another situation that causes a mess. This confuses the wounded hero, who doesn't understand why the rescued victim keeps creating problems.

The wounded hero and the rescued victim often come to resent each other for the very reasons they were attracted in the first place. They resent being stuck in their wounded cycle, but their wounded part doesn't see the path for them to unfold into their greatness. The wounded hero doesn't understand why the rescued victim can't change, as the wounded hero easily sees the solution, but the rescued victim isn't interested in healing their wounding or this perpetual cycle.

The most likely wounded synergistic pairing for this archetype is the wounded hero, who is the oldest in an alcoholic or emotionally unavailable household, and the rescued victim, who has a lot of insecurities but is also passive-aggressive in getting their needs met.

The Wounded Hero Archetype

The wounded hero is lost in their own wounding: that of needing outside validation for their sense of worth. The wounded hero needs to find people and situations that need fixing, and when they come upon someone who is needy, they pull out all the stops. If the wounded hero is single, they go from one relationship to the next fixing problems. Once they fix all the problems with one person and are no longer needed, or the rescued victim develops strong boundaries, the wounded hero looks for other people and other situations to help.

The wounded hero does lots of things to rescue the victim and fix a situation. They expect the rescued victim to love them even more, even after the hero gets burned out. When the rescued victim doesn't acknowledge or treat them any better, the wounded hero becomes resentful and says things like, *I'm trying to be nice doing all of these things for you. I expect you to treat me better because of all of the efforts I've made to help you.* Alternatively, the wounded hero becomes the martyr, doing all of these things selflessly. Without good boundaries and self-care, they burn themselves out in the process.

> *The wounded hero is a lost soldier always looking for someone to save from distress; in doing so, they hope to save themselves.*

Rarely will the wounded hero voluntarily move on from the rescued victim when there are still problems to fix. The hero sees rescuing as their life's mission, so the last thing they want is to be relieved of duty or abandon their post. In many ways the hero is trying to save a wounded part of themselves.

Wounding Origins of the Wounded Hero

The hero often comes from a family where there is a sense of being loved but no one ever hears "I love you." This emotionally unavailable family often has some kind of drama or ongoing unresolved issue that feels chaotic to the wounded hero. Usually the oldest child, the wounded hero tries to be the fixer wherever they go. Siblings of the wounded hero look to them with either admiration or resentment. The hero sees that it is their job to try to fix the family and make it as functional as possible. The hero gets used to adjusting and adapting to many different out-of-control or unpredictable situations, which is their training ground to be the hero to many as an adult.

Wounded Tools of the Wounded Hero

The wounded tools that the hero learned from childhood trauma include:

- being controlling
- overcompensating
- being lost in fixing and protecting
- feeling hurt when others don't accept help
- wanting to be seen as the hero to hide internal shame
- feeling angry when things don't work out
- feeling resentful
- enabling others
- acting in a passive-aggressive manner
- having poor self-care and a lack of boundaries

THE RESCUED VICTIM ARCHETYPE

The rescued victim carries a lot of wounding around issues of self-love and self-worth. This wounding plays out in their not being able to hold on to a job, having broken relationships, and generally sabotaging their life. The rescued victim doesn't have a sense that they are part of the problem, as they feel victimized by life. They continually turn over their own sense of power to the wounded hero or the persecutor, or both.

The rescued victim doesn't always see what the wounded hero does for them because they are lost in their own wounding and expect to be rescued. After all, they aren't used to taking care of what they need, so they don't know the efforts the wounded hero has to make to do the rescuing. As a result of this and for other reasons, the rescued victim burns through many relationships.

The magical thinking and chaos of the rescued victim's self-sabotage keeps them from seeing the underlying wounding that perpetuates the drama.

The rescued victim finds a wounded hero who is either a basically good person or a narcissistically wounded, persecutory, or abusive person. Ironically, the rescued victim eventually pushes away any goodness that their hero does to make their life functional, because the victim knows chaos, not stability. The rescued victim begins to resent what they perceive as the hero's control or dominance, and will become passive-aggressive toward the hero, as their inner child wounding doesn't want things to be functional. Sometimes the rescued victim sees the wounded hero as a persecutor or very controlling. It is the construct of the devil and the angel: the victim usually seeks out both in order to stay in their wounded place.

Wounding Origins of the Rescued Victim

The rescued victim comes from a chaotic or disorganized household in which their needs were not met, or they didn't feel validated or seen. But unlike the wounded hero, they don't have any sense of responsibility to fix or take care of any of this drama. Instead, the rescued victim just goes along with things and is buffeted about like a small boat being tossed around in the ocean. They are reactive, not interested in planning, and then, when things go wrong, they either blame themselves (*poor me*) or, more likely, find a persecutor or situation to blame. They feel others don't understand them, but when others try to get to the root of the issue, the rescued victim pushes this help away because they don't want the drama to end. The rescued victim is often the middle or the youngest child in the family.

Wounded Tools of the Rescued Victim

The wounded tools that the rescued victim learned from childhood trauma or wounding include:

- feeling like a victim
- wanting others to see the chaos, hoping that someone will step in
- seeking attention, which then feels like love
- creating chaos to deflect attention from the real issue
- perpetuating the drama triangle
- unconsciously sabotaging
- feeling resentful
- acting passive-aggressive
- escaping into a fantasy life
- getting lost in dependency
- having poor self-care and a lack of boundaries
- unplugging from responsibility

SYNERGISTIC WOUNDED PAIRING—TROY AND MIA

Troy and Mia are a typical wounded hero and rescued victim pairing. They met at a community garden where they both rented plots for the summer. Troy liked that Mia brought her daughter along to help. Soon they began spending time together and helping each other garden. Troy was a handy guy, and he began doing repair work around Mia's house. They soon started dating. Mia felt relieved because her father was out of state and she couldn't afford to pay for the repairs. She was also overwhelmed by her ex, Logan, who used abusive and threatening language toward Mia, especially when it came to their daughter. Mia worked two jobs but always struggled with money; she sometimes bought things she couldn't afford.

Troy had had a steady job for over ten years, and he didn't have any debt. With all of Mia's issues that needed to be addressed, Troy was in full-on hero mode. He was reenacting his own wounds of needing to fix and control in order to have a sense of value and worth. He didn't see that he was overstepping and taking over Mia's life; he just saw that he was solving problems and making things "better."

Mia, the rescued victim, gratefully accepted Troy's help, which then fed into his need for validation and a sense of accomplishment. Troy and Mia didn't consciously realize that they were feeding each other's wounded needs. Their synergistic wounding was activated at this point, and they began to fill a need to satisfy their familiar childhood roles. Between their mutual attraction and synergistic wounding, Troy and Mia got into their relationship quickly.

Mia was getting her needs met, and her life was more functional, at least for the moment. Over time, she became dependent on Troy to fix and solve her problems, and Troy enabled her so that she didn't have to learn how to fix and solve her problems on her own. She felt protected, and Troy subconsciously liked her dependency; he felt needed. All of this felt right to both of them, and their friends and family were happy for them. From the outside, their relationship looked functional.

Mia's ex, Logan, her daughter's father, played the role of the persecutor in the drama triangle. He was a mean man who was jealous and could be vindictive. He didn't like the idea of Troy being in his daughter's life. Logan often threatened to take Mia back to court over parenting time or how much he was paying her in support. He harassed her, and would not bring back their daughter on time when he had her. Troy saw all of this and felt helpless. The more he felt out of control, the more projects he did around Mia's house to have a sense of control over something. He even started to give her money.

In the drama triangle, Mia and Troy felt that they were both aligned against Logan. This began to complicate and muddy their relationship, and their discussions were frequently about how to outmaneuver Logan so he wouldn't hurt Mia again. Troy was beginning to feel that he got more than he was looking for with this drama triangle, but he loved Mia. Mia felt trapped by the situation, and didn't see the role she played in continuing the drama triangle.

When Mia didn't set boundaries with Logan, he would take more. When Logan would become "big," Mia would back down. Troy would then feel protective and step in, trying to control the situation to protect Mia, but Troy could not be around when Logan stopped by. This pattern kept recycling, and none of them were happy.

Mia saw herself as a victim of the situation and in conflict with persecutor Logan. Troy saw Mia as a victim of circumstance; he didn't see her lack of boundary-setting. They were both getting their needs met but in a dysfunctional way. They were lost in their own woundings and playing this out unconsciously.

The STARR Reset for the Wounded Hero
and the Rescued Victim Archetypes

If you recognize your relationship in these archetypes, know that the STARR Reset will be a learning curve for both of you, but it is not impossible. This work is about teaching you to be consciously aware and to see when, where, and how your emotional wounding comes forward. If you think you enact the wounded hero or the rescued victim, see if you can take in the following messages to help you heal.

Stop—People who are either the wounded hero or the rescued victim are entrenched in their roles. They can't see how their emotional wounding comes out because they are so lost in the drama of it all. The challenge for the wounded hero is to see that what they are doing is ultimately not helpful, which is in strong contrast to their original intention. The rescued victim needs to have a flash of insight into the pattern they are in and how they keep giving away their power.

Think—If you are the wounded hero, your challenge is to not rationalize or intellectualize the situation, as in, *If I don't take care of it, no one else will.* This keeps you caught in the rescuing loop. Observing how you are hurting instead of helping your partner would be eye-opening.

If you are the rescued victim, your goal is to observe and analyze why you don't use better boundaries as a way to address your issues. You need to consider why you like to depend on someone else to fight your battles or solve your problems.

You both need to ask yourselves what you want, and how you want your lives to look and feel.

Act—If you are the wounded hero, you can describe to the rescued victim all of the things that you are going to continue to do, but you can also detail things that you would like your partner to do for themselves. When your partner hears you talk about boundaries, they will feel nervous and uncertain, which could trigger feelings of abandonment.

If you are the rescued victim, you may have tried to take care of your own issues in the past, but without strong, consistent boundaries, maintaining this stability is hard. You can talk with your partner, and even your persecutor, describing your feelings using "I feel" language without explaining *why* you feel the way you do. In other words, simply state your feelings.

Both of you need to employ strong boundaries within yourselves and with each other for this process to work and be healthy.

Reset and Repair—Once you both have identified your feelings and what you want to do about them, you can start the repair process by listing things you need to claim and clarify or apologize for.

The wounded hero can say something reassuring, such as *I'm going to be there for you. I love you. I know you are very strong, and I believe in you. I'm going to try to pull back from always stepping in and trying to make things better for you. This will be hard for me, as helping is what I know to do. I'm going to work on learning new ways to express my love and concern for you other than fixing, rescuing, and controlling your life.*

The rescued victim can begin to own their strength instead of always leaning into the hero. They can say something like, *I feel grateful for all of your help. I am going to try to do more things for myself so that I can feel good about my own efforts. I am starting to feel my own power, and I'm learning to speak my truth.* This may be hard for the hero to hear because they may take it personally, almost as a rejection. But this is a boundary statement, not a statement of rejection. The one who is used to being rescued is taking more responsibility for their life and moving away from always relying on others. The hero will have a hard time giving up control, but this boundary statement will help the hero and the rescuer. Both are learning how to be responsible for their own feelings but in different ways.

Healing the Wounded Hero

If you identify with the wounded hero, you need to know that you are a good person and that all of your efforts have indeed made things better. The hero is playing out inner child wounding, which will not heal until boundaries are put in place. Stop the cycle; stop acting to automatically fix and rescue. Your hero skills will still be needed, but instead of deciding that someone needs you, let that person reach out to you. Follow their lead and respect their journey. Observe your life and your relationships, and see where you have overstepped or did too much in order to make things better. Use wise discernment and practice better internal and external boundaries.

Ask yourself: Have I overstepped my bounds trying to be the hero? Have I gotten upset when others have not done what I said so that they would be OK?

If you connect to the energy and expression of the hero, say this intention for your wounded inner child:

I know that even though things were chaotic or out of control when I was growing up and I tried to make them better, I don't need to continue to do that in my adult life. I am safe and loved, and I trust that others are able to take care of themselves and ask me for help when they need it. I am a good person and am surrounded by loving family and friends. It's OK to be me and not do things for others all the time.

Healing the Rescued Victim

If you identify with the rescued victim, you can stop giving away your power by claiming and stating your truth. Set boundaries with your hero by saying, *Let me see how far I can get on my own, and I will let you know if I need some help.* By setting this boundary, you are letting yourself and your hero know that you are going to work hard at taking care of yourself. You may indeed need your hero to step in, but this process will help you move away from being dependent on the hero's help. Set boundaries with your persecutor or persecutory situation by making boundary statements to protect yourself.

You may find yourself resisting change because you don't want to give up this familiar role. If you recognize this, watch out for trying to make the wounded hero into a persecutor in order to keep them engaged in the cycle. It is not unusual in the drama triangle for the victim to make the same person their rescuer and persecutor, alternating how they perceive the other's actions and how they treat them. This is manipulation on the part of the rescued victim.

Ask yourself: Have I relied too much on the hero to rescue me? Have I gotten lost in depending on the hero's help? Do I escape into a fantasy life or sabotage things so the hero will have to come back? Have I given away my power to a persecutor so I don't have to feel my strength?

If you connect with the energy and the expression of the rescued victim, say this to your inner child:

I am very strong and capable. I no longer need to believe that I am stuck with someone persecuting me or rescuing me. I know that at times I like when people step in to help me, because this reminds me that I am loved. But I am learning how to see and feel this love in ways other than people doing things for me. I am loveable, and I am capable of setting good boundaries and making grounded decisions. Creating stability in my life will help me heal.

The STARR Reset—Troy and Mia

As Mia became stronger and better with internal and external boundaries, she became tired of the push-pull dynamic with Logan. He would do anything to cause trouble or chaos, and Troy always wanted to step in and rescue. But this time was different. Mia realized, through her introspective work, that Troy wanting to defend her and getting upset was not helping their relationship. She was caught between Logan and Troy. Mia decided to use her new skills and apply the STARR Reset.

Stop—Mia reached her personal threshold and said to Troy, "I don't want this drama to continue with Logan, as it's affecting our relationship. I want it to stop, and I have some ideas."

Think—Earlier Mia had asked herself what she wanted to do in this situation. She didn't want the drama with Logan anymore, and as much as she appreciated Troy's efforts, she didn't want him to keep stepping in. Mia realized she needed to speak her truth with Logan and set firm boundaries. She also needed to declare a boundary with Troy. She needed to step up and protect herself, to own her truth, and to stop pushing this off onto Troy to fix for her.

Act—After realizing the boundaries she needed to set, Mia said to Troy, "I really appreciate how you look out for me and want to fight my battles, but I need to speak my truth to Logan."

Feeling apprehensive, she then told Logan, "I feel disrespected by your actions toward me, and I only want to communicate via text. You can no longer show up at my house unannounced, wanting to see our daughter." Mia reached deep inside for her strength to give this message to Logan. Predictably, he said that she wasn't going to tell him what to do. This set Mia back, but she remembered that manipulative people rarely honor boundary statements because it goes against what they want. Mia knew she had a tough road ahead with Logan, but she was prepared.

Reset and Repair—Mia said to Troy, "I love you, and I'm glad we are together. You are helping me to find my inner strength. I know you've always supported me, and I'm stronger for it."

Troy, seeing how hard she was working on her issues, said, "I love you, too, and I am so proud of how you are standing up for yourself. I always knew you could."

Mia was able to apply the STARR Reset because she had prepared herself to do the work. This was a complicated dynamic, as Mia first had to have clarity within herself about what she wanted and didn't want. She found her internal clarity, boundaries, and strength by understanding her wounding and how it kept showing up in her relationship.

Mia was not responsible for Troy's or Logan's boundaries, only for her own. She had to come up with boundary statements for the two men. She expressed her boundaries with Logan and will need to continue to do so, as manipulators rarely take "no" as a complete sentence. She also had to let go of her victim narrative.

Mia and Troy now have a more solid relationship with just the two of them. Mia became more responsible with money once she realized that she can take care of herself. She demonstrated that she was capable so that Troy could see she wasn't always the victim in distress. Through Mia's consistency, Troy sees that he doesn't have to help her as much.

The wounded hero and rescued victim pairing is, for the most part, a loving connection. There is a lot of goodwill, and a genuine desire to help and for things to work out. This couple can get along very well and have a productive life together if they both heal to a degree where their wounding does not play out in such a loud way. They will be able to have a respectful connection with good boundaries and a healthy regard for the other.

LOOKING INWARD

How does the synergistic wounding of this couple remind you of your own wounded struggles within yourself and with your partner? What were some of the inner child woundings that you connected to? How does this match with your own story? What was activated inside of you when you read how this couple worked on their communication using the STARR Reset? Record your impressions in your notebook, as this will help you heal your wounded patterns.

CHAPTER 10

The Blame-Shame Game Archetype

*Sometimes we are just the collateral damage in
someone else's war against themselves.*
—LAUREN EDEN, "COLLATERAL DAMAGE"

The Blame-Shame Game archetype is represented by one or both partners not taking responsibility for their actions and directly or indirectly blaming and shaming the other. It is easier to point fingers than it is to own what one has done to someone else. Frequently these partners use absolutes in their accusations, such as *you never* and *you always*. They mirror to the other that which they cannot own themselves.

Shame = I am bad.
Guilt = I did something bad.

The Blame-Shame Game Pairing

Partners who play the blame-shame game often feel depleted and victimized because there is rarely a resolution to their situation, nor do they always want one. The blame-shame gamer chooses someone with low self-esteem or someone they can boss around. Both feel less-than and try to gain emotional traction by putting the other down so they feel greater-than. Someone who blames others is afraid take a hard look at themselves. They usually have a high level of shame or self-criticism that is projected onto others.

Blame-shifting is when someone says or does something wrong and then dumps this onto someone else so they don't have to take responsibility. They might apologize, sort of, and then push the blame back, not wanting to take responsibility. *I'm sorry I did this, but you always . . .* People who blame-shift have difficulty accessing their own emotions, rarely take ownership of their behaviors, and are reluctant to admit any faults.

The most likely synergistic pairing for this archetype is one who has a low sense of self, feels justified in their behaviors and thoughts, and then projects this onto their partner and one who has low self-esteem and gives away their power.

Wounding Origins of the Blame-Shame Game Archetype

The blame-shame gamer didn't start out blaming others, but they learned that it was easier to use this wounded tool to protect themselves from other family members than it was to own their choices and apologize. They grew up in a controlling or judgmental household, where arguing and emotional turmoil were always present. The child's feelings were ignored or dismissed, and they struggled to know how to fully express their emotions. Inner child wounding develops from this family dynamic when the child is blamed for things they did not do. The child then develops a defensive posture to emotionally survive in the family and not get swallowed up by the projected shame.

In this type of childhood family, showing humility and being apologetic are seen as weaknesses, leaving the child open to direct criticism from others. Any attempt at showing empathy or forgiveness is seen as an undesirable trait, and the family dynamic ridicules (shames) this out of existence. To them, an apology represented vulnerability and weakness.

This family dynamic is often *enmeshed*, which means everyone is in everyone else's business and judging them. This creates wounding in two ways: one, the child doesn't feel they have any right to set a personal boundary (resulting in not feeling safe), and two, the child begins to criticize themselves or others because this is what was modeled or projected onto them.

The blame shifter blames how they are as an adult on situations that happened in childhood. They hide behind this victim wounding instead of looking to heal it and move on with their life.

Wounded Tools of the Blame-Shame Game Archetype

The wounded tools that the blame-shame game archetype learned from childhood trauma or wounding include:

- pointing fingers—finding fault in others' imperfections
- holding back and testing behaviors
- stewing old hurts
- blame-shifting

- giving half-hearted apologies with strings attached
- orchestrating situations to feel victimized
- staying defensively guarded
- shutting down
- not taking ownership, and pretending that they are not at fault
- projecting insults at others, even when unprovoked

Synergistic Wounded Pairing—Mary and Kurt

Mary and Kurt are a typical blame-shame couple. The blame-shame game provided a good cover for them to avoid dealing with their core issues, as they were always looking for the next target to blame. Pointing fingers at one another or others was a great way to deflect and distract, and it set up a victimhood dynamic between them. They each felt victimized by the other. Mary blamed Kurt for why she was upset, and he blamed her reactions and yelling for why he was upset. He would try to overpower her with his bigness and yelling, but she would just yell back, trying to match his energy.

They would pass the buck instead of saying, *Yes, I made a mistake, and I'm sorry*, and asking what the other person would own about their choices. They didn't want their blame-shame game to end; if it did, they wouldn't know how their relationship would change. Staying in the cycle was easier for Kurt and Mary, even though they would say that they were tired of it.

Mary didn't want to be overtaken by Kurt, so she would defend her ground. Inside, though, she would go into a shame spiral and tell herself how bad she was and that what Kurt was saying was true. After most conversations, she felt worse about herself, and she was tired of his half-hearted apologies

(*I'm sorry, but . . .*). Initially, Mary wasn't a blamer, but she saw that Kurt blamed her a lot, so she started giving it back. They were in a vicious cycle.

Their projected blaming and shaming sounded like this: *You never help me out, Kurt. I always have to do everything myself. Why can't you treat me like you do your best friend? Well, Mary, I would help you out, but you don't treat me like a friend. You're always yelling at me.*

Kurt grew up in a household where yelling was normal and shaming others was used as a weapon. He learned how to shame others to get them to submit to him. If he was caught red-handed about something, he would lie or otherwise get the attention off of himself. Mary grew up in a household where her parents yelled. This scared her, so she would become smaller and lose her voice. She felt things were her fault even when they weren't. Kurt's inner child wounded tool of shaming and blaming matched Mary's inner child wounding of feeling less-than.

THE STARR RESET FOR THE
BLAME-SHAME GAME ARCHETYPE

If you recognize your relationship in this archetype, be honest about it and begin to forgive yourself. You don't need to shame yourself or someone else anymore.

Stop—The stopping process is not easy. Most people get so used to saying mean things to themselves and their partners that they think it is normal behavior. The first step in healing is to recognize when you do this. When you are about to blame or shame someone else or yourself, you can literally stop yourself mid-sentence. Stay with it and keep practicing.

Think—If you are the blame-shame giver, think about how you feel and what you want to do instead. What do you think led to your feeling defensive and wanting to shame or blame-shift? Why did you say or do something that blamed or shamed your partner? What do you think are the wounding experiences from your childhood that led to this behavior? See if you can determine what the triggers are that precede your blaming and shaming.

If you are the one being blamed and shamed, think about how you feel when you hear this from your partner. What is going on inside of you at the moment when you see or hear this familiar blame-shame cycle? What would you like to communicate to your partner? Think about other ways your synergistic wounding has drawn you to someone who blames and shames.

Act—If you are the blame-shame giver, begin to talk with your partner about what you think you are doing. If you are on the receiving end, ask yourself why you put up it. See if you can work through these issues in conversation with your partner. This acknowledgment may be hard at first, so start with small things. This may be a real stretch, but use the intentional communication tools you learned in chapter 7 to begin the conversation. Talk about what keeps happening, and work toward your reset and repair.

Reset and Repair—The repair process works best if the one blaming and shaming can humbly and vulnerably give their partner a heartfelt apology right away. *I'm sorry I just said that. This is what I meant to say.* Acknowledge the emotions you feel to let your partner know what is going on inside of you (not to justify or defend your choices). Resist the urge to put up your defenses again with another blame-shame attack.

If apologies are hard for you, read Heartfelt Apologies in chapter 7 again. Your consistency will help your partner feel reassured that you are trying to repair this destructive cycle because you see how damaging it is. Make an internal boundary commitment to yourself that it is your intention not to blame or shame. If you feel strongly about this, tell your partner this is what you are going to try to do for yourself and the relationship. Recognize when you blame-shift, and stop this behavior. Write out your commitment to yourself going forward.

Healing The Blame-Shame Giver

The blame-shame giver's wounded inner child carries deep hurts and projects them onto others. This behavior is seen in their comments, such as *Really? You're going to do that again?!* or, *Why can't you ever do this the right way the first time?!* These comments might seem rational and logical to the blame-shame giver, but the receiver hears them as shaming, ridiculing, and hurtful.

You may not know if you are blaming and shaming others. If you don't know but suspect you are, ask those around you, in a moment of bravery, for their feedback. If you do blame and shame, it will not take them long to come up with examples. With humility, thank them for their feedback, as this knowledge will help you heal.

In your notebook, write out mean things you say to yourself or your partner every day. Next to each item, write out what you would like to say instead. You may be amazed at how much of a bully you have been. *Get this for me. No! I told you I wanted that! Why can't you listen to me? You are so stupid sometimes. No, I'm not going to do that, that's ridiculous! Why did I do that? I'm so stupid!* (This is an example of shorthand language that you learned about earlier.)

You don't need to lash out at yourself or your partner. I recommend that you follow the HEAL process steps in the *Healing Your Lost Inner Child Companion Workbook* to help you learn better ways to communicate to this wounded part of you. Over time, your awareness of how, when, and why your inner child shows up to blame and shame others will help to heal this cycle.

If you connect to the energy and expression of the blame-shame giver, say this intention for your wounded inner child:

I know that as a child I experienced situations where I was shamed by others or blamed for things I didn't do. I know now that I don't need to blame or shame others like I once was. I am learning that my worth and value come from just being myself. I am perfectly imperfect, and every day I am working on honoring myself. Going forward, I will own my thoughts and deeds, and am asking the same from my partner.

Healing the Blame-Shame Receiver

The partner who carries the energy and expression of this inner child wounding will need time to work through the trauma from the deep core wounding of being blamed and shamed for things when they were a child. This wounded inner child learned to be hypervigilant and on guard all of the time, waiting for the next blame or shame attack. They are defensive and on edge because they are trying to avoid being hurt again.

On the other hand, many people who are on the receiving

end of blaming and shaming normalize the little cuts and microaggressions, becoming immune to them. These hurts then become background noise, and the receiver doesn't realize how they are being hurt emotionally.

To begin healing this inner wounding, use clear and loving language with your inner child. Say that you are going to set boundaries with others so that if something begins to happen like what happened in your childhood, you, the responsible adult, will step in and take care of the situation. Let your inner child know that it doesn't need to be on alert for criticism all of the time.

When you receive blame or shame, see if you can make an "I feel" statement right away, and include a boundary statement if needed. (We make a boundary statement for ourselves first, then for the other person.) This sounds something like, *I feel really hurt and humiliated when you say that it's my fault the car keeps breaking down. I feel that you are making all of this my fault. I will own that I'm not the best at maintaining the car, but I'm trying my best. The reality is that I need help going forward to keep the car in good shape.* Boundary statements are not magic; just because you stated your truth doesn't mean that your blame-shame partner will give up their defensive posture. They may be too lost in their own wounding.

Ask yourself: What are the wounding experiences from my childhood that led to this behavior? Write out your commitment to yourself going forward.

Be patient with yourself and your partner, and give this cycle time to heal. The inner child will hold on to the blame-shame defenses for a long time because this is how the child emotionally survived in the family of origin.

If you connect to the energy and expression of the blame-shame receiver, say this intention for your wounded inner child:

I know that I am a good person and that I try to do my best, but I'm not perfect. I know that I don't deserve to be treated with disrespect and blamed for things I didn't do. I will find the courage within myself to stand up for myself when I need to, and set healthy boundaries in all of my relationships. I will use healthy responses to express how I feel.

THE STARR RESET—MARY AND KURT

Kurt finally began to hear what Mary had been telling him for a long time: that he was constantly blaming and shaming her. He began to recognize when he was starting the cycle. He saw when he was being manipulative or pointing out what Mary was doing wrong. He also realized that he would say something just to upset her and then go into a victim space. He began to understand that when he thought he was apologizing, he was actually shifting the blame back onto her. Through doing his own work, he saw how he would shame her to make her feel smaller so he could get what he wanted. He felt remorseful for his past behaviors.

Here is how the STARR Reset played out for Kurt and Mary.

Stop—Kurt's personal threshold came when, after years of Mary telling him she hated how he spoke to her, he finally heard himself; he recognized his habit of shaming her during a conversation and said to himself, *I'm not going to do this to her anymore.*

Think—In an instant, Kurt remembered all of the ways he used to shame her, and this flooded his heart. He thought of ways he could express his feelings to her in a way that didn't make it all her fault or turn her into the bad guy. Kurt was tempted to shut down, walk away, or blame her for why he did things, but he knew that wasn't right. This new skill was hard for him to learn, as he didn't have the right words. He wrote a symbolic letter to help him craft a message that Mary could hear and that didn't use shaming language.

Act—Kurt said to Mary, "I was going to start blaming you for everything that's wrong at home and project all of the things I'm worried about onto you, but I don't want to do that to you anymore. I'm going to work on owning my feelings, and come up with better ways to tell you what's going on inside of me."

Feeling surprised, Mary said to Kurt, "I know you blame me all the time for things that aren't my fault. I usually feel awful after we talk, even worse than before."

Kurt said, "We are both hurting, and I'm going to try not to do this to you anymore. I'm not going to be perfect at it, but I'm going to try." Mary was tempted to tell Kurt a list of offenses he had done to her because she saw him opening up and becoming vulnerable, but she stopped herself.

Reset and Repair—Kurt said, "I'm really sorry for how I've treated you, and I love you."

Mary held back all of the things she wanted to talk about and resolve. Instead she said, "I'm sorry, too, and we are going to figure this out together because there's more good in our lives than bad."

Kurt asked for a reset because he was ready to stop the cycle. He was ready to admit to himself that he no longer wanted to treat someone he loved that way. He had to find a sense of humility and culpability to get to this point. He continues to work on slowing down and using respectful language.

At the end of our lives, it's not the things we have done that we regret, it's the things we haven't done, especially when it comes to heartfelt apologies.

Mary realized that her inner child wounding got triggered whenever Kurt became big and loud. She saw how this wounding had lain the groundwork for her to be with someone like Kurt. She didn't want a repeat of her childhood, of shrinking and being silent. She realized that she didn't need to shame or blame Kurt in turn to feel powerful.

Mary is working on healing her inner child by using boundary statements to protect herself instead of being defensive all of the time. She is able to stop herself from going into her shame spiral, and instead uses gentle words of affirmation to ground herself.

Kurt and Mary are both good people who were letting their wounded parts do all the talking. They love each other, and they learned that they had gotten into some very bad habits. Now they no longer attack each other. If Kurt or Mary feels the urge to blame, they will say, "I really want to blame you for something that I don't want to own. But this is my old wounding, and I'm making a conscious choice to own my stuff and not hurt you."

Looking Inward

How do Kurt and Mary remind you of your own wounded struggles within yourself and with your partner? What are some of their inner child woundings that you connect to?

How does this match with your own story? What was activated inside of you when you read how this couple worked on their communication using the STARR Reset? Record your impressions in your notebook, as this will help you heal your wounded patterns.

CHAPTER 11

The Scorekeeper Archetype

Every day is like survival. You're my lover, not my rival.
—CULTURE CLUB, "KARMA CHAMELEON"

The scorekeeper archetype pairing is one in which there is love and connection, but each partner wants to have their position in an argument taken seriously and know that their perspective has been considered. This couple has a decent relationship outside of the fact that they get into discussions that are centered around specific unresolved issues in the relationship. I have heard couples say, *We get along fine until this comes up!* This couple's synergistic wounding searches for a sense of balance and justice. They wait for some kind of vindication, which is rarely produced.

THE SCOREKEEPER PAIRING

The partners in this couple are well matched, meaning that they both have their guard up and have trained the other to be defensive, even if the partner was not that way originally. They experience the relationship as unequal, and they track examples of inequality with scorecards, ready to play at any hint of a quarrel. They stuff their frustrations about important issues, and save up their measured disdain to use in distracting trivial issues, such as *Who left the butter out on the counter?* and *The garage door is always left open, and I always have to shut it.* Rarely are these things the real issues. The real issues need to be discussed, but they avoid these emotional landmines, as each can feel the weight of the topics and the portentous outcome.

Focusing on something other than the real issue is called *displaced anger.* Displaced anger is when we are angry about one thing but find another thing on which to focus our anger. For example, a parent may start to yell at the kids when something that happened at work is the real issue. The kids may not be perfect, but whatever they are doing, it isn't equal to the degree of anger the parent expresses.

Your hurt inner child feels the need to stay defensive and loaded up with evidence in order to prove the injustice of a situation.

Displaced anger covers up the core issues in the relationship. Examples of core issues are when one or both partners consciously ignore that they have not been sexually intimate in years, or that one has a gambling issue and the other turns away from or enables this reality. Or, they both know something is wrong with their child developmentally, but neither wants to admit it or get help for the child. All of these sensitive issues are more important than yelling about who left the butter out all night, but fighting about the butter is easier because it is not as serious. By ignoring important discussions, this couple stays in a pretend world with well-worn grooves, and they refresh their scorecards every time they go in for a fight.

The most likely synergistic pairing for this archetype is one who feels criticized and insecure but hides this insecurity, and one who finds fault in everything because they have trust or anxiety issues. Typically, both are strong-willed individuals who stand their ground.

Wounding Origins of the Scorekeeper Archetype

The adult who needs to keep a scorecard comes from a household in which they had to defend themselves in both small and profound ways. Overall, they did not feel listened to. Alternatively, they grew up in a family where they had to act strong even if they didn't feel strong.

This family was loving but emotionally unavailable, disconnected, and scattered. Certainly nothing of significance was discussed, because the parents had neither the time for nor the interest in this level of communication. They were often self-involved and took a hands-off approach, letting the siblings figure things out. Many issues were swept under the carpet, and family members, including the parents, looked the other way when bad things happened.

The child in this emotionally unavailable household never learned how to communicate feelings deeper than surface problems because they learned nothing was acknowledged, anyway. The parents, being emotionally unavailable, did not see or hear the child's distress, so the child kept trying to get a sense of justice, often shouting into the wind. Sometimes the child was criticized and judged unfairly and so began to do this to themselves. They then began to project this criticism toward others.

Without a steady force in the house claiming right or wrong, the child learned to present an impassioned strong defense to one parent, hoping it would convince them to step in and mediate differences with their siblings. When this failed, the siblings would take out their frustrations on each other by holding petty grievances, establishing turf, and keeping score. Siblings in this household felt they were on their own and did not feel like a cohesive unit. Because of the lack of recognition of right or wrong, the child learned to keep score of the wrong-doings to maintain a sense of internal control or to feel that they weren't going crazy.

The child in this household was confused as to why no one else saw the level of dysfunction in the family; they just saw problems swept aside and everyone moving on. When someone brought up a problem, they were called crazy for making an issue out of a situation. This gaslighting behavior further reinforced in the child the need to fight for justice, as no one saw or named the glaring issues and the injustices.

This wounded inner child carries a banner that screams, This Is Wrong! This Is Bad! This Is Unjust!

One or both partners in a scorekeeper relationship probably grew up in such a household and does not feel heard or validated as an adult. This perpetuates the problem in which one partner keeps looking for a sense of validation and justice. The butter and the open garage door are not the core issues for this couple, but arguing about them helps them to avoid the real issues, just like what happened in their family of origin household. Their wounded dance is carried forward from their childhood.

Wounded Tools of the Scorekeeper Archetype

The wounded tools that the scorekeeper learned from childhood trauma or wounding include:

- overusing examples of issues going back years
- hiding internal shame by being defensive or projecting
- criticizing themselves and then projecting that criticism toward others
- fighting for justice even when there isn't an injustice per say
- carrying hurts that are hard to let go
- arguing over ridiculous or annoying issues to avoid the real issues
- recycling arguments to beat the other person down
- keeping a scorecard to use as a tool of manipulation
- showing "exhibit A" so that a judge and jury will decide the winner

SYNERGISTIC WOUNDED PAIRING—DANIEL AND JEREMY

Daniel and Jeremy are a typical scorekeeping couple. They were always ready on a dime to bring out folders of evidence proving wrongdoing on the part of the other. Neither Daniel nor Jeremy felt heard, and neither would let go of an issue until their opinion was acknowledged and confirmed. They frequently brought up the past in their scorekeeping. *This is just like the time when you . . .*, or, *Remember that time when this happened? Well it's happening again!* They were always ready to present to some off-camera judge how and why they were right and the other was wrong.

When one throws a rock, the other throws a boulder.

Daniel and Jeremy both saw their scorekeeping as a way to prove that the other was confused or wrong. Jeremy would bring up an issue that he was upset about, and Daniel, stunned that they were even talking about it, would blow it off. Jeremy would then be offended that Daniel tried to dismiss the issue, and they would both get louder and louder. Not wanting to talk about the real issue, one of them would switch to a distraction topic, and then they would argue over their version of the butter discussion. They spent so much time defending their positions that they couldn't see how lost they were in their wounding.

Well-worn score cards are rarely discarded by the wounded inner child, as they are a pernicious means of defense.

Neither Daniel nor Jeremy wanted to give up their scorecards because the scorecards protected them from what they didn't want to talk about. They were used to talking over each other and not being good listeners, so they both felt disrespected. They didn't want this dynamic to end, though, because then they wouldn't be able to create diversions from the core dysfunctional issues.

THE STARR RESET FOR THE SCOREKEEPER ARCHETYPE

If you recognize your relationship in this archetype, the most important thing you can do is to begin to listen to one another and stop keeping score.

Stop—First, put down your scorecards and stop the cycle of preparing the evidence. Stop, observe, and ask yourself if you really want to get into the issue about the butter being left out. Chances are there are issues that you want or need to discuss that you have been avoiding by tracking these trivial issues.

The real issue isn't the butter or the open garage door; it's that one or both doesn't feel seen or heard.

Think—Think about and discern what is happening within you. You may be tempted to prepare evidence and strike back with mean words or displace your anger onto an unrelated topic, but you know that will not take you both to a good place. You also know the familiar patterns and the frustrating back-and-forth discussions that go nowhere. During this stage of the reset, it is important to think about what you are getting out of defending your turf and the harm that such discussions are doing to your relationship. Each time you bring out your scorecard, you are reenacting old hurts and trying to right a wrong, but you are doing so in a destructive way. By continuing this pattern, you reinforce that it is OK to keep using these old arguments to hurt your partner instead of trying to work through things in a calm, rational way.

This new way of communication is a better road map to follow than the one your inner child designed for you.

Act—Once you have slowed down your communication, ask your partner if there are things they would like to talk about that you have not been receptive to in the past. Are there things you do that annoy your partner? Are there things the two of you have been ignoring but that are serious issues in your relationship?

You have probably had to talk about matters of importance before, but for whatever reason, you just got it over with. You have the skills for these talks, so see if you can be more intentional with your words. Set aside the time to talk about important issues; you will both feel better about yourselves and the outcome. You will have a renewed sense of the strength of your relationship and that you are on the same team. You *can* work through issues productively. Remember, you both probably want similar outcomes. You are learning how to communicate your feelings and thoughts to reach that shared outcome.

Reset and Repair—Repairing this pattern will greatly improve your daily quality of life. The repair work involves a new way of communicating the annoyances of the relationship while asking for a level of respect. It is not about anyone "winning" the round, which is impossible anyway. What I say to couples is to slow down your communication. Say what you mean to say, in the best way you know how, the first time. When we rush through conversations, we end up having to redo the talk and clean up whatever we initially said in a not so-good way. The goal is for you both to feel that you were seen and heard by the end of the conversation.

Set aside your evidence and speak in "I feel" language that relates your emotional range. Paraphrase back what you hear the other say. An example of this is, *I feel discouraged when you completely disregard what I have said about leaving your shoes out in the middle of the hallway. Going forward, I need you to put your shoes away, which will help me feel respected. I need you to repeat back to me what you just heard me say, please.*

You can also begin a reset conversation with *I own that I do this; knowing and hearing what you are willing to own will help me feel connected to you*. I know you probably don't use this sort of language now, but this will go a long way toward helping you each to feel joined in the conversation and, in time, let your guard down. Remember, this is about both of you feeling honored and respected, and fostering a deeper connection between you.

If you have old hurts and examples of injustice that you want to bring up, I encourage you to do some symbolic letter writing to clarify your feelings. This will help you come up with a concise way of speaking with your partner about what you are upset about instead of defensively blasting off a scorecard.

Healing the Scorekeeper

If you relate to this synergistic wounding, reference the triggers list and wounded responses in chapter 2 and determine which unhealed part of you shows up in your adult relationship. What does this part need from you? What is it looking for from your partner? The harder step is determining whether it is your adult self trying to get through to your partner or your inner child trying to find justice with someone from your childhood (parents or siblings). It may be a little of both.

The inner child will not go away just because you don't want to acknowledge this part. By taking the time to hear the distress of the inner child, you will be able to hold your impulses and not react so much to the annoying things that happen. You will be able to listen to your partner and ask them to listen to you.

Your inner child will feel a sense of relief if you slow down and speak with intention, because all parts of you will begin to feel heard, validated, and honored. You will still annoy each other—that is just how living with someone else is—but now you will have more tools to use to make your relationship as functional as you can.

If you connect to the energy and expression of the scorekeeper, say this intention for your wounded inner child:

I am free and open in my relationships, and I trust those around me to listen and respect me and my feelings. I know that I can set healthy boundaries when I need to and that I am worth fighting for, but not everything is a fight. I am learning to trust in myself and others. My words have meaning and value, and I'm learning to speak my truth in a loving way and not hold on to past hurts or keep score.

The STARR Reset—Daniel and Jeremy

Like most couples, Daniel and Jeremy tried to have an equal separation of duties around the house, but the reality is that people fall into their routines and avoid those things they don't like to do. Daniel felt that Jeremy would do just a few chores inside the house and then say, "Well, I take care of everything outside." But whenever Daniel looked around outside, he saw that not much was being done. Daniel would go to Jeremy with his scorecard and point out all of the things that he, Daniel, was doing and what Jeremy wasn't doing. Jeremy would get offended and dig in because he didn't like household chores, whether inside or out, and didn't think it was necessary to keep things "showroom ready" all of the time. Then, as a way to deflect, Jeremy would bring up things that Daniel didn't do years ago as evidence that Jeremy didn't need to help inside.

Daniel felt exhausted and didn't know how to get through to Jeremy. They would go to opposite sides of the house and not talk for hours, each stewing in righteousness.

Stop—Daniel reached his personal threshold and knew something needed to change. He didn't want to continue trying to convince Jeremy by using the same tactics he had used in the past, so he changed course. Daniel decided to stop his old pattern.

Think—Daniel thought about all the ways he had used his scorecard in the past. He would bring evidence to Jeremy to appeal to Jeremy's intelligence and convince him to help. If that didn't work, he would get mean with his words, hurling accusations of injustice to show his frustrations. This time he thought of a creative approach. He decided to join Jeremy help with things Jeremy liked doing.

Act—One day Daniel helped Jeremy do some work outside that was challenging for one person to do. Jeremy appreciated Daniel's help. He said, "I like it when you're out here with me. This is fun to do together."

Daniel said, "I like it, too, and I can do more things like this with you." Feeling brave, he added, "I would be willing to help you more outside if you would help me more inside the house. How you feel now is how I want to feel. I like it when we do things together; I feel closer to you."

Reset and Repair—Jeremy saw what Daniel was doing. He started to get defensive and said, "Oh, I get it. You're out here helping me because you want me to help you inside!"

Daniel said, "Yes, that's part of it, but I also like helping you, and I know you like my being outside with you. I would love for you to help me with some chores in the house that I don't like doing by myself. Can you do that for me? I love you. I want us to feel connected and more like a team."

Jeremy said, "OK, I love you, too, and I will do more of those things inside that are important to you. I know you work hard to make things nice for us, and I think I sometimes take it for granted. I need you to show me how you want the chores done, because I don't think I do them the way you like."

Some might say that Daniel was being sneaky or manipulative, but working outside and doing chores that he didn't like to do was a stretch for him. He also knew that Jeremy loved when he was outside with him. He knew that this act of service would appeal to Jeremy's love language and fill him up. But he also wanted Jeremy to get the point, because his other efforts weren't working. He was trying to communicate in a new way with Jeremy, and it got through.

Daniel and Jeremy needed to be honest with each other. They were both doing chores, but neither one was consistent and both felt isolated, so neither of them felt that chores were getting done. Once they admitted this, they made progress on healing this pattern. They both committed to better follow through with the chores. They got out of their pattern and addressed how they felt. Both walked away from this discussion knowing and feeling they were heard. They each had to set aside their scorecards and defensiveness in order to get through a fairly simple conversation. If they hadn't used their new skills, the talk they had would have just dipped into a well-worn groove with a disappointing outcome.

After they each did some therapy work, Daniel and Jeremy agreed not to keep score anymore. They saw how destructive this pattern was and that they truly love each other. They needed to have someone point out their relationship dynamics so they would understand what was happening. They can now make conscious choices of how to discuss these issues. They no longer look for distraction topics, and if they start to go down that road, one of them gently reminds the other that they are no longer doing things that way.

A reset doesn't always have to be formulaic and robotic. You need to be creative in how you stop your cycles and communicate your needs. Daniel and Jeremy still have their struggles and are sometimes tempted to pick up the scorecards, but Daniel broke the cycle and got his partner's attention. They graduated to the next level in how they communicate and look at things.

Sometimes the best conversations are the simplest ones, especially when we speak from the heart with the intention of joining with the other.

LOOKING INWARD

How does this couple remind you of your own wounded struggles within yourself and with your partner? What are some of the inner child woundings that you connect to? How does this match with your own story? What was activated inside of you when you read how this couple worked on their communication using the STARR Reset? Record your impressions in your notebook, as this will help you heal your wounded patterns.

CHAPTER 12

The Mindreader and the Accused Archetypes

I'm in the dark. I'd like to read his mind, but
I'm frightened of the things I might find.
—'TIL TUESDAY, "VOICES CARRY"

The mindreader and the accused archetypes are common in wounded pairings. The mindreader is a person who makes up stories about what other people think, feel, or how a situation will play out. They make accusations that their partner is thinking or feeling a certain way. One or both partners of this synergistic pairing spends more time in their head imagining what the other person is thinking or feeling than they do talking with their partner or others to learn what is actually going on. The mindreader uses their fears and insecurities to complete a story about the other that is usually not warranted. The mindreader is often an overt controller.

Both the mindreader and the accused bring forth the energy and expression of the victim in this synergistically wounded relationship.

Mindreading is a fear response in the absence of trust.

The mindreader archetype occurs when one has an over-active, anxious energy that spills over onto the other. The mindreader's concerns are not in balance; their accusations are all about calming themselves down with no regard for the accused. The accused is buffeted about by the mindreader's projected fear, and the stories the mindreader makes up have only a few elements of reality or the truth. Like most couples, the partners in this wounded pairing didn't start out this way, but the framework for their back-and-forth arguments and the broken trust issues were already there.

The most likely synergistic pairing for this archetype is one who has anxiety issues and one who tries to calm the other down as a codependent caretaker, fixer, or rescuer.

The Mindreader Archetype

The mindreader, who does not trust and who makes up stories, usually has anxiety issues along with inner child broken trust issues that exaggerate the stories even more. They use accusations as weapons to gain dominance or control over their partner. They look for anything that reinforces their fear-based fiction so that they can say "gotcha" to their partner. This is a form of gaslighting; they hope their partner will agree with them, which would complete the cycle and confirm their worst fears. The mindreader usually comes up with worst-case scenarios; rarely do they imagine everything working out well and that others are happy. The behavior is self-sabotaging, keeping the mindreader in the energy and emotional space of the victim.

Mindreaders are convinced that their invented falsehoods are firmly rooted in reality.

It is natural to wonder how other people feel, but mindreading is a whole different level in that the mindreader creates an entire movie. For example, say the mindreader has trust issues and always looks for ways their partner is cheating on them. They check their partner's phone, keep track of their schedule, and obsessively look for something that their partner has done wrong. If their partner is late or the routine is interrupted, the mindreader will make up elaborate stories of the what, when, why, and where regarding the "cheating" partner. It is easier and safer for them to make up a story than to just ask. They are not open to what they could hear from their partner, because then they may have to admit they were wrong. If they do ask their partner, they don't believe the answer they receive.

The mindreader has a fundamental broken trust issue that feeds a need to create stories, giving them a sense of control.

Why does the mind make up stories like this? The mind likes to be informed and active, so it will spin a fictional story from a few bits of truth or fact to fill out the narrative. This fiction, which is rooted in emotional wounding, then becomes "fact." The mindreader believes these stories because they fit with the wounded narrative that aligns with their fears.

There is a difference between a mindreader and a partner who comes from a grounded place to ask a question. The mindreader says, *I can tell by the way you look today that you are mad at me. I just know it; I can tell right away. What did I do now?* A grounded partner says, *I notice that you don't seem like yourself today. Is everything all right?* The mindreader projects an insecurity and looks for an answer that confirms a fear; the inquiry is self-serving. The grounded partner looks for an answer because they care how their partner feels; their question is altruistic.

> *Projections of fears and insecurities feed into the made-up elements of the storytelling.*

Broadly, the mindreading partner is a conflict avoider. Making up stuff and staying in a state of not knowing is easier because then the wounded inner child feels in control. Talking the mindreader back to a grounded reality is often difficult.

Wounding Origins of the Mindreader Archetype

Children who develop the mindreading wounded tool come from a variety of family backgrounds. There is no one set of circumstances that fosters an anxious or fearful child. Most anxiety disorders are genetic and thus hard-coded, so mindreaders have to learn how to manage their symptoms and develop healthy coping skills.

Many adults learned how to play out their anxieties as children by watching or hearing their parents deal with anxious situations. Parents who were distant, narcissistically wounded, depressed, anxious, addicted, or emotionally unavailable created the child's need to practice mindreading so they could figure out their parents. In their attempts at feeling close to their parents, such children make up stories as to why one parent doesn't spend time with them, for example. The mindreading child may think, *Well, Dad is busy with work, and that's why he doesn't play with me like other kids' dads play with them. That's OK, because I think he loves me.* Or, *Mom is really sad today. I don't know what I did, but I probably did something that upset her.* These children then carry this mindreading skill into their adult lives.

> *The mindreader distorts a few kernels of truth into a convenient story that feeds their fears.*

The mindreader grew up in a household where they learned not to trust or believe in themselves, so they relied on others to shape their sense of self and their reality. If household events were upsetting, they learned to look to others for reassurance. They learned to rely on their imagination to make up fear-based stories, which kept them in a highly anxious state. When they told others what they felt and believed, the story they had created was so far from reality that they were called crazy or out of their minds. They became highly defensive, mistrusting themselves and others. As a result of this negative reinforcement loop, the fear-based mindreader stayed in their head even more, making up new scary stories that frightened them and kept them in a state of anticipatory anxiety.

> *Making up stories helps the mindreader feel safer because they think they know how someone feels or how something will work out. They feel in control.*

The mindreader grew up fearful of not knowing everything, so, as an adult, they need to know what is going on in every situation in order to feel a sense of safety. They use their mindreading skills to fill in the gaps so the story will make sense to them. This pattern developed at a young age and carried into adulthood.

Wounded Tools of the Mindreader Archetype

The wounded tools that the mindreader learned from childhood trauma or wounding include:

- using mindreading to determine what is going on
- shutting down and not trusting
- controlling things to avoid surprises
- making up stories about how the other feels so that it "makes sense"
- putting themselves down and not trusting themselves
- impulsively looking for reassurance and not taking responsibility for emotions
- using a few facts to create an elaborate fiction that they then believe
- accusing others of not telling the truth or finding inconsistencies that "confirm" a falsehood
- being all or nothing in relationships

THE ACCUSED ARCHETYPE

Partners who are on the receiving end of made-up stories are often emotionally unavailable conflict avoiders. They are accused of having feelings, thoughts, or behaviors that may or may not be true. Their synergistic wounding of not feeling good about themselves matches with their partner's made-up accusations. They accept this mindreading arrangement because they don't want to talk about how they feel, anyway. Their wounding vacillates between indifference and outrage at the mindreader for trying to intrude into their thoughts. This back-and-forth wounding cycle drives the relationship further into the ground. If the accused tries to talk about their feelings, their partner will say, *No, that's not how you feel; this is how you feel.*

The accused sometimes wants the mindreader to know what they are thinking so they don't have to express their feelings or work at the relationship. When their mindreading partner isn't able to accurately read their mind, the accused responds passive-aggressively by giving the silent treatment, shutting them out, or sulking.

Mindreading is not intuition;
it is a projection of fears or insecurities.

If you are in a relationship with a chronic mindreader, know that this is a coping skill for them, a wounded tool they use to make unknown and scary situations feel safe. You will not be aware of when your partner makes up a story until they state the story as fact. For example, they will say, *I know that you are mad at me,* when you are not. When your partner makes up a story without consulting you, you feel left out, disregarded, disrespected, and gaslighted. Their accusation is based on assumptions, and no one likes to be told how they feel; it is disrespectful.

If you don't know if you are in a relationship with a mindreader, ask yourself these questions: Are you often on the defensive, having to explain yourself? *Where were you? What were you doing?* Does your partner tell you how to handle things because they know you won't do them the "right" way? Are you told how you think and feel? When you say how you feel, does your partner turn it against you or say that it isn't true? All of these are signs that your partner does some level of mindreading and is possibly an overt controller.

Mindreading is a vicious cycle for couples to get into. The mindreader believes that the made-up story is fact, with the accused guilty until proven innocent. This accuse-and-defend contest creates division and animosity in the relationship. The mindreader is saying to the accused, *I do not respect you enough to ask you a question directly. I don't know how you are going to react, so I'm going to avoid this altogether and just proclaim that this is how you think and feel.* The accused has to work hard to stay grounded in their own reality and not get lost in the mindreader's gaslighting.

If you recognize your relationship in this archetype, know that you are beginning to heal just by recognizing this pattern. You both have the potential to move into a new way of relating and to heal old ideas of how to have a good relationship. You can learn to speak your truth, and your partner can learn how to hold this truth for you. Be gentle with yourself as you make your way toward creating a new paradigm.

Wounding Origins of the Accused Archetype

The childhood family of the accused is one in which the parents or caregivers are controlling, emotionally unavailable, or detached. A caregiver's addiction or a preoccupation with work, illness, or other stressor plays a factor in the distraction away from feelings. The parents tell the children how they feel and what they want instead of asking them. It is easier for the parents to decide these things than it is for them to engage with their children, have a discussion, and get feedback.

The children in this household don't have a vote and are rarely given options as to what they can do. They are rarely asked how they are doing, and when they are asked, they don't have access to many feeling words because this isn't encouraged or modeled. The parents or others then fill in the blanks for them. The children don't necessarily want to hide feelings, they just never learned how to express them. If they do express their feelings and are then told that is not how they feel, they begin to doubt their feelings. They learn that it is easier to let others guess how they feel, whether the guess is right or wrong.

The parents may be caught up in their own issues or feeling their emotions in a big way. When this is the case, the children don't have the space to express themselves. The parents take all of the energy with their outbursts; there is no place for the children to have emotions. When the children feel emotional neglect or abandonment, they will say, *If you loved me, you would know how I feel.* They interpret others' mindreading or guessing as expressions of love or concern.

These children feel lost, unnoticed, and unacknowledged. They reach a point where they have outbursts of emotion because no one pays attention to their needs and wants. They grow tired of others telling them how they feel and being incorrect. When they have enough energy, they overcompensate, defend themselves, or correct others. They desire connection, but they don't know how to express their feelings or ask for what they need.

Wounded Tools of the Accused Archetype

Wounded tools that the accused learned from childhood trauma or wounding include:

- looking the other way when people assume things about them
- having inconsistent feelings about being told what they think or feel
- harboring anger and resentment toward the mindreader
- being passive-aggressive and avoiding conflict
- lying so as not to trigger the mindreader's anxiety
- adapting to fit whatever story the mindreader believes, neither confirming nor denying
- overcompensating in order to prove innocence
- carrying the responsibility for their partner's moods, whether anxious or calm

SYNERGISTIC WOUNDED PAIRING—CHRIS AND KELLY

Chris and Kelly are a typical pairing of the mindreader and the accused. Both had symptoms of anxiety and were conflict avoiders. They talked about issues in their relationship, but they relied more often on their ability to "read" the other and so make up stories.

Kelly was the more frequent mindreader. She would watch Chris's facial expressions, body movements, tone of voice, and word choice so she could piece together a story that matched a fear she had. She invested a lot of time and effort into thinking about what he was not telling her, and she projected her fears onto him. Chris sometimes did this to Kelly, but most of the time he enabled her anxieties by putting up with her behavior. They both guessed at what the other thought and felt.

For years, Kelly had been jealous of the women Chris worked with. She had met them at work events, visited with them at house parties, and liked them, but she didn't trust them. She was nervous that Chris would be tempted to have an affair. She began to question him as to who was in the office that day, what they were wearing, if he noticed them, whether he talked with them in the break room, how long he stood at their desks, if he was working on any projects with them, and so on.

Kelly began to make up stories daily about what Chris thought and felt about these women, and what they thought and felt about him. Chris had never cheated on her, but he dutifully answered her questions because he saw how upset she was. Kelly completely lost herself in these made-up stories because of her anxieties and broken trust issues from childhood. It got to the point where she put a tracking app on Chris's phone and demanded that he check in with her throughout the day. If he didn't respond to one of her texts, she would keep calling his phone till he answered. When Chris got home, Kelly would go through his phone and track back all of his phone activity to see what websites he searched, what he looked at during the day, and what numbers he called. If she found anything out of the ordinary, she would get angry, make up stories, and hurl accusations and insults at Chris. When she didn't find anything, she would look back through his old phone (which she kept), as she was certain she missed something there.

Chris didn't like being accused and having to defend his behaviors every day, but when he tried to talk with Kelly about it, she got even angrier and said that this proved he was having an affair. Chris wasn't in a relationship with Kelly, he was in a relationship with Kelly's wounded and highly anxious inner child.

Both Chris and Kelly were synergistically wounded by her high anxieties, his enabling, and their shared conflict avoidance. They did not address issues head on and instead used indirect methods to try to figure out what the other was thinking or feeling. In their childhood families, they both learned that situations involving emotions were not to be discussed, and if they were, they would result in great distress.

There was more unspoken in this relationship than there was discussed. When Chris and Kelly did talk, they argued about the stories they had made up, so miscommunication and defensiveness consistently derailed the relationship. They spent more time avoiding direct communication and instead made up stories about the other.

THE STARR RESET FOR THE MINDREADER AND THE ACCUSED ARCHETYPES

If you recognize your relationship in this archetype, know that it will take hard and consistent work to start making a change. If you are the mindreader, you need to stop this behavior and stop avoiding talking about things. One way to do this is to recognize when you start to mindread and then stop it in midthought. This thought behavior is ingrained into your daily life, so it will be hard at first for you to see the problem and then recognize how often you do it. It will take practice. Keep trying.

Stop—Stopping thoughts is hard to do, as the mind is like a machine: it gets into a groove. The mind likes order and routine as well as novelty and puzzles. Getting your mind out of the habit of mindreading will take conscious effort. If your partner has pointed out that you do this, pay attention; they aren't making this up.

Think—Once you decide to stop this mindreading pattern, think about how it can be different. For example, the mindreader wants to go on vacation, but in the past his partner always said no. He decided to book the tickets without asking her first and then ask for forgiveness later. *She never wants to spend the money, so she probably doesn't want to go. I really want to go, so I'm going to go ahead and book the tickets.* To avoid future storytelling, he can think, *I don't know if it is true that she doesn't want us to go on vacation this winter, but she keeps talking about how we don't have money for extra things. I'm going to ask her instead of making up a story to fit what I want.*

Act—Write out all of the stories you make up and tell yourself for your own comfort. For each one ask yourself, *Is this really true, or is it something I think may be true?* Confirm whether the stories you made up were true or not. Don't keep going through life working off of false premises.

Reset and Repair—This new way of relating will feel strange for both of you. You will feel unsure about your new roles and new way of communicating. If you work at it, you will use more direct language in your conversations than you have for years. At first, the direct questions will sound or feel confrontational, but this is not about confrontation. Ask each other questions to confirm, deny, or clarify. There is a learning curve here, so take your time, slow down your communication, and speak and listen respectfully. Know that you both are learning a better way to conduct your relationship, and admit that the old way wasn't functional.

You may have a backlog of questions that you want to ask your partner to clear the air. *Do you really think I'm foolish? Do you not want to move out of this house?* Don't ask all of your questions at once. Take your time as you clear up the misconceptions you have been carrying for a while. Ask, for example, *Are you OK with us going on vacation this winter?* Even if the answer is no and you were right, at least you know for sure instead of spending time inside of your head imagining the answer.

Healing the Mindreader

If you make up stories based on a few facts, then you cheat yourself out of living your life based in reality. You create a version of your life that dovetails with your wounding. If you do not speak directly with your partner or your friends about these issues, you will deny yourself a more fulfilling and less stress-filled relationship.

If you consistently need an immediate answer from someone else to calm yourself down, you are using them as a coping tool instead of developing a healthy, functional response.

If you have made up a story about someone, resist asking them to reassure you. For example, if you texted a question and they didn't get back to you right away, resist the urge to keep on bugging them for an answer, even if your anxiety goes off the chart. Learn to rein in the urge to get instant reassurance, and tell yourself that you will get an answer when they are ready or able. Practice using functional emotional response tools with your inner child self instead of enabling this wounded part, which is the part that impulsively and anxiously tries to get an answer. You may need to talk with a therapist to get at the root of the anxiety and to learn more coping skills, because this can be a deeply entrenched behavior.

You may be doing well with getting out of your head and not making up stories, but now and then you go back to old habits. When this happens, gently guide yourself out of this mental habit. If you feel brave, tell your partner about it. For example, *Today I made up a story that you were mad at me. Is this my imagination, or are you upset with me?* Your partner can clarify, but I do not advise you to go to your partner all of the time for reassurance, because this behavior is just as destructive as the storytelling.

Establish some boundaries within yourself by saying, for example, *I'm not going to make up stories about my partner or my friends. The only fact I know is that they were going to call me back at a certain time and they didn't. Anything else I make up comes from fear. I don't need to make up a fiction to fill in the gaps in order to reassure myself. I don't need to obsessively try to contact my partner or my friend and bug them. I am learning ways to calm myself down and self-soothe to help me through times of uncertainty.*

If you connect with the energy and expression of the mindreader, say this intention for your wounded inner child:

I know that when I was growing up I had to keep tabs on my mom and dad to make sure they were OK and that things were not spinning out of control. That is not my life today. I can trust that I am safe in my relationship and that I have loving friends and family in my life. I know that feeling anxious is just a FEAR of mine and that I can Face Everything And Recover. I am safe and loved.

When you move out of a mindreading mode, you will feel vulnerable, exposed, and like you are flying without a net. This just means that trusting is new to you.

Healing the Accused

If you are the accused, look at some of the reasons why your partner feels the need to make up stories. Are there things that you do or don't do that cause them to make up stories? Are you up front with your thoughts and feelings, or do you close down so that your partner has no idea how you think or feel, leading them to resort to their stories? See if you can open up when your natural inclination is to shut down. This will help your mindreading partner to move away from their mindreading behavior. When you understand more about the behavior, you will know what you need to stop so that you don't keep contributing to the cycle.

Answer the following questions in your notebook. Why do I withhold feelings from my partner? Why don't I share more when I know they want to know how I feel? What is it about my inner child wounding that still influences this continued behavior? What does my inner child need to know so that they feel safe to share more? Once you have some insights, try to be more forthcoming with your thoughts and feelings so that your partner doesn't have to work so hard to fill in the blanks.

If you have tried to work on these issues on your own and are not getting very far, a therapist may help you navigate through this pattern and heal the underlying wounding. Until the core wounding of the broken trust issues and low self-worth are addressed, they will keep presenting in the relationship.

If you connect to the energy and expression of the accused, say this intention for your wounded inner child:

Every day I can be myself and celebrate my thoughts and feelings. Each day I am learning new ways to calm and reassure myself. I know myself more than anyone else on this planet, and I give myself permission to speak my truth. I am learning to respect myself and others, and I use healthy boundaries to keep myself emotionally safe in my relationships. I love and trust myself.

THE STARR RESET—CHRIS AND KELLY

One day, when she couldn't reach Chris at work, Kelly made up a story that he and Sharon, the office manager, were at a hotel having sex. Kelly called Brian, who worked with Chris, and asked where Chris was. Later, Brian told Chris that Kelly had called, was really upset, and was looking for him. Chris was extremely embarrassed that Kelly's anxiety and storytelling, which he had been trying to manage discreetly, had spilled over into his workplace. It had all become too much; he had reached his personal threshold. Chris decided that things had to change. He tried the STAR Reset for the first time.

Stop—Chris felt embarrassed that his buddy had to chase him down because his wife was having a semi-panic attack as a result of her out-of-control anxiety. He couldn't ignore the severity of the problem anymore; no matter what he tried, it didn't work, and Kelly wasn't feeling any better.

Think—Chris loved Kelly very much and had tried to accommodate all of her requests. He thought he was helping her by containing and managing her anxiety and their relationship, but he was enabling her, ultimately making things worse. When Brian asked Chris what was going on, Chris realized that this was a bigger issue than he had thought, and he couldn't play the game anymore.

He decided that he needed to talk to a therapist to help him understand what was going on with Kelly and their relationship.

The therapist helped Chris understand how their wounded cycle had gotten out of control, that his behavior was enabling Kelly, and that he had become Kelly's number one coping tool. Chris realized his part and how highly dysfunctional it was. Therapy and symbolic letter writing helped him come up with the language to talk with Kelly about her anxiety.

Act—Chris said to Kelly, "I know you are worried that I have inappropriate conversations or a relationship with a woman at work, but I don't, and I'm not. I realize that when I give in to all of your requests for where I am and what I'm doing, I am not helping you; it just makes the problem bigger. I'm going to work on doing a better job of being patient and setting boundaries with you, but I need your help by talking with someone about your anxiety. My therapist says we can develop some next steps together. I realize I can't help you on my own. Ultimately, you need to help yourself."

This was a lot for Kelly to hear. She couldn't imagine giving up all of her wounded coping tools, such as relying on Chris and using the mindreading and controlling behaviors that she had developed to manage her fears. She was upset and embarrassed, as she didn't think it was that bad. She started yelling at Chris and tried to shut down the conversation by turning it back on him, making it his fault. She told him that he didn't love her and that this proved he was sleeping with Sharon.

Chris stayed steady. He said, "I know this is hard for you, but I'm not going anywhere. I will still tell you what's going on when I'm at work, but we need to come up with a better solution together, because your anxiety is getting too big for the both of us. This is too much for me." This got Kelly's attention, but she wanted to storm out of the room. Chris asked her to please stay so they could talk about it some more. Once Kelly calmed down, she asked if Chris could still check in with her during the day. Chris agreed but with some changes. He told her that if she would go to therapy with him, they could work out a plan.

Reset and Repair—Chris said to Kelly, "I love you, and I respect that you have anxieties. I want to do my part in our healing journey."

Kelly said, "This is really hard for me, but I love you and don't want to lose you. I am fighting every urge to make up a story right now about how you are hurting me on purpose. I hate the fact that I have all of this anxiety. I need your help, but I also know I need to help myself. I will go to therapy with you, but I'm scared."

Chris said, "We are going to get through this together, sweetheart. I'm here for you."

Chris and Kelly are learning how they co-created and fostered the synergistic wounding in their relationship. They are also learning internal and external boundaries. Kelly is learning new ways to cope with her anxieties, and no longer uses Chris as her main coping tool. Chris trusts that Kelly is learning how to manage her anxieties. He is learning that setting boundaries with Kelly models a productive behavior, whereas in the past he had seen this as turning his back on her. He feels stronger and better about himself and the relationship when he sets boundaries. Following their reset, they both have a whole new set of tools to use in their relationship. They are making it work one day at a time.

LOOKING INWARD

How does this couple remind you of your own wounded struggles within yourself and with your partner? What are some of the inner child woundings that you connect to? How does this match with your own story? What was activated inside of you when you read how this couple worked on their communication using the STARR Reset? Record your impressions in your notebook, as this will help you heal your wounded patterns.

CHAPTER 13

The Fabulist and the Enabler Archetypes

You can't hide your lyin' eyes, and your smile is a thin disguise.
I thought by now you'd realize, there ain't no way to hide your
lyin' eyes. Honey, you can't hide your lyin' eyes.
—EAGLES, "LYIN' EYES"

The synergistic pairing of the fabulist and the enabler is a common coupling. The fabulist lives in an illusion of their own making, while the enabler chases after them to determine what is real or fake. They each have inner child wounding that attracts the other and keeps them together.

The fabulist is prone to lying, is a master of illusion, and has to work hard at keeping track of their lies. The fabulist creates a sense of control and conflict avoidance through lying, and is not interested in stopping this behavior. The enabler has a long history of enabling codependent behavior with addicts or chaotic, disorganized people. The enabler doesn't see that they are part of the problem; they see themselves as the helper, the fixer, the rescuer, and the one to rehabilitate the wayward.

*The couple who are not honest with each other
are not honest with themselves.*

The inner child wounding of both partners shows up in their adult relationship as codependent behaviors, such as controlling, avoiding, enabling, being sneaky, omitting the whole truth, hiding, and lying. Addictions, specifically anonymous sex and gambling, often show up in these pairings. These forms of addiction involve dissociation, risk, and chance, which match the fabulist's need to deceive and control others (and themselves). It is easier for them to live in a fabricated illusion than in reality; they feel they can more easily navigate their life and manipulate with their illusions.

Sometimes both partners have addiction issues. They keep feeding this cycle, wanting the party to never end. They ignore their family as it falls apart, neglecting their children, jobs, and responsibilities. The couple in this type of pairing resists any discussion of moving away from what they know. They don't want to access their real feelings, and are afraid that if they speak their truth, their partner will get mad or leave them.

*The fabulist tries to keep track of their lies,
while the enabler chases after the truth.*

The fabulist and the enabler get into self-destructive and self-sabotaging cycles that are subconsciously driven. Their subconscious wants to heal their inner child woundings, so it sets up situations that invite the couple to face reality. Not wanting to face reality, however, they will avoid it by creating distractions away from whatever is about to crash and burn. For example, if a couple is facing bankruptcy, the fabulist will borrow money from family so they don't have to face the bankruptcy, and they do not tell the enabler. The fabulist will create a distraction and ignore their life crashing all around them in order to deny the reality that is staring them in the face. When such deceptions are revealed, they create deep trauma in the relationship. Lies built on top of lies become deep layers of trauma that the couple will have to work through.

The fabulist lives in a false narrative that they are better, cleverer, and can out-think and out-maneuver everyone else.

Sometimes a major life event, such as the death of a close relative, a job loss, or an affair that is revealed provides an opportunity for the couple to wake up, as it would be hard for the fabulist to avoid something so bold. Such a rare occurrence of honest recognition is a crossroads for this couple. They can choose to go back to their old ways of lying and avoiding, or they can choose a path toward being open and honest with each other. When one is ready and the other is not, they will likely go back to their old ways, as the one who is not ready will be too threatened by this bright light focused on their dysfunction. It is hard for someone who is used to living in deception to suddenly live with accountability.

The most likely synergistic wounded pairing for this archetype is one who is a codependent enabler and one (or both) who has narcissistic or manipulative traits. They are each plugged into the wounding of the other. The enabler typically caters to the narcissist's whims, deceptions, and distractions so that neither one has to face reality. They both are lost in the illusion of their own making.

THE FABULIST ARCHETYPE

The fabulist can hold the energy of chaos; in fact, they thrive on risk and chance. They tend to be catastrophic, or all or nothing, in their thinking. This extreme is the result of having too little experience working things through, talking reasonably about difficult topics, and creating a sense of balance within themselves. The fabulist assumes that if the difficult issues are brought up and dealt with honestly, then the situation must be bad, and therefore the outcome will be even worse. They scurry away from serious conversations, afraid of culpability and responsibility.

The fabulist's dishonesty and conflict-avoidance pattern usually predates the relationship. It may be connected to past failed relationships, family of origin woundings, or their personality characteristics. Their partner does not know about their lying, at least at first.

The fabulist may commit infidelities in the form of sexting, flirting, or full-blown emotional or sexual affairs. People who have affairs want to minimize their betrayals as something other than an infidelity, saying, for example, *I don't like saying the word "affair."* But any behavior that one person doesn't want their partner to know about is an infidelity. People will say to me, *We don't meet in person, and we have never had sex; we are just playing.* I will ask, *If your partner were sitting right next to you, would you show them these texts?* One hundred percent of the time the answer is absolutely not. Whatever the case, an infidelity is a betrayal of the trust within the relationship.

Wounding Origins of the Fabulist Archetype

The fabulist generally comes from an addicted or highly dysfunctional household. They learned the skills of lying and avoiding early on in their family of origin so that they could navigate a chaotic household or one or both parents' addiction. They were not bad children, but they learned that telling a lie was easier than facing up to a truth or dealing with out-of-control rage. They learned that, by lying, they could avoid uncomfortable situations; control chaotic situations; and temporarily avoid blow-ups with their family, teachers, or friends. If their lie was discovered, it was easier for them to ask for forgiveness and then move on. This manipulation became their go-to wounded tool, using it not only for big lies but also small, inconsequential lies. If they were asked why they lie, they would honestly say they don't know.

Honesty and accountability are kryptonite to the fabulist.

There may have been loose boundaries in the household, or one or both parents were not faithful or had multiple marriages. These children learned at a young age that if something didn't work out in a relationship, you don't have to work hard to make the relationship functional; you can just leave, manipulate others, or escape into your own reality.

An adult who grew up in a household with addiction learned to avoid their feelings and reality by escaping into alcohol, drugs, overeating, gambling, overworking, preoccupation with sex, or excessive shopping. They learned that it was easy to get lost in another reality and fool themselves into thinking that everything was OK.

*The fabulist manipulates their reality with
magical thinking, furthering a false narrative.*

The parents in this household created chaos or disorga-
nization, and rarely discussed topics of importance. When
such topics were brought up, it was at the last minute, there
was a lot of tension, and decisions were made hastily. This
further increased the level of drama in the household. The
children learned that whenever big topics were discussed,
they were full of emotion and so best avoided. The theme
of conflict avoidance filled this household, becoming much
more elevated as the tension built to the point of a huge
explosion.

Some fabulist adults grew up in loving and stable families. I
believe some people have a personality that is prone to lying if
it serves their inner child wounding. Their inner child doesn't
want to upset or disappoint others, which is similar to conflict
avoidance, but they also look for acceptance and validation.
They say whatever they think the other wants to hear in order
to be told they are good. This temporarily rescues them from
feelings of shame or insecurity, but the underlying wound is
still there.

Most adults who are prone to lying and are aware that they
do so can tell you when they started this behavior. It begins
with something as small as lying when asked if they did their
homework. If they lied and said yes, their parents' smiles
were all the reinforcement they needed to feel better about
themselves, so they continued to lie.

You can see from these examples that there is a wide range
of family-of-origin household dynamics that can contribute
to a person's dishonesty, manipulation, or avoidance as an

adult. Not everyone who grows up in such an environment is destined to become a dishonest person with their own chaotic household, but if someone has a predisposition in their personality to become this way, there is a good chance they will do so.

Dishonest folks rate their lies as little or big.
They don't see either one as bad or hurting others;
lies are just a means to an end.

Wounded Tools of the Fabulist Archetype

The wounded tools that the fabulist learned from childhood trauma or wounding include:

- being sneaky
- lying to cover up feelings of being less-than
- lying to cover up their core shame
- seeing lies as means to an end
- spending a lot of time tracking lies to manage relationships
- using new items, situations, or relationships as a way to distract from feelings
- ignoring realities that are too difficult to face
- avoiding conflict at all costs in order to be seen as good
- distrusting others even when there is no reason to
- manipulating reality to feel in control

THE ENABLER ARCHETYPE

The enabler synergistically pairs with the fabulist in many ways. They subconsciously choose someone who is an addict or has emotional wounding that creates chaos in order to replicate what they had in childhood. The two situations may not look the same, but the dynamic is the same. The enabler brings their illusion of control and rescuing to try to lock things down, but it never works. They are linked to the addict or the chaotic situation because they cannot imagine another way of life.

The enabler looks the other way or takes the lying partner back after they are caught in a deception. They desperately try to catch the fabulist in their lies, attempting to recapture what they see as their perfect time together before the lying. As much as the enabler doesn't like the lying, they are part of the problem by forgiving the lies and saying, *That's OK. I will be with you anyway.* The enabler feels they are smart enough to figure out this problem so that they can reclaim and rehabilitate the person they thought they fell in love with.

They outwardly say that they want the truth, but the louder message is that putting up with their lying partner is easier than facing the dishonesty and dysfunction in their relationship. They are coaddicted to the dishonest person's lying behavior. The wounding of the enabler doesn't see the wounding of the dishonest partner. They are each lost in their pain, living in their own illusion.

The fabulist and the enabler are both in a wounded illusion, and neither wants to face reality.

Wounding Origins of the Enabler Archetype

The enabler grew up in an environment where they didn't learn to trust themselves and looked to others to determine their reality. They probably grew up in a household with addiction or emotional chaos. They learned that it is OK to stay in a relationship even when their partner doesn't treat them very well. As an adult, the enabler carries this misplaced loyalty through friendships, partnerships, and work life. They often work for dishonest or dysfunctional people; this feels right to them because of their low self-esteem. Their broken trust issues create feelings of anxiety, which they use to control or monitor others as a way to cope. They constantly give their power away, and when they discover this, they feel bad, which contributes to their toxic shame bank. The theme of the victim shows up in the enabler.

Wounded Tools of the Enabler Archetype

The wounded tools that the enabler learned from childhood trauma or wounding include:

- giving power to others even when it is not warranted
- making excuses for others
- excusing the inexcusable
- paving over feelings of betrayal
- fixing, rescuing, and caretaking
- focusing on others, not on themselves
- having low self-esteem and self-worth
- feeling empty inside
- overcompensating
- overcontrolling
- tracking, monitoring, and obsessing over the fabulist's behavior

SYNERGISTIC WOUNDED PAIRING—KYLE AND MEGAN

Kyle and Megan are a typical fabulist and enabler pairing. They looked cool on the outside but were in a constant state of fear. They did not trust, and they both needed to feel in control, which often came out as passive-aggressive behavior or covert control. Neither of them liked conflict, because the other partner would learn about their feelings if conflict arose. Holding their cards close to the vest was better, because then neither partner would know the other's true feelings on any one issue. If they revealed too much to the other, the partner might one day use this against them. They both lived in a state of risk and chaos built on a foundation of wounded deception.

Kyle and Megan are not wealthy, but they had been living as if they were. They used the distractions of sex, new cars, boats, vacations, parties, and impulsive buying to transfer attention from the real issues to the shiny and new. They lived their lives focused on illusion, where there was excitement and drama, not on a mundane, boring reality.

Megan and Kyle were in an elaborate dance of deception, with each other and themselves, that disguised their pain.

Megan, the fabulist partner in this relationship, tended toward addiction. She started with lottery scratch-offs, and eventually worked up to swinging by the casino. She engaged in anonymous sex with random men, which numbed her feelings and helped her feel attractive and wanted, letting her escape for a time. She would get a dopamine hit from acting out and then settle down for a while.

Megan self-sabotaged and lied because she didn't feel worthy. She felt that Kyle was too good for her, and she held her breath waiting for him to say he was leaving for good. Kyle had threatened to leave her many times but then always forgave her and took her back. She tried her best to test or break up the relationship before he did. Neither of them were conscious of their wounding.

Doing something detrimental to the relationship and then asking for forgiveness later was easier for this couple than being honest up front.

Kyle was more risk averse than Megan. If he had been on his own, he wouldn't have spent so much money, but he indulged Megan when she acted out because he loved her. He even took a second job to make up for the money she spent gambling and purchases they made to distract themselves from their lives. When Kyle would stumble across one of Megan's deceptions, he would get mad and feel the edges of betrayal, but never enough to stand up for himself and set a boundary. He didn't trust his gut enough to set strong boundaries.

Kyle had a lot of anxieties, and he tried to monitor Megan's behaviors as a way to feel safer and more in control. He was, in fact, a coaddict. He believed that if he could control his own behavior and Megan's, then he could control her addictions to spending money, gambling, and anonymous sex. He would try to do end runs around her to discover her lies instead of dealing with core issues and setting functional boundaries.

When Kyle sensed that Megan was lying, he didn't trust this sense, so he made up stories about her behaviors, essentially lying to himself. He wanted to keep his idea of Megan wrapped in shrink wrap, making excuses for her as fast as she lied. He was lost in his own enabling illusion, just like she was lost in her addiction. Kyle had what I call *complicated betrayal,* or multiple betrayals. This meant that he would have a longer road toward healing once he began to be honest with himself and realized the depth and chronic nature of the betrayals in their relationship.

Coaddicts get caught up in the recycling pattern with the addict. Both are lost in their wounding.

Kyle knew Megan lied to him, but it was easier and emotionally safer to stay in the illusion than to face the hard truths about their relationship. Both of them would do whatever they could to avoid seeing their real feelings, paying the bills, and dealing with sickness and addiction. When they did have to deal with these issues, it was often haphazard, disorganized, and reactionary. One of their main goals was coming up with creative ways to stay in denial.

Both Kyle and Megan have deep inner child woundings whereby they feel flawed, damaged, and broken, on top of the repeated relationship traumas from the deceptions. At some level, they both feel they don't deserve better. Their adult distractions had kept them from seeing or feeling their wounded inner child reality. They preferred instead to continue to bring on the new and novel, the chaotic and disorganized, to convince themselves they were OK. If their outside world had new, exciting, and shiny things in it, they must be OK and not screwed up.

This couple was on a self-destructive path because they had to either keep promoting all of the lies between them or face the consequences of their choices. But avoiding and distracting themselves from reality was not sustainable in the long term. It is a wonder that this synergistic pairing had any sort of connection. Kyle and Megan were so synergistically wounded that neither could see how incredibly toxic their relationship was.

THE STARR RESET FOR THE FABULIST
AND THE ENABLER ARCHETYPES

If you recognize your relationship in one of these archetypes, you need to stop the dishonesty and chaos. This will not be easy, as these behaviors are woven into the fabric of the relationship. Dishonesty on top of chaos is a volatile combination, so you will need to remove some of this fuel first so you have some stability.

Fabulists don't always know they are lying, or if they do recognize this, they underestimate how much they lie, omit the truth, or minimize details about a situation. When I ask a fabulist if they want to lie, they will say no, but they will also say they don't know what their life would be like if they didn't lie. They are afraid to speak their truth because they fear their partner's reaction. The enabling partner will say things like, *Just don't do it anymore.* But if it were that easy, the fabulist would probably have stopped a long time ago. An abrupt stop to this behavior is not reasonable to assume.

Stop—Stopping the behavior for each of you means recognizing what you are doing. If you are the fabulist, you will need to reach a personal threshold, where you have had enough of lying and deceit. This is harder than it sounds, as lying is your main way of relating to the world. Sometimes something dramatic needs to happen for you to want to stop.

If you are the enabler, you will also need to reach a personal threshold, where accepting the lying and manipulation is more painful than putting your foot down and saying *no more.* You will have to get to a point where you are tired of trying to rehabilitate your partner, where you have had enough.

Think—This step is the hardest because it will feel the most foreign to this couple. If you are the fabulist, think about all the ways you use deception to get what you want instead of being upfront and stating your needs or concerns. If you are the enabler, think about all the ways you ignore the lying behaviors and how you perpetuate the problem.

You may get to the thinking stage of the STARR Reset process and not go any further out of fear. You may feel, at a deep level, that if you proceed to act, you will not be able to go back. The reality is that you both will have to practice using these new skills, and find the words and the courage to move to the next step.

Act—Once you have discerned how you feel, begin to use intentional communication techniques to bring up difficult issues with each other. One partner may not be in the same place as the other; just because you are excited and want to talk about these things doesn't mean that your partner is. Stay with it.

If you are the fabulist and feel you can't stop lying, at least acknowledge what your partner says, and try to be more honest and forthcoming. Your partner won't expect a huge change; they just don't want to second-guess you all of the time. Know that your partner misses feeling close to you and wants to have a grounded discussion in which they feel heard.

If you are the enabler, know that your partner isn't going to want to be held accountable for their lies. If you try to get them to admit and apologize, you will be in for a battle. Instead, when you realize you have been lied to, focus on your feelings and the effects the lying has on you. Focus on your boundary statements and speak your truth, even if your dishonest partner can't admit any wrongdoing. If you can communicate your feelings and feel heard, then that is a success. You may not resolve anything, but you are learning to communicate in a more functional way.

With practice, your partner will know where you are headed when you want to have a discussion. However, this can be good or bad. It can be good because they won't be thrown off about the process and can (begrudgingly) talk with you about things. It can be bad because now that your partner knows that you are trying to get them to be present and emotionally available, they may become even more defensive or do bigger things to distract and get you off track. With any of these approaches, you are learning to be persistent and patient. Any relationship worth having is worth fighting for.

The fabulist may feel attacked when being held accountable, especially if they are not ready to own the choices they have made.

Reset and Repair—Now you can begin working on resetting, reconnecting, and repairing the damage. You may need a therapist to help navigate the relationship traumas, specifically the losses and betrayals you feel. There usually is a grieving process that you have to go through to get to the other side. You are grieving the loss of the trust that you once had. You are grieving the time that was wasted on all the lying, deception, and distractions. You may even grieve the loss of money, opportunities, and quality of life if your lifestyle has been propped up with deception.

If you are the enabler, you may feel a great deal of shame that you ignored and put up with all of this behavior in the past.

For the reset and repair to work, the most important tools to have in your relationship are honesty and transparency, and the biggest keys you both need to move past this wounding and behavioral pattern are humility and radical vulnerability.

You will need to set your egos aside, trust in each other, and get help from professionals to help guide you through this transition.

Healing the Fabulist

If you are a chronic fabulist, the habitual behavior of hiding the truth and avoiding conflict has been with you for a long time, and it will be extremely hard to break. You can begin by making a heartfelt apology to your partner, which will let them know you are aware that this is a problem in the relationship. This act of humility goes a long way toward repairing your relationship, which has probably been pretty chaotic. Through your ownership of your part of the problem, you let your partner know you are willing to work with them on the hard issues. Take your time as you heal this wounding, and be patient with yourself.

Without the lies, the fabulist feels exposed and vulnerable.

If you connect with the energy and expression of the fabulist, say this intention for your wounded inner child:

I know that when I was growing up, things felt out of control and I didn't always feel emotionally or physically safe. It was easier to lie and avoid making someone mad than face the consequences. Today I don't need to continue that pattern, as I am now learning how to honor myself and those I love. Today I am choosing to speak my truth and know that I can get through any difficulties with my

*partner when I am available with humility. I don't need
to manipulate others to get my needs met. I know that I
am a good person, and I deserve to be honest with myself
and others. Each day I will try to say more honest things
than dishonest things. For today, I forgive myself for those
behavioral choices, and each day I'm learning to love
myself more.*

Healing the Enabler

If you are an enabler, look at how you have contributed to or
enabled the dishonesty in the household. Your partner may be
avoidant with their lying, but you may be avoidant with your
denial that this situation is really bad. You may have lulled
yourself into making excuses for your situation because you
just don't want to deal with your partner's games anymore.
Have you set boundaries within yourself and with your partner,
or are you continuing any codependent enabling behaviors?

Look at what causes the chaos in the relationship. What
distractions do you create that contribute to the chaos? How
can you step up and take responsibility instead of going into
a victim space, avoiding, and letting things crash and burn?

It is important for you to remember that your dishonest
partner has had this behavior for most of their life, and that
it probably began before they were twenty years old. Lying is
part of their emotional protection system. Most likely, your
partner does not lie purposely to hurt you. Hopefully, in time,
they will learn and feel, at a deep level, that they do hurt and
manipulate you when they are dishonest. As you face your
own truths, be gentle with yourself, and do not blame yourself
for your partner's behavior. Do not feel that you "should have

seen this before." You don't need to shame yourself into a healing space.

If you connect to the energy and expression of the enabler, say this intention for your wounded inner child:

I work hard every day to create a loving expression of myself to give to the world. I know that in the past I have made choices that put others' needs before my own. I also know that I have overlooked people or situations that have hurt me. Each day, I am learning to give to myself first, then to others. Through strong boundaries, I am learning to speak and honor my truth. I trust and love myself.

THE STARR RESET—KYLE AND MEGAN

Kyle suspected that Megan was having an affair with a man she works with, but he didn't want to believe it, so he kept ignoring the signs. He noticed how she always had her phone with her and would not give him the password. He also noticed that sometimes her errands took longer than they should.

Megan felt justified in her behaviors, and Kyle didn't feel that he deserved any better.

Megan had gotten lost in her desire and the thrill of chasing after married and unavailable men. Her sex addiction had gone beyond anything she ever thought she would do, and she felt out of control. One day, she was going to meet up with a man at a hotel. She walked through the lobby and over to the elevator, which had mirrors on the outer doors. As she stood waiting for the doors to open, she saw herself for the first time in a long time. She saw that she looked tired and desperate, not at all how she pictured herself. She froze, then turned around and left the hotel.

Later that night, Megan and Kyle started to get into an argument about where she had been and why she hadn't come home when she said she would. She was about to launch into deflecting, defending, and getting mad at Kyle, but instead she broke down. She didn't want to go into her old routine of making up lies to cover her tracks. Megan had hit her personal threshold. She wanted to reset her life and her relationship. Kyle had never seen her cry like that before. He didn't know what to do. First she just cried and wouldn't say what was wrong. Then, between her sobs, Megan said she "couldn't do this anymore." Kyle thought she meant she wanted a divorce.

Stop—Megan had reached a breaking point. She was now facing a part of herself that she wasn't proud of and didn't like very much. She was tired of running and had hit her rock bottom, her personal threshold.

Think—Megan said to herself, *I can't do this anymore. I don't like what I have made of my life.* She knew she had to stop her behaviors and addictive cycles, and that she and Kyle couldn't keep going like this. She didn't know what needed to happen, but she knew some kind of reset had to occur, because she was so tired of feeding her addictions. She thought she was more powerful than they were, but now she realized that she wasn't.

Act—Megan said to Kyle, "I don't know what's wrong with me, but I can't do this anymore. I'm tired. I know I love you, but I think I'm addicted to sex and gambling, and I can't keep this up. I need you to help me. I'm tired of lying to you all the time."

Kyle started to yell at Megan. "I've been trying to tell you this for years! Why don't you ever listen to me?" Megan was verbalizing everything he had been telling her and everything he had been feeling, but this was the wrong reaction for him to have at that moment. Megan buried her head in the pillows, crying harder. Kyle was frozen hearing Megan sob. He was upset with her, but he also felt compassion for her and wanted to rescue her.

Reset and Repair—Kyle was stunned by how hard Megan was crying. He stopped yelling when he saw that she wasn't fighting back. In a moment of compassion he said, "I don't know how to help you, but I want to. I have been trying to talk with you about these things for years, but I guess you weren't ready. I love you so much."

Megan said, "I love you, too, but I think I'm really screwed up and I can't help myself anymore. Am I going to be OK? Are we going to be OK?"

Kyle said, "I'm here for you, baby. We've been through a lot, but we can get through a lot more."

Megan and Kyle got to a point where they could both acknowledge and recognize their behaviors. Megan, tired of the exhausting chase of feeding her addiction, had reached her breaking point. She, like many addicts, had reached an internal point of surrender, when the addict realizes that they are powerless over the addiction. Kyle was a coaddict and lost in his own process, so he couldn't have helped her see this. It needed to come from deep within Megan.

After they went through their STARR Reset, Kyle told Megan that he could now see that, in the past, he had tried to manage her world by keeping tabs on her and seeing if she was lying or not to give himself a sense of control. This behavior was his wounding, not hers. Kyle was clear with Megan that he loved her, but he was learning, through boundary setting, what was his work to do and what was hers. Kyle had to admit that he couldn't control Megan or her addiction.

Knowing that Megan was consciously aware of her addictions was reassuring to Kyle, as this told him that she was trying. It also helped him understand her behavior and how he was lost in this, as well. Kyle learned more about his coaddict enabling role and no longer tries to control things or clean up their messes with money or rescuing. He is patient with Megan even though he still catches her in lies. Kyle is beginning to realize the extent of the layers of betrayals in their relationship, and sometimes he gets overwhelmed. When he does, he asks for some reassurance and loving from Megan. They exclaim their love for each other.

Megan began therapy. One of the first things she did was to join some twelve-step groups to work on her addictions. She had to admit she was an addict and couldn't control the addictions. She also began to tackle her lying. When she and Kyle would get into arguments, Megan was the one who would say, "Wait a minute, we need a reset. I just lied to you. Let's start over." Kyle joined support groups for coaddicts and codependents.

I encouraged Kyle and Megan to reassure each other by saying, *We are going to get through this together, and I love you.* This is not a magic fix, but what they are saying is that they are a team and no one is going to abandon the relationship. They check in with each other by saying, *I'm being transparent with you; are you being transparent with me?* This reminds them of their shared goal of honesty with themselves and each other.

If you can't imagine saying this to your partner, then ask yourself why. There may be too much damage done to the relationship from the chronic lying and mistrust. Or you may be too lost in the game of your own illusion. If you think this is the case, please carefully read "Should I Stay or Should I Go?" in chapter 18.

Looking Inward

How does this couple remind you of your own wounded struggles within yourself and with your partner? What are some of the inner child woundings that you connect to? How does this match with your own story? What was activated inside of you when you read how this couple worked on their communication using the STARR Reset? Record your impressions in your notebook, as this will help you heal your wounded patterns.

CHAPTER 14

The Bickersons Archetype

Darkness cannot drive out darkness; only light can do that.
Hate cannot drive out hate; only love can do that.
—DR. MARTIN LUTHER KING JR.

The synergistic pairing of the Bickersons[1] archetype is that of two people who use yelling and argument as their main form of communication. On the surface they look like a couple who just yell at each other a lot, but their pain is deeper than what the yelling reveals. They have forgotten how to be civil toward each other, and often forget what they were arguing about; they just know they are hurting. Generally, these are two proud people who each have a strong sense of self outwardly but are

---

1. From Wikipedia: the Bickersons was a radio comedy sketch series that began September 8, 1946, on NBC in the United States, moving the following year to CBS where it continued until August 28, 1951. The show's married protagonists, portrayed by Don Ameche and Frances Langford, spent nearly all their time together in a relentless verbal war. Source: Wikipedia.

deeply wounded underneath. They are not mean people, they are just hurting and defensive.

Each partner feels that they are right and doesn't want to back down. When they have backed down in the past, they felt weak and vulnerable. Sometimes their partner uses this "weakness" against them by taunting them or throwing their words back at them. Then one or both go into a shame spiral, which reinforces the need to stay defensively guarded and distant. Both carry the emotional energetic signature of the hurt victim.

This couple keeps up the yelling, arguing, and making snide remarks as a way to communicate their feelings or opinions about the most mundane topics. This volume feels normal to them, and they are used to throwing mud at each other. They argue about unimportant issues, so they would be hard pressed to remember any of them down the road. But in the moment, it's front page news because this is the focus of their displaced anger.

Displaced anger is when we are angry about one thing but focus our anger on another issue that is less on target and more neutral. This couple has mastered displaced anger. They raise the volume by threatening divorce or harming themselves or others. Their statements become more dramatic over time in their attempt to be heard, seen, and validated.

He triggers her, she triggers him.

There is a testing component to this wounded pair, which is another way they create dramas to yell about. They didn't learn how to express feelings or ask for what they needed in childhood, so they subconsciously test their partner to see if they really love them. In other words, they will think, *I'm going to do this to see if they are paying attention. If they love me and really know me, they will see what I'm trying to say.* This is a set-up designed to get their partner to show some love to them without their having to ask for it. Of course, the partner doesn't know anything about this test; they are just going about their life. When the partner inevitably fails this unfair test, the testing partner feels hurt, neglected, ignored, and sad. In their mind, their worst fear has come true: their partner doesn't love them. Then the cycle starts all over again with the yelling, feeling hurt, and attacking.

Week-long fights persist when the relationship is fractured and nothing is ever talked about or resolved. There is wounding on top of wounding.

THE BICKERSONS PAIRING

You learned in chapter 7 about a pairing in which one is the logical (thinking) partner and the other comes from an emotional (feeling) place. This dynamic often plays out with the Bickersons. (To clarify, it is not always the case that females are the feeling ones and males are the logical ones. Being logically or emotionally aligned is not gender specific.)

If the feeling partner tries to communicate using emotional language, the logical partner will say that their feelings don't make sense. The two will then go back and forth, both of them becoming louder as they try to get their point across (as if volume helps with understanding). The emotionally connected partner will use their feeling words over and over, hoping the other will eventually understand that they simply want validation and acknowledgment. Of course, the logically connected partner wants the same thing: validation and acknowledgment. They use different approaches to make their points, and both are valid, but they cross over each other. They are reluctant to back down, and each wants to have the last word. Sometimes, out of exasperation, one will agree just to get the argument over.

Oddly, sometimes the Bickersons' yelling becomes a form of emotional intimacy. There is only a small amount of tenderness in this relationship, and rarely any sexual intimacy. One way for them to feel close to each other, to stir up passion and vulnerability, is to fight. When they exchange curse words or cut deep with an insult or snide remark, they get a reaction. This response is the intimacy, the payoff, the connection that they are missing. They then keep insulting or yelling, looking for the next reaction that tells them their partner is engaged. When their partner is engaged they feel connected, thus continuing this ongoing cycle.

Do you create emotional intimacy in your relationship in healthy or unhealthy ways?

Even though this couple wants intimacy, they keep each other at arm's length, never letting the other get too close. This is what I refer to as a *bubble boundary*. They create a wall of words to keep their partner out, but at the same time they want them in. By engaging in this confusing push and pull, they complete each other's dramas, as they are synergistically wounded. They deeply understand each other and want to be together, but they don't know how to do this in a healthy, functional way.

The Bickersons want to resolve their issues, but they don't have the communication skills to do so. They use the wounded tools they learned from what they saw and learned growing up. Their synergistic wounding chose a partner who would understand their unique form of communication. As their relationship progresses, the issues between them never get resolved. Many Bickerson couples are OK with that.

Unfortunately, many open-ended problems develop that are either set aside or linked to other issues, thus becoming a bigger issue. The issue has to grow to a crisis for the couple to make a decision. At that moment, under duress, the couple is able to come together and make a joint decision. When they put their heads together, their last-minute crisis resolution skills are often productive.

The most likely synergistic pairing for this archetype is one who is narcissistically wounded and finds their mirror in a partner, and one who is insecure enough to be manipulated into being dramatic with them, someone they can spar with and keep up the yelling and bickering.

When your partner's inner child wounding comes out, you are no longer interacting with your adult partner, you are interacting with their hurt and lost inner child.

Wounding Origins of the Bickersons Archetype

Growing up in this household, the children had to work hard to be seen and heard, as the parents were busy doing their own thing. This was a loving home, but when conflicts came up they were not resolved, just shoved away and ignored. There was never a sense of closure with disagreements, and this open-ended non-resolution of conflicts led to a backlog of unresolved issues. Resentment would set in, and the toxic pressure of not discussing these conflicts would build. The parents yelled and the kids yelled, causing a very loud household.

The children would try to work out disagreements with each other, but this never went well because they had no frame of reference from the parents for how to come to a resolution. When yelling back and forth did nothing, the kids would start to physically fight, take things from each other, or destroy possessions out of frustration. Their ability to resolve conflicts regressed to a pre-verbal stage of development because talking about it didn't do any good.

The child in this household learned to manipulate others to get their needs met or to see if others were aware of their hurts, such as setting up tests to see if anyone was paying attention. When the parents or siblings failed the test, the child would get angry, pout, slink off, and go into a victim space. They equated the response, or lack thereof, to how much someone cared for them. The child's distorted way of creating a sense of self-esteem and self-worth became wrapped up in other people's level of attention instead of the child creating a clear sense of self within. A child from this household would say that they never felt acknowledged by the parent from whom they wanted the most attention.

Wounded Tools of the Bickersons Archetype

The wounded tools that the Bickersons learned from childhood trauma or wounding include:

- being the loudest one in the room
- arguing for the sake of arguing

- staying defensively guarded so as not to feel vulnerable
- not backing down until the other agrees with them
- being the victim in relationships to get what they need
- displaying passive-aggressive testing behavior to keep people guessing (*if you really love me you would . . .*).
- making big or dramatic statements to get attention
- feeling seen as a result of any kind of reaction from someone else
- not showing weakness but secretly wanting others to see their pain

SYNERGISTIC WOUNDED PAIRING—VALERIE AND TRISTAN

Valerie and Tristan are a typical Bickersons couple. They were always going at each other and yelling. It was a wonder that they stayed together given the relationship volatility, but like most synergistically wounded pairings, they were each getting something out of it. Even when they were speaking normally to each other and not yelling, there was an unspoken tension between them, like a simmering pot about to boil over. They didn't look at each other with kindness in their eyes, instead showing the weariness of resentful, long-unresolved battles.

One or the other always found something wrong with the house, the car, the kids, the dishes, and so on. They seemed to look for things to be upset about, and yelling was their main mode of communication.

Speaking in normal tones is boring
for the Bickersons pairing.

Both Valerie and Tristan carry the wounding of the victim but in different ways. Tristan was sexually abused as a nine-year-old boy, and Valerie grew up feeling neglected by her emotionally unavailable parents. They both felt that their life circumstances had not been kind to them, and they looked to each other as kindred spirits to make them feel better. They were on a search for the deep, heartfelt validation that they never received from their childhood family. They both thought the other could provide it, but they only mirrored each other's wounding. They were trying to fill up this hole inside, but they were going about it in all the wrong ways, and neither was emotionally grounded to provide a strong, loving safe place for the other.

They both mirrored the wounding of the other,
getting lost in the pain.

Tristan has some PTSD symptoms from his sexual abuse history, for which he receives individual therapy. He often created barriers to physical, sexual, and emotional intimacy with Valerie because of this sexual trauma wounding. He slept on the couch most nights, and she in their bed. He sometimes stayed awake as a test to see if Valerie would come down and try to get him to come to bed. When she didn't, he would feel very sad, like he did when he was a boy, and sometimes cry from the feelings of rejection and abandonment. Valerie was looking for Tristan to step up and recognize her emotional needs, but neither have enough healed parts to meet the other's requirements.

THE STARR RESET FOR THE BICKERSONS ARCHETYPE

If you recognize your relationship in this archetype, you first need to stop the yelling. This sounds easy, but it is a big ask for the Bickersons couple. They say that they don't know how to talk and that all they do is yell.

Stop—Stopping this behavior will be hard for both of you, as it feels natural to get big and loud when you are upset. It will take time to move away from this destructive behavior to a new way of relating to someone you love. The first thing to do is to recognize when you are yelling, and immediately interrupt yourself.

Think—Once you have learned to recognize when you are yelling, discern what you think and feel about your relationship. Think about which feelings stand out. If you need help to determine your feelings, read over the feelings chart in appendix A. How do you feel when your partner yells at you? How do you feel when you yell back? What do you want to transform in your relationship? Do you want to get out of the back-and-forth arguing? Do you want to feel closer? Do you want to learn how to be kinder to each other? Once you have clarity with your feelings, you will be able to speak clearly and affirmatively with your partner.

Make intentional choices about how you would like to proceed with the relationship. This will help you to create a road map for healing. This isn't about changing your partner, it is about transforming the hurt and pain inside of you so that you can communicate reasonably with your partner. The only way out of this dysfunctional dynamic is to change how you respond to your partner.

Act—Once you understand your feelings, find the courage to ask for what you need from your partner. This may be a big stretch, because you and your partner are not used to speaking about your tender feelings so directly. You can also come up with a boundary statement (see chapter 19), such as, *I feel disrespected when you say that I always do something or that I never do something. I feel demeaned by this, and I need you to not say those things to me. Going forward, I need you to communicate in a more respectful way.*

Reset and Repair—You both have spent a large part of your relationship thinking about everything the other isn't doing. Try to shift that perspective by making a list of those words and deeds your partner does that add to the quality of your life in general. There are probably many things your partner does that contribute to the functioning of the household, or for you personally, that you may take for granted. For example, your partner buys certain foods you like, or they work the family schedule around a certain hobby or sport that you like.

Create softer edges around your relationship by acknowledging what is right instead of always what is wrong or missing.

Take in these moments, and don't discount them by saying, *Yes, they got me this, but they don't do these other things I want.* That is unfair and demoralizing to your partner. Take small steps, and thank your partner for doing those small things. This says to your partner that you see what they do for you and that you are honoring and thanking them. This could sound something like, *Thank you for making sure I can play with my team tonight. I appreciate how you listen to my needs.* Work on changing your communication patterns so the two of you can begin to be nicer to each other.

You can begin this change by picking something to discuss that isn't a red-hot issue, one that you feel you can discuss in a reasonable way. For example, if the two of you haven't been able to come to a consensus on putting up shelves in the laundry room, the conversation might sound like this: *I know you want shelves in the laundry room, but I don't, and we keep arguing about it. Can we come to a place in the middle, where you get what you want and I get what I would like? I don't want to argue about this anymore, and I want us both to be happy.* This beginning dialogue isn't going to bring about world peace, but it is a start.

Successful compromise is about both of you feeling that your needs were heard and that there is reciprocity, balance, and fairness in the discussion and resolution. In our example, you both agreed that the shelves will go up in the laundry room, but only after you heard your partner's reasoning and they heard yours. Acknowledging the feelings and perspective of the other brings a sense of mutual respect to the discussion. You each have to give up a little to get a little of what you want. If there is no resolution at the end of the discussion, say, *I know this is a difficult topic, but I want you to know that I love you and that we will get through this together.* With this, your partner knows that you are trying and that you want to achieve the best outcome possible.

Healing the Bickersons

Healing the Bickersons couple may require more intensive work, as I cover in *Healing Your Lost Inner Child*. Understanding and healing your own wounding will help you to become more emotionally available to your partner. If you work on understanding and recognizing your triggers, you will be able to see the specific coping skills you need to work on for when your partner activates a wounding within you.

For example, if your partner uses accusatory language, such as *you never* or *you always*, go deeper within and figure out what this trigger is connected to in your past. Does this language feel shaming and disrespectful? Does it feel like something you experienced as a child? Do you feel like your partner speaks to you as a child? Check in with yourself to understand what is getting activated within you when you are talked to in this manner. It could be that, like most of us, you just don't like being spoken to in that way!

Be still and ask yourself, *Is this how I want my relationship to play out? Is there another way I can express myself?* Things won't change just because you want them to. You will need to be brave in your relationship to shift the energy between the two of you. By being more conscious in your choices, you will feel more in control and will signal to your partner that you are ready to move out of the dance the two of you have been in for quite a while.

If you connect to the energy and expression of the Bickersons, say this intention for your wounded inner child:

Even though I get scared when things happen that are out of my control, I am learning new ways to express my feelings other than yelling. I know that I can receive validation and be heard when I am emotionally available to myself and others. I am learning that I can trust others to hold my truth, and that I don't have to manipulate others to agree with me.

THE STARR RESET—VALERIE AND TRISTAN

Valerie and Tristan had some kind of disagreement on a daily basis. Their arguments were so familiar and regular that they could almost choose them off a menu board. In the past, they had each tried to stop this cycle, but they didn't have the functional tools they needed and would fall back into their routines. It wasn't fun, but it was familiar.

One day Tristan said to Valerie, "See, you are doing this again. I told you, don't leave all of this stuff on my workbench. How many times . . ."

Valerie, not one to back away, launched into a tirade of all of the things Tristan did that were disrespectful to her. She said, "Yeah, well, I have to pick your clothes up off the floor every day. I hate it. Why can't you do something so simple?" Neither one ever answered the other's question or addressed the issue; they would just exclaim their grievances to each other and wait for the next time to bring up something they were upset about.

They were usually at their worst on Monday mornings, when both felt stressed about getting ready for work and packing up the kids for school. They would start bickering at each other. "I told you, stop leaving your clothes on the floor." "Well, you left the garage door open again last night, and the cat got out. Now I have to go find the cat." This was regular Monday morning mayhem for Valerie and Tristan and their family.

Their eldest, Martin, was twelve years old. One day, as Valerie was packing up their school backpacks, he said to her, "Why do you guys yell all the time?"

Valerie, taken aback, said, "I don't know, honey, we just do. That's what we do."

Martin then went to his dad and said, "Why do you and Mom yell all the time?"

Tristan looked at Martin and wanted to yell at him for being disrespectful. Instead, he said, "I don't know. Why don't you ask your mother?!"

That night, after the kids were put to bed, Valerie was exhausted and wanted to zone out by watching TV. Tristan said to her, "You know, Martin asked me why we fight all the time."

Valerie said, "He asked me the same thing."

Tristan asked, "So, why do we?"

Valerie responded, "Look, I don't like our arguing, but you never listen to me. I feel I have to do everything, and you never help." She has just reached her personal threshold. She didn't know it, but she about to call for a reset.

Stop—Valerie was exhausted from the back-and-forth bickering. Having reached her personal threshold, she said, "OK, I know where this is going, and I don't want to do this again tonight. We need to just stop this cycle now. We need a reset. Let's start this conversation over."

Think—Valerie knew that they were not going to get anywhere if they continued down this familiar path. She knew that if they did, she would just dump all over Tristan and he would do the same to her. She stopped the conversation and asked for a reset. She didn't know what to say next, but she knew she didn't want to continue the cycle. She wasn't happy, and she thought that saying *stop* would be enough.

Act—Valerie said, "I don't know how to get us out of this cycle, but I'm tired. I don't want to keep going back and forth with you."

Tristan said, "Well, I don't know how, either. All I know is that you won't listen to me and that you tell me I don't listen to you. I feel rejected by you."

Reset and Repair—Valerie, enjoying this moment of civility, said to Tristan, "What if we just agree to disagree?" But she didn't like that, so she added, "If you stop, I'll stop, or at least I'll try."

Tristan didn't know what she meant. He said, "Do you mean that if I stop yelling at you, you won't yell at me?"

Valerie said, "Yes, like a truce."

Then, out of the blue, Tristan asked, "Do you even want to be married anymore?"

Valerie sat in silence, longer than what was comfortable for Tristan. Finally, she said, "Yes, I do—at least, I think I do. I don't often feel close to you, and sometimes I wonder if I love you anymore, but for right now I want to stay married." Stunned, Tristan wasn't expecting an honest answer, as he had asked the question rhetorically. He wanted to go back to their familiar bickering because he knew how to do that.

He didn't know how to navigate these uncharted waters, but he gave it a try. "OK, I hear you. I asked a question, so I guess I should have expected an answer. I love you, even though I probably don't act like it. I love you, our family, and our life together."

Valerie said, "I like all of that, too, but I don't like the arguing. Maybe some part of me has fallen out of love with you, and I don't know if I can get that back." Silent now, they both sat in the heavy air of words expressed that couldn't be taken back.

Valerie finally said, "Here's what I can try. I will try to be kinder to you, but if you start yelling at me, then I will shut down and yell back."

Tristan knew that this conversation was nothing like any other talk they had ever had, even when they were dating. He said, "OK, I can respect that. I will try my best, but I'm not going to be perfect."

Valerie replied, "Neither am I. I don't know what I'm doing with this, either, I just know that we need to stop having these same arguments over and over, and get out of this cycle."

Valerie and Tristan had a lot of work to do if they were going to repair their relationship. She put him on notice that she wasn't going to love him unconditionally if he kept arguing with her. She wasn't an angel, either, but she expressed her feelings and interrupted their back-and-forth bickering.

After both had individual therapy and tried some new communication techniques, Valerie and Tristan decided to separate. Their battles over the years had taken too great a toll on both of them, and Valerie, especially, was simply worn out. Neither could find the energy or desire to continue on together. Tristan was devastated. He thought Valerie could have hung in there with him, bickering till the end. It's important to honor that, even with their individual emotional wounding, Tristan and Valerie tried to make their relationship work before separating. In the end, though, years of fighting had worn away any goodwill left between them. They divorced, and both continued to receive help for their underlying wounded issues.

It is hard to hear about couples who don't work out. There is something in the human spirit that inspires us to want people and situations to succeed. The fact is, some couples take the opportunity to work on their issues early on, and some neglect the relationship until it dies.

I have found that when deep traumas such as childhood sexual abuse and emotional neglect are present, they can cut to the person's core and, ultimately, their relationship. Valerie and Tristan both had inner child trauma wounding issues that were left unchecked and unhealed for many years. They both realize the individual work they have ahead of them, but they are ready to heal. Uniquely for this couple, they will probably be able to heal better apart than if they had stayed together.

LOOKING INWARD

How does this couple remind you of your own wounded struggles within yourself and with your partner? What are some of the inner child woundings that you connect to? How does this match with your own story? What was activated inside of you when you read how this couple worked on their communication using the STARR Reset? Record your impressions in your notebook, as this will help you heal your wounded patterns.

CHAPTER 15

The Oversharer Archetype

Strong minds discuss ideas. Average minds discuss events.
Weak minds discuss people.
—SOCRATES

The oversharer archetype describes a person who can't sit on a juicy tidbit; they have to tell someone or they will burst. When they feel scared or uncertain, they share confidential information about their partner to see what someone else thinks, because they do not respect their relationship or trust their own opinion. Of course, telling secrets out of turn is never helpful for a relationship.

The secrets that I share make me look big in the eyes of others but small in the heart of my love.

Sharing a partner's secret with a third person and then asking them to give their opinion is a boundary violation. These sorts of boundary violations are about fear or manipulation.

Such violations are used as a set-up, as a way to say to their partner, *See, I told you that was a bad idea; even my friend agrees with me.* This cycle is reinforced with repeated betrayals of trust.

When the oversharer talks outside the relationship, they are trying to figure out what is going on in a situation and get support for their point of view. By doing so, the oversharer conveys to their partner that their opinion doesn't matter and that this outside person's opinion has more value that the partner's. Unfortunately, this is one of the most common behaviors that can happen in a relationship, and it is incredibly destructive. The oversharer is in the control position, a two-against-one sort of situation. When their partner finds out, they are left feeling shamed, vulnerable, defensive, and on their own.

An example of oversharing is telling your parents or a sibling personal information about your relationship or partner. This is often more damaging to the relationship than sharing with a friend. If the oversharer shares a confidence with their parents, for example, then the betrayed partner may be uncomfortable or embarrassed at every holiday family gathering the couple attends. The parents may pass judgment on the partner or the couple, or worse, give unsolicited advice. When a family member or friend interjects themselves into the couple's private issues, then there are three people in the relationship.

THE OVERSHARER PAIRING

I believe that many people who overshare are, at some level, trying to talk through confusion or shock because they don't understand why their partner feels a certain way, for example, or why they want to participate in an activity, or why they have a particular belief about something. Sometimes the oversharer shares with friends or family in order to shame their partner or to get others to be against the partner. Sometimes the over-sharing partner is just a gossiper and can't hold anything in.

The choice to share a secret may come from a place of good intention, but in most cases, the partner feels hurt and be-trayed on learning of the sharing. For example, the one partner wants to try something new in the bedroom, or the one has an illness they don't want anyone to know about, or the couple is trying to work through the aftereffects of an affair. Any time the oversharer shares confidential information about these types of private situations, the oversharer's partner will feel hurt and betrayed. It is a violation of trust that erodes the connection between the partners.

Oversharing could be called just plain gossiping, such as when the oversharer talks about what their partner has said about their job or workplace, or what they have said about one of their friends. What the oversharer doesn't know is all of the people that those friends or family know. Something the oversharer thinks is a small bit of gossip about their partner's workplace could reveal information that jeopardizes or exposes someone else in the workplace. Gossiping could be the oversharer's way of expressing concern and wanting their friend or family member to help calm their fears, but it is nevertheless a betrayal of the trust in the relationship.

Gossip: If the person you are talking about was sitting next to you, would you want them to hear what you are saying? If not, you are gossiping.

Often the betrayed partner doesn't know what to do to stop the oversharing partner. They have tried talking with them and describing how they are hurt by this action, but the oversharer gets a lot of out of sharing juicy gossip.

Sometimes when betrayals are made, the one partner is trying to get back at the other partner because of something the other partner did. I especially see this happen in the case of an affair. After the affair is discovered, the betrayed partner will say, *Well you hurt me, so I'm going to hurt (shame, humiliate, punish) you by telling my good friends what you did.* This bit of revenge may feel good in the moment, but it is one of the most damaging things a partner can do. Once this information is shared with family or friends, it forever changes how those people think of the betraying partner, and will impede the work of moving through and healing the betrayal. This is a wicked situation, as both partners are deeply hurting. If you are tempted to do this, step back, take a breath, and ask yourself what you would gain by saying this about your partner. How would it help your relationship to heal?

I want to hurt you so you are just as miserable as I am.

The most likely synergistically wounded pairing for this archetype is one who is emotionally insecure and one who is confident but private. They support each other in different ways, but they are not always on the same page with their decision-making. The insecure person doesn't trust themselves and goes outside of the relationship for advice, thus hurting the private partner.

Wounding Origins of the Oversharer Archetype

The oversharer's childhood household was one in which everyone was in everyone else's business, a state called *en-meshment*. There was little privacy, and if someone tried to hide something or keep something a secret, all members of the household would go out of their way to expose the secret. Private information wasn't kept private, so family members either learned to shut down and not say anything to anyone or made it a point to out someone's secret.

The parents didn't acknowledge any of this behavior because they were also enmeshed in the dysfunction. There wasn't a lot of trust in this family because of all the betrayals and microaggressions of confidences being broken. Children learned that if they went to a parent for help and asked the parent not to tell anyone, the parent shared it with the other parent, other relatives, or worse yet, the household in general. When family members randomly brought up this private issue, the child was caught off guard, feeling highly vulnerable as toxic shame washed over them.

Such betrayal of trust was normalized in this family of origin, where no child or parent had a sense of where they ended and another family member began. Everyone was in everyone else's business, and the child had fuzzy or nonexistent boundaries. The child did not learn how to calm themselves down, and the parents were lost in their own wounding and not able to give comfort when a trust was betrayed. It was easier for the child to go to someone outside of the family for support and comfort. In doing so, they learned that others were more sympathetic than their own family. They would reveal their own secrets as well as what was going on within their family. This is one example of how sharing secrets can begin.

Wounded Tools of the Oversharer Archetype

The wounded tools that the oversharer learned from childhood trauma or wounding include:

- telling confidential secrets
- not respecting boundaries (blurred lines feel like closeness instead of disrespect or smothering)

- doubting and second-guessing themselves
- hurting someone else if they are hurting
- sharing secrets to rely on others to calm them down or get their approval
- getting back at their partner by sharing their secret
- feeling powerful or getting revenge from telling stories
- disrespecting someone's feelings to get their own needs met
- gossiping about a secret because they are worried

SYNERGISTIC WOUNDED PAIRING—EMMA AND BILL

Emma and Bill are a typical oversharer couple. Bill secretly gossiped confidences that Emma shared with him, and Emma was hurt and embarrassed when she found out. They love each other, but Bill had poor boundaries. He would bring friends or family members into their relationship by revealing intimate confidences.

When Bill got excited with new information and couldn't keep the secret, he violated relationship boundaries. This shows a lack of internal and external boundary setting and is a form of enmeshment. Sometimes he felt nervous about what Emma had told him, and he excitedly told his best friend, Adam, whom he has known since he was a boy.

Bill's inner child emotional wounding didn't have the internal support to contain or hold Emma's personal information or secrets. He didn't know where he ended and someone else began. This was also a betrayal and a violation of trust. When Bill shared his and Emma's secrets with Adam, he felt reassured and less worried when Adam gave him feedback. There were many reasons why Bill thought it was OK to share these secrets, but it was unwanted exposure for Emma.

Bill's oversharing reminded Emma of how she used to share her feelings with her mom, who would then tell Emma's dad. Her dad thought it was weird that Emma had feelings that didn't make sense to him, and he would mock or shame her feelings. Deep emotional scarring and betrayal by her mom and dad effected Emma's need for secrecy and safe emotional boundaries.

Once a betrayal happens, the wounded inner child goes into a defensive, shut-down mode.

Once she met Bill, Emma thought she could finally feel safe and open enough to share her emotions, but Bill turned out to be just like her mom. She felt incredibly hurt at this betrayal, but Bill felt justified in getting Adam's opinions about what was going on in their relationship.

Feeling powerful was important to Bill, as he always felt insecure growing up and didn't get the attention or acknowledgment he needed. His older sister, who had many illnesses growing up, consumed the family's attention, and Bill was pushed off to the side. Sharing secrets gave Bill a sense of being important, but it was a false sense of identity.

THE STARR RESET FOR THE OVERSHARER ARCHETYPE

If you recognize your relationship in this archetype, the betrayal of trust needs to stop if you want to repair and create a deeper connection with each other. If you are the oversharer, you need to stop this behavior. Each and every time you tell a secret, you are tearing away at your commitment to your partner.

Stop—If you are the oversharer, you probably get rein-forcement from sharing secrets with people outside of your relationship. Stopping this behavior will be an abrupt change, and you may not know what to talk about with your family and friends. To stop the oversharing, you must first learn to recognize when you are starting to do so. This is the hardest part of the healing process.

Ask yourself what you get out of telling a secret to some-one else. Is it the thrill of doing something you know you shouldn't? Is it for revenge? Something else? How do you feel afterward? Do you feel a momentary satisfaction and then feel bad that you betrayed your partner's trust? Do you feel that you are gaining a level of control or dominance over your partner by telling their secret? Do you feel like you are trying to even the score? Are you trying to get more people on your side?

If you answer yes to most of these questions, you can heal the underlying wounding so you don't feel compelled to tell your partner's private information. You may need to work through resentments or anxiety issues before you can heal the relationship. Just stopping the behavior will not be enough to heal this wounded pattern. If you feel you can stop overshar-ing and heal this behavior, then move on to the next step of thinking about what your feelings are and why you overshare.

Think—How do you feel about your relationship? Do you want to work on the issues between you and your partner? If you were betrayed by your partner in some way and involve other people in order to shame your partner, ask yourself why you are doing this. If you have a bad habit of sharing things your partner has told you regarding their work or other people, then ask yourself if you overshare to feel important with other people.

Consider how you would like your relationship to feel in the future. Consider that you and your partner could reconnect, feel closer, and be more deeply bonded if you decide to stop oversharing with family and friends. When you keep your partner's confidences, you are conveying to them that you respect them and your relationship. You send a message that they are important to you and that you want to feel closer to them.

Act—When you choose not to share a secret, you show that you have self-control and can manage your feelings even when you are resentful and anxious. This self-regulation is an emotionally mature adult skill that is learned over time.

When couples come to therapy after one of them has overshared personal or private information, both partners hurt but for different reasons. The betrayed partner feels exposed and hurt, but the oversharer doesn't see why it is a big deal and quickly comes up with excuses. Of course, when the oversharer disagrees that this is even a problem, their minimizing or rationalizing makes the hurt even deeper.

When you both agree to no longer hurt each other in these ways, the healing within the relationship can begin. It will be hard to go through the STARR Reset or even get to the Act step if either of you are defensive in your communication. There has been a betrayal of trust, and two wrongs don't make a right.

Apologies do the heavy lifting to help couples get out of the ditch of continual fighting and back on their path.

Reset and Repair—The next step is to work on repairing the damage that has been done by the oversharing. The oversharer needs to give a heartfelt apology because they must acknowledge that there was a break in trust. Even if the oversharer was betrayed first, an apology will help to reset and get the two of you grounded back into your relationship.

An example of a heartfelt apology sounds like this: *I'm sorry I told my friend that you were unfaithful to me. I am hurting, and I guess I wanted to make you hurt somehow. I know this is wrong, just like your having an affair was wrong. I don't know if I can forgive what you did. Going forward, I will not go outside of our relationship to share information with others while we are working together on our relationship.*

It is key that the two of you acknowledge that you are working on the relationship. Apologies given and accepted reset the energy and the conversation. By honoring this commitment to work on the relationship, you are saying to each other, *We know this is a tough time, but we want to make this work.*

If you share your private struggles with someone else after you have reset the relationship, you will only erode whatever trust you have rebuilt between you. If you want your partner to open up to you during the rebuilding phase, you need to keep their confidence. You both need to be honest with each other during this time.

A note about privacy comes up when couples need to work out an agreement regarding access to online accounts and phone and app passwords. This can be a tricky subject for couples who want a level of privacy and still be open with each other. You will need to negotiate what feels comfortable and safe for each of you, which could be on a case-by-case basis. If you are reluctant to share your passwords with your partner, ask yourself why. Is it related to your partner's trustworthiness, or is it a past wounded issue coming forth? If your partner is reluctant to share passwords with you—especially to financial accounts—you will probably need to understand the reasoning behind this decision.

You can reset the energy between the two of you by offering heartfelt apologies and maintaining confidentiality.

Healing the Oversharer

Most people have things they do not want discussed outside of their relationship, and some partners do not want the other to talk with anyone about any of their issues. That being said, one way we process difficult topics is to talk about them with friends and family. If one partner doesn't ever want anything to be discussed with family and friends, then I recommend that the couple seek counseling, separately or together, so that they have a safe, confidential, neutral place to talk about their issues. There needs to be an outlet to emotionally process sensitive topics safely in such a way that each partner feels respected. Containing the problem just between the couple often leads to one or both talking about the issue behind the other's back anyway, defeating the purpose of the confidence boundary.

I have seen couples come in after the oversharer has exposed their partner's affair. The partner who had the affair feels as hurt by this violation as the oversharer feels betrayed by the affair. They are both "walking wounded." The oversharer feels justified in the sharing, while the other reluctantly accepts the fact that they deserve public shaming at some level. Once this has happened, then it is done; you can't take back confidential information you have overshared. You can say to the person you disclosed the information to, *I told you something the other day that was a confidence between my partner and me, and I shouldn't have. My partner and I are working on our issues, so can I ask you to keep that just between us?*

Going forward, you can choose to set a boundary of exclusivity and confidence between you and your partner in which you both agree that you will not involve other people in the resolution of the hurts in your relationship except for outside professional counsel. The hurts back and forth need to stop in order for the relationship to heal.

In the case of infidelity, I highly recommend both partners have individual and couples therapy to help them work through the trauma and toward a resolution. Both partners have complicated emotions around an infidelity, and most couples do not have the skills between them to navigate through this maze.

The more transparency you have in your relationship, the greater the level of trust you create in the relationship.

If you connect to the energy and expression of the oversharer, say this intention for your wounded inner child:

I know that I don't always know what to do when I hear things that shock or scare me, and that I need to tell someone else so I can calm down. I am working on honoring myself and my partner and not sharing our secrets. I am learning to trust my partner and myself. We are working to strengthen our relationship so that we feel safe and whole. Each day, in every way, I am developing a deeper bond with my partner, and I feel more connected to them.

Keeping Secrets from Each Other

It is normal to have thoughts, feelings, and fantasies that you don't want anyone, not even your intimate partner, to know about. Lots of people keep such feelings and thoughts to themselves, never revealing them to anyone else.

Many people tell me about secret, often sexual, fantasies they have, and say that their partner would never understand. Their own private world gives them pleasure, relief, or escape. Over time, they start to feel brave and begin hinting to their partner that they could get into a fetish or enjoy some kind of "scene." You may have tested the waters to see how your partner would react if you were to share your secret fantasy. Who knows? Maybe your partner would think it is OK and that such indulgence could deepen your relationship. Or they may think it is awful and can't believe you would like such a thing. Either way, you are in control of this information. If you think you are the only person who would like such a thing, you would be surprised. Couples who can hold and respect what their partner likes, even if one doesn't like it themselves, can go the long haul and have a deeply loving relationship.

The caution here is to know that for anything so intimate and vulnerable to be revealed, you need to have a very strong commitment to each other and trust the boundary system within yourselves and the relationship. You can begin such sharing by saying, *I'm going to tell you something in the deepest confidence. It is not to be shared with anyone else.*

If I can share my deepest private longings and desires with you, and you respect and hold them with me, my heart will feel loved and supported by you.

Sharing with Permission

It is unrealistic to think that partners will never talk about relationship issues with friends or family. Sometimes we need a trusted person as a sounding board to talk to about our emotional pain and troubles in our relationship. This type of sharing necessitates a negotiation up front between you and your partner.

The easiest rule to follow is to first ask your partner if it is OK for you to talk with a family member or friend about something private. This way, you and your partner can negotiate what is OK and not OK to discuss. Be as specific as you can. For example, your partner asks permission to talk about your situation, and you say, *Yes, it's OK to talk about how hard things are on all of us because I'm out of work and we are strapped for cash.* Or you may ask your partner if you can talk with your mother about your money troubles, and your partner says, *Yes, you can talk to your mother about our financial situation. I just don't want you talking about our sex life with anyone or how I can't perform sexually like I used to.*

Negotiating what is OK and not OK to talk about may be new for you, but it prevents pain and suffering later. You need to be specific with sensitive topics and put a fine point on what is to be discussed so that your partner knows specifically what is OK to be shared and with whom. Openness in a loving relationship doesn't need to be one hundred percent, but it should be pretty close.

You are free to tell your own story.
Telling someone else's story is
a betrayal of trust.

If your partner is the oversharer, let them know that you will now set boundaries with them and that you are renegotiating what is OK and not OK to discuss with others. Begin to feel a sense of safety and trust building within you both as your bonds of loving commitment deepen.

If you connect to the energy and expression of the partner of the oversharer, say this intention for your wounded inner child:

I know that each day I am trusting and loving my relationship. Even though I have been hurt in the past, I am taking it one day at a time and expanding the trust and love in my heart so that I feel safe, loved, and protected by my partner. Our commitment to each other grows and expands each day, unfolding to our greatest potential.

THE STARR RESET—EMMA AND BILL

Emma knew that Bill shared information about their relationship with Adam, and she wasn't upset about it most times. The two men have a brother energy between them, and she likes Adam. She remembered that she noticed Bill's habit of oversharing when they were dating, but she didn't stress about it. She ignored this red flag.

As time went on, though, Emma felt that Bill revealed too much about both their personal life and her work, and she finally had enough. She wasn't angry; she was just worn down and defeated knowing that her husband talked about things that were personal and shouldn't be shared. She was angry at herself for not saying something earlier, because now the oversharing was out of hand. She tried to talk about it with Bill on multiple occasions, but he deflected or became defensive and tried to talk Emma out of her feelings.

If you have to explain to someone why or how they hurt your feelings, they do not respect you.

Emma explained to Bill why his oversharing hurt her feelings by saying, "It hurts me when you share personal stuff with Adam."

Bill responded, "I'm just talking with him. He's my buddy. We tell each other things all the time. I can't believe that you are hurt by this. I'm not being hurtful. And besides, you like Adam!" Emma knew they were headed toward the same argument they always had; it was just a different day.

Stop—Emma had reached her personal threshold. She realized that Bill's oversharing was too much, and she was tired of being disrespected. She calmly told him that they needed to stop this back and forth about the issue.

Think—Emma thought about all the times she had tried to convince Bill that his oversharing and how he treated her hurt her, but he never heard her. She was confused as to why he didn't listen and take in her message. She thought about how she felt disrespected and embarrassed by his disclosures.

Act—Emma said to Bill, "I know you don't think this is a big deal, but to me, your talking with Adam about things I feel are between you and me is too revealing. You also tell Adam about how I'm struggling at work, and it's too much. I feel exposed and used."

Bill said, "Em, that's just how I am. I need to talk about this stuff, and I do so with Adam. What's the big deal?"

Emma said, "I know that's what you do, but it isn't right. And you're not hearing how I feel. You keep being defensive."

He said, "Well that's just what I do. I'm going to talk with Adam; he's my best friend. I tell him everything."

Emma was tired of trying to tell Bill how she felt when he wasn't listening to her words. She said, "I know that's how you are. I just don't want you to say personal things about me or us to Adam anymore." Bill saw that she was going to keep this up, so he asked her what specific things she didn't want discussed. She said, "I don't want you telling Adam that I'm not interested in sex anymore; that is too embarrassing for me. That should be just between us."

Bill said, "OK, I won't talk about that anymore."

Emma was glad that Bill heard her, but she didn't think he was getting the point about how she felt. She said, "I'm glad you are not going to talk with Adam about our sex life anymore, but the bigger point is, I don't think you show me respect." Bill just thought Emma didn't want him talking with Adam about their sex life, but he wasn't getting what the bigger picture of what she was saying. She said, "This is what I need you to hear: When you tell others something deeply personal to me without my permission, I feel violated. I think it's more important for you to impress or tell juicy gossip than it is to understand how demeaning and hurtful that is to me."

Bill said, "OK, I think I hear what you're saying. You don't like me sharing any personal stuff, and when I do, you feel disrespected."

Emma gratefully said, "Yes, Bill, yes, that's what I've been trying to get you to understand."

Reset and Repair—Emma wanted to go on, but she remembered what she learned about having discussions with men and how they get overloaded, so she said, "I love you. Thank you, Bill."

Bill said, "I'm sorry, Em. I love you, too."

Bill and Emma came up with a list of specific topics that were OK and not OK to share with others. They both agreed that if they slipped up, they would tell the other right away. For example, Bill once had to say, "I need to let you know that I told Adam about what happened with your boss." He then used the heartfelt apology technique to repair this betrayal. He followed this up by saying, "Going forward, my promise to you is that I will not share this information anymore."

Emma and Bill learned how to use the STARR Reset and the sharing-with-permission technique. Bill likes the permission technique more than he thought he would, as it created guardrails for him to know what he can talk about. He told Emma that talking with her first about what is OK to share helps him feel closer to her, which in turn helps him to feel more in control and internally stronger. All of these steps are helping to heal his inner child wounding.

Bill's friend Adam doesn't fully understand why Bill no longer shares everything with him, but Bill knows that his marriage to Emma is more important than his friend knowing all the details about their relationship. Emma feels a greater sense of safety in their relationship, which helps her inner child wounding to heal. She told Bill that her little girl inside is happy that she can share things with him and know that the information is safe.

Emma still needs to do more internal work so that she can better maintain boundaries and express her feelings to Bill, now that she knows that he will respect her need for privacy. Like all couples, they can do what they are ready to do and are a work in progress. Their synergistic wounding is still active, still expressing and responding to each other, but now they have more functional tools with which to navigate this landscape. They continue their dance.

Looking Inward

How does this couple remind you of your own wounded struggles within yourself and with your partner? What are some of the inner child woundings that you connect to? How does this match with your own story? What was activated inside of you when you read how this couple worked on their communication using the STARR Reset? Record your impressions in your notebook, as this will help you heal your wounded patterns.

CHAPTER 16

The Bad Boy and the Good Girl Archetypes

We got married in a fever, hotter than a pepper sprout.
We've been talkin' 'bout Jackson, ever since the fire went out.
—JOHNNY CASH AND JUNE CARTER CASH, "JACKSON"

The bad boy and the good girl are the classic pairing of one partner who goes against convention and breaks free from restraints, and one who seeks a rebel. This pairing is often seen in adolescents and younger adults, but it doesn't stop there.

Please note that while the archetypes in this chapter reference the bad boy and the good girl, the synergistic wounded pairing can play out in any gender combination (e.g., bad girl/ good boy).

The good girl who dates or marries the bad boy is in for an exciting and exhausting roller coaster, as the bad boy is usually charming, smart, colorful—and dysfunctional. This is the frat boy, the man-child, the one who can't be contained.

This relationship is layered with drama from the beginning. As you have learned, there is an emotional payoff for both parties in any synergistically wounded relationship.

Over time, even though the relationship is filled with excitement, it becomes tiring for the good girl. The fascination and pull is still there, but now there are battle scars to show for all of the adventures. Underneath the bad boy exterior is a person who is defensive, insecure, and lonely. The bad boy rarely apologizes and will rationalize why he shouldn't have to; he feels he is above that. He will sabotage things if others get too close, even when he knows he shouldn't. The good girl is left holding the bag with the unhealed, unresolved issues that the bad boy laughs off and disregards. The lack of emotional vulnerability in this pairing is demonstrated in black and white, and everyone can see it.

One of two scenarios plays out with this pairing. The first is one in which the good girl looks back over all the times she has tried and failed to control or manage her bad boy, so she just gives up. She learns to make herself smaller to fit into the bad boy's world. The other is one in which the good girl has had enough of the chaos and threatens to leave. In most cases, she doesn't want to leave because she is still magnetically attracted to the bad boy, but she is tired of being the only adult in the relationship. She is tired of the drama and wants off of the roller coaster. When she says she is leaving, she is trying to get the bad boy's attention so he will stop the destructive behavior. This rarely works, and when it does, it is because the situation has turned dangerous or deadly. This sounds dramatic, but the point is that things have to be really bad for the good girl who is tired of this dance to finally leave, or for the bad boy to change his ways.

The most likely synergistic wounded pairing for these archetypes is one who is the chasing partner, has low-self esteem, and wants to feel better about themselves, and one who outwardly demonstrates what is perceived as strength, what the chasing partner desires. The bad boy tries to hide his wounding as much as the good girl projects onto him someone that he is not. Both are living in an illusion.

THE BAD BOY ARCHETYPE

The bad boy archetype is as old as time. He is the one who cannot be constrained or told what to do. In many ways, it is easy to understand the wounding of the bad boy. Not wanting to be constrained, he rebelled against his family, who tried to keep him in line, and he broke free. Alcohol, drugs, and other addictions help to fuel the unpredictability and the chaos off of which the bad boy lives.

The bad boy has tremendous insecurities that he hides with flashy things or bravado. He tests people to see what impresses them and if he can manipulate them. Rarely does the bad boy have close friends or people who are stronger than he is. He zeros in on a good girl, becoming clingy and needy and isolating himself from others. She interprets this as true affection, but often it is just his wounding playing out.

The bad boy rarely grows out of this behavior; he just gets older, broken down, and tired. Later in life, he doesn't have the energy to be the rebel. He regales others with his incredible tales of dramatic moments as he becomes a shell of his former bad boy self, with sagging tattoos, broken relationships, and a mountain of debt to show for it all.

At best, the bad boy can become a huge success, often an entrepreneur. At worst, he scrapes by, continuing to spin in past dramas and regaling others with tales from his glory days. As the bad boy gets older, he will do anything to keep the party from ending. Even when others have moved on, he will try to recapture a place in time when he "had it all."

Wounding Origins of the Bad Boy Archetype

The bad boy grew up in a household where he did not feel honored or respected. He might have had a loving home, but most of the time he did not feel loved. He was always told what to do and called out for doing something wrong. This created feelings of shame, insecurity, and being less-than. He began to overcompensate by rebelling to feel a sense of power and control.

The bad boy typically chose authority figures—parents and teachers—to fight back against. The parents didn't know what had gotten into him and were at a loss as to how to control him. Of course, the more they tried to control him, the more he rebelled. Grounding him and taking away privileges, phones, and cars only enraged and emboldened the rebelling child. Sneaking out, breaking curfews, doing drugs, and drinking alcohol became the norm for the adolescent. Siblings tried to keep him in line, but the rebel didn't want to follow rules.

Typically, one of the parents was controlling and authoritarian and the other was enabling and quiet. The rebel played the parents off of each other to get things from each of them. This triangulation became a destructive family dance that created chaos in the entire household.

Wounded Tools of the Bad Boy Archetype

The wounded tools that the bad boy learned from childhood trauma or wounding include:

- rebelling against authority
- doing things to manipulate and get a reaction
- being defensive and shutting down emotionally
- not caring about the consequences of actions
- acting out in a big way to hide feelings of inadequacy
- being unable to apologize or own any shortcomings
- lashing out in anger and putting up walls so others can't see their internal shame
- sabotaging good things to reinforce low self-esteem

THE GOOD GIRL ARCHETYPE

The good girl chases after the bad boy, even after she is told that the bad boy is not good for her. Going after someone who does not make the best choices tempts and excites her. She doesn't have a strong sense of self and looks to others to define her world. She is attracted to others who are daring and exciting, or who need to be fixed or tamed. She herself isn't bold and rebellious, but she wants to be with others who are perceived to be courageous and reckless.

The good girl thinks that any guy who is not a bad-boy type isn't going to be a "real man." Her friends give her attention when she is dating a bad boy, and peer pressure is intense. She confuses toxic masculinity for positive or healthy masculinity. She doesn't have the clarity to know the difference, as it is her wounded parts that are running after the bad boy. She sees the bad boy as a challenge to be conquered; she feels that she can tame him and that he will then rely on her.

When the good girl meets the bad boy, her parents try hard to talk her out of the relationship. The parents are beside themselves as to how it got to this point. What did they do so wrong that their child wants to date or marry such a bad boy? No matter how much the parents try to talk the good girl out of this, she will not give up. She is rebelling against the parents, just like the bad boy rebelled against his. The bad boy is her forbidden love, her sweet revenge against her parents.

Often the good girl becomes trauma bonded with the bad boy, and it becomes the two of them against the world. They see everyone as being against them and telling them what to do. This perpetuates the core wounding they both carry. Some good girls who don't have a strong sense of self will stay on the roller coaster ride of exciting times and demoralizing attitudes, only to later feel lost in the regret of their decisions.

Remember that this synergistically wounded pairing can occur in any gender pairing.

Wounding Origins of the Good Girl Archetype

The good girl's family dynamic is similar to that of the bad boy's. She didn't feel understood or acknowledged as a child, and her parents kept a tight control over her comings and goings. The more control the parents exerted, the more the good girl found ways to get her needs met, often through passive-aggressive behavior. This created a lifelong pattern of codependent behaviors and the avoidance of facing problems and issues directly.

The child in this household needed to be seen and heard, but her parents were too self-centered to consider her needs. They were more interested in controlling her so they didn't feel anxious or so they looked good to others. The child learned how to maneuver around and manipulate her parents. As a teenager, she figured out her parents' weaknesses and what they would not like. She learned how to throw them off-center and gain control. As a form of rebellion, she wanted to connect with a bad boy who would shock them. Part of her wanted her parents to be put off by the bad boy, and part of her wanted her parents to prove how much they loved her by protecting her from herself.

Wounded Tools of the Good Girl Archetype

The wounded tools that the good girl learned from childhood trauma or wounding include:

- trying to save, rescue, or control someone else
- accepting someone who never apologizes or is abusive
- getting needs met indirectly
- feeling misunderstood
- feeling a victim of circumstance
- ignoring or laughing off the destructive life choices of her partner
- overcompensating and making things better after her partner self-sabotages
- being passive-aggressive

The bad boy and the good girl have much in common. In particular, they both often come from a strict or controlling upbringing. Their emotional wounding is displayed differently, but they are similarly wounded at their core.

Synergistic Wounded Pairing—Jimmy and Alicia

Jimmy and Alicia are a classic example of the bad boy and the good girl. They were not bad people, but they made bad choices. They had big fights and dramatic reconnections.

Jimmy was a rebel as far back as any family member could remember, and he couldn't imagine being any other way. Alicia was always attracted to bad boys but didn't understand why. She liked watching the "show" and wondering what the bad boy was going to do next. Jimmy's bad-boy antics and chaos distracted Alicia away from her own sad, lonely, angry feelings.

Alicia and Jimmy always had stories to tell about each other. *I can't believe he did this! Can you believe what she said about me?* Their stories became legendary—tales of bar fights, drag races, shoot-outs, and other hold-my-beer moments. All of this was entertaining, fascinating, and thrilling in the beginning. As they became their own reality show, family and friends wondered what in the heck they were going to do next.

Alicia was never as wild as Jimmy, but she liked to have a good time, which encouraged Jimmy to continue his outrageous behavior. Sometimes she tried to control or contain him, with disastrous results. She would let him do whatever he wanted and then get pissed off, go into a victim space, and blow up at him. Jimmy would rebel, dramatically demonstrating that Alicia wasn't going to tell him what to do. She saw his behavior as the problem; she didn't recognize her role in their codependent dance.

When both partners are deeply wounded,
finding a strong footing for the relationship
to grow and heal will be a struggle.

Jimmy was an unpredictable live wire who, in his prime, was destructive and dangerous. Keeping people guessing was like oxygen to him. When others tried to get him in line, he felt like he was being asked to give up part of his personality and identity. Jimmy primarily drank alcohol but occasionally used drugs of any kind as a way to intensify his experience, making it more fun for him. He was a legend in his own mind, and he had to keep up his reputation.

THE STARR RESET FOR THE BAD BOY AND THE GOOD GIRL ARCHETYPES

If you recognize your relationship in this archetype, know that your and your partner's inner child woundings are similar in many ways. You both have an underlying wounding that contributes to your insecurity. You both act out in your own ways, one overtly and the other covertly. There is great opportunity for healing here, but you both have to bring in humility in order for the STARR Reset to work.

Stop—Start by being honest with yourselves and each other. Most likely only one of you will have enough of this cycle and reach your personal threshold. The first step is to share how you each feel and acknowledge that one or both of you want the problem behavior or the roller coaster to stop. Recognize the highs and lows of the problem and how you would ideally like this to be healed.

Think—Think about what you want to say now that you know more about how you feel and can see these cycles you both get into. If you know a little about what your partner's wounding is, use your words to ask how they feel, because you don't know for sure. The problem has been going on for a while, so there is a backlog of frustration and confusion. Take your time as you go through the next steps.

Act—Say to your partner, *I know sometimes we get into situations that feel out of control, and I think it's fun for us to a point.*

But I feel overwhelmed by this problem, and I don't want to be on this roller coaster anymore. I love you, but this is really hard. See how your partner responds and if they recognize the problem. Understanding where they are will determine your next steps.

If they are oblivious and don't want to talk about the problem at all, you will be on a solitary journey of self-discovery. If they are compassionate and recognize that this is causing you distress, then you will have something to work with. If you both agree that there is a problem, then the goal is to work toward repairing the relationship. Do not expect that your partner will stop the problem behavior altogether, as that will be almost impossible. What you can hope for is that they understand how you feel. Once you have established this, then you can work on some specific behaviors that relate to the feelings you have.

For example, your partner goes out to bars with their friends, comes home after you have gone to bed, and you wake up, which interrupts your sleep cycle. The next day, compose yourself and think of the words you want to use to express your feelings. If you launch into being mad at them, they will get defensive, feel justified in their behavior, and the two of you will be back to square one. Make a different choice this time. Be grounded when you ask if now is a good time to talk, then tell your partner how you feel when you are consistently woken up at one o'clock in the morning.

Do not expect a conversation like this to go well the first time around. You will need to be patient and persistent. The two of you have spent a fair amount of time creating an elaborate dance, so it will take a while to work in a new pattern. Stay with it, and show your partner that you are serious and that you are going to stay on topic no matter how much they try to get you off track. By not backing down, you are stating a boundary, your truth. Hopefully, your partner will see your efforts and join with you. But manage your expectations, as the rebel is not one to be told what to do or think.

Reset and Repair—Model for your partner how you are sorry for things you have done that have contributed to the cycle. For example, you were so frustrated with his chronic late homecoming that all you did was yell at him because you didn't know what else to do. Say, *I'm sorry for yelling my frustrations at you instead of managing my emotions and coming to you calmly to let you know how I feel so you could hear me. I miss feeling close to you, and I want us to work though things. I love you.* Practice this openhearted communication so you both can break down the barriers and connect more deeply.

Talking like this will not feel natural to you; you may want to keep yelling at your partner instead of staying calm. Your partner may ridicule you for this "therapy speak" and say that you just got it out of a book. This language will sound weird, but you have to start somewhere, and what you have been doing hasn't been working. Something has to change.

When you stay calm, you are in control.
When you yell, you lose control and will
be more likely to make bad choices.

Apologize for your wrongdoings, then ask your partner what behavior choices they will own and apologize for. They might say nothing, but they heard your request. Your partner is now aware that you no longer want to play this game. They hear your frustration and that this is no longer fun for you. Knowing this may scare your partner, because they will start to feel the shift that is occurring within you and the relationship.

I don't recommend trying to go over and over your feelings and these behaviors too much in the first go-around. Your partner has heard you; you have planted the seed. You can come back and restart this discussion later.

You know that you and your partner deserve a more fulfilling relationship. You know that you don't have to keep on playing out these wounded dramas with each other. This process will take time, but the two of you are worth it.

Healing the Bad Boy and the Good Girl Archetypes

For this relationship to start to heal, the bad boy, who is the alpha in the relationship, has to be on board. He has to be willing to set down his defensive acting-out behaviors so that he can be more emotionally available to his partner. He has to see that he may lose his partner if he doesn't change his behaviors. The good girl has to be willing to stop enabling her partner so that they can both own their own feelings and behaviors.

I recommend that each of you in this unique pairing write down what you think are the problems in the relationship in language you can use in a discussion. This is because the bad boy may not see any problems, since he is getting all of his needs met. Writing down what each person sees as the problems in the relationship is a starting point for a discussion to help you come a little closer together on what the real issues are.

I also recommend that you both write symbolic letters describing how you feel about the relationship and what you would like to see happen. After this, look over your list of problems again. Would you like to reword anything you wrote down so that your partner can better hear you when you are ready to discuss them? Are you planning to say these things in the most loving, kind way you know, using "I feel" language?

Once you both have a list of the issues in the relationship, come together with an understanding that you will both respectfully listen to each other. Agree that this discussion will not be a personal attack but about how you both feel and see as the problems. If you feel that what they are saying doesn't make sense, just sit there and listen anyway. If there is one issue that you both agree is a problem, focus on that one issue. Begin to talk about it using "I feel" language, and see how far you can get. Remember to bring in the STARR Reset steps if you begin to get off track.

You may need a therapist to walk you through your wounded expressions, as you may be so entrenched in your individual perspectives that you won't know how to move forward. The bad boy may be so dominant that his partner cannot reach him.

If you connect to the energy and the expression of the bad boy or the good girl, say this intention for the wounded inner child:

I know that I have worth and value, and that it's OK to be direct with my feelings. I have people in my life who are safe to talk to. I can show them how I feel, and they will not hurt me. I don't have to keep on rebelling or manipulating others to prove my worth, feel in control, or know that I have strength. Each day I am learning how to be kinder with myself so that I don't have to self-sabotage my life.

The STARR Reset—Jimmy and Alicia

Alicia is still emotionally attracted and attached to Jimmy and doesn't want to give up the relationship. But she eventually tired of the cycle and is now working on healing herself. She wants Jimmy to stop doing destructive things so that they can have a normal life, but Jimmy doesn't ever want to be seen as normal, ordinary, or common. He tries hard to be the enigma, not wanting his emotions to be seen or known. His self-destructive, sabotaging behaviors are meant to form a smoke screen so that others don't see his true self or his underlying pain.

Their fourteen-year-old son, Jacob, was smoking weed, his anxiety was getting worse, and his grades were failing. When Alicia tried to talk to Jimmy about Jacob, Jimmy would walk out of the room, ignore her, or say, *Here we go again.* Talking about Jacob was hard for Jimmy, because he wanted Jacob to be a kid and have fun. (Jimmy has always wanted to be a kid and have fun). He knew at some level that Jacob was like him; he didn't want to see his son's wounding because it mirrored his own. Alicia needed to put the STARR Reset into action.

Stop—Alicia reached her personal threshold and knew she had to make a change. She said, "Jimmy, we can't keep doing this. We need to talk, and you need to participate in this conversation with me. We need to restart this conversation."

Think—Alicia knew that if she and Jimmy stayed at the house to talk, he would find all kinds of distractions and ignore her. She knew she had to change something so that they could get a little further in the discussion.

Act—Alicia said to Jimmy, "Let's go take a walk." After some balking, he agreed, and she led them on a walk away from their close neighbors' house. She knew Jimmy would start talking with them and then they wouldn't get anywhere in the discussion.

Alicia said, "Jimmy, I know you don't think Jacob has a problem, but he does. He looks up to you, and when you say that his smoking weed isn't a problem, he smokes even more."

Jimmy said, "Well, I don't think it's a problem. What's the big deal?"

Alicia said, "His grades are bad, he has no motivation, and he says his anxiety is worse. From what I've read, it could be because of how much he's been smoking."

Jimmy said, "Well, what am I supposed to do? If he smokes a little bit, that's fine. All of our friends do."

Alicia said, "I need you to take an active role in helping me talk with Jacob. Right now it's just me trying to reach him, and it's not working, I can't do this alone. I've been trying to get you to help me, but you keep on ignoring me and this situation. I'm tired, frustrated, and I feel all alone."

Jimmy heard Alicia and what she was saying, but he didn't know what to do or say. He said, "Well, I'm just a screw-up. What do you want me to do?"

Alicia said, "Jimmy, the first thing I need you to do is to acknowledge my feelings!"

Reset and Repair—Jimmy said, "OK, I'm sorry that I'm not doing what you want me to do and that you're angry at me. If I talk with Jacob, will you be happy?"

Alicia said, "I'm more frustrated than angry, and I also feel alone. And yes, I need you to talk with him."

Jimmy hugged her and said, "I'm sorry that what I do frustrates you. And I don't want you to feel alone."

Alicia said, "Thank you for hearing me this time. That means a lot to me. I love you, Jimmy."

Jimmy said, "I love you, too, and I'm lucky that you put up with me and all my craziness."

They were trying, but Alicia and Jimmy struggled with their communication. Jimmy continued to hear Alicia's words as telling him what to do, criticizing him, and shaming him. He would go into a hurt victim space and get defensive.

It took a great deal of effort on Alicia's part to get Jimmy to hear what she was saying. For the longest time they had to use the paraphrasing technique, with Jimmy repeating back to Alicia what he heard her saying. Jimmy hated this, but he loves Alicia and saw that she was hurting, so he tried. He told her he felt like an idiot and weak talking that way. She held his hand, looked him in the eyes, and told him she loved him and that it was going to be OK. For a moment, Jimmy's heart melted enough to let her in.

Alicia worked on boundary setting, understanding how her wounding shows up, and her role in continuing their reality show of a relationship. She went as far in her healing work as she was ready, willing, and able to. She will need to continue to be the driver in discussions with Jimmy. She will have to stand her ground and be persistent, as Jimmy participates in the conversation only by following Alicia's prompts; he does not actively participate, he just tolerates the discussions. They still have a long road ahead of them, but they can make it, and hopefully Jimmy will become open to talking with a therapist so that Alicia doesn't have to work so hard on her own.

Alicia and Jimmy are still together. Jimmy is a watered-down version of his old self. He still drinks, says outrageous things, and now just talks a big game instead of carrying out destructive behaviors. Alicia lovingly obliges, and she tries to set boundaries and speak her truth. Jacob is in counseling to help him with his anxiety and pot use. Alicia and Jimmy's relationship works for them.

LOOKING INWARD

How does this couple remind you of your own wounded struggles within yourself and with your partner? What are some of the inner child woundings that you connect to? How does this match with your own story? What was activated inside of you when you read how this couple worked on their communication using the STARR Reset? Record your impressions in your notebook, as this will help you heal your wounded patterns.

CHAPTER 17

The Tug-of-War Controller Archetype

Attempting to constantly control everyone and everything around you is not only exhausting, it is also futile. The only real power you can achieve in this life is being in control of yourself.
—ANTHON ST. MAARTEN

The tug-of-war controller archetype is where one or both partners want a level of control or dominance over their partner, situations, and the relationship as a result of broken or damaged trust issues. How this control is demonstrated varies greatly, but the root of it is their attachment wounding from childhood. A controlling person partners with someone who, at least on the surface, doesn't need as much control. Opposites attract.

We all have a basic need for a sense of control and safety within ourselves and our relationships, which is a good thing. Most people are able to have a balanced feeling of control over their lives, but trouble develops in relationships when the need for control comes from a wounded place and manifests in a distorted way. In these situations, the desire for control comes from a place of fear. The core wounding often predates the relationship.

Nobody said this would be easy,
but we can have fun trying.

The most likely synergistic pairing for this archetype is two people who both have broken trust issues, but the issues show up differently. The degree of control they employ matches the degree that they do not trust a person, situation, or outcome. Most likely, each partner grew up learning how to navigate around difficult personalities and became experts at conflict avoidance. Sometimes broken trust issues develop in adulthood following an affair or other betrayal. Anxiety issues are prevalent with this pairing.

There are three themes to this pairing: an overt and a covert controller; two overt controllers, or what I call the *lightning bolt pairing*; and two covert controllers.

THE OVERT CONTROLLER

Most overt, or direct, controllers are what I call the soldiers, protectors, fighters for justice, and champions of the underdog. They don't want anything bad to happen to anyone, so they are on high alert and ready to go at a moment's notice. They are who you call in a crisis. But they can also look at everything as a crisis response situation when it is not.

Overt controllers insert themselves into situations, making themselves indispensable so that family or friends rely on them for advice or help. This is self-serving for the overt controller's wounding, and they love it. It reinforces their need to establish a sense of order, and they become judge and jury, deciding right and wrong. The overt controller feels proud or justified in their controlling behaviors.

The overt controller does not respect their partner when they impose their sense of right and wrong on them. They also keep themselves locked in this overcontrolling paradigm, where they have to find new situations to levy a judgment for their own sense of self-worth. This also becomes a dysfunctional coping skill for anxiety; they can't control things that are out of control in their own life, so they will control others.

THE COVERT CONTROLLER

If you think you are not controlling, look at the ways you get your needs met. Do you ask for things directly, or do you find a way to get those needs met without negotiating or compromising with your partner? If the latter, you are probably using the wounded tools of the covert, or the passively dominant, controller. Ironically, the covert controller doesn't see their behaviors as controlling at all; they see themselves as trying to keep their sense of self amid the tug-of war dynamic. They see the overt controller's behaviors as the problem. The covert controller sees themselves as the "good" one in this pairing, as they are trying not to lose themselves to the overt controller.

The covert controller does things indirectly so as not to be like the overt controller. However, their covert controlling attempts can be perceived as passive-aggressive or conflict avoidant, such as delaying making a decision or refusing to be intimate. The covert controller is offended, or even ashamed, if this is pointed out, because they don't see themselves that way.

Both the overt and covert controller wounded styles more clearly manifest when people are under stress. At these times, the need to control or lock down an outcome is of primary importance so that things don't get out of control. The disparity in perspective between the people in this partnership sets up the tug-of-war and is played out over small and large issues, with both keeping score. If either partner feels they are being slighted, they will even the score using their unique wounded tools of attack. This restabilizes their sense of balance and restores their sense that their needs are being met. They regain a feeling of control inside, and their inner child wounding is satisfied.

In spite of all of the back and forth, the tug-of-war pairing is often fairly functional in a dysfunctional way, because their wounding synergistically integrates with the other. Both know the language of how to codependently adapt and adjust within the other's dynamic.

THE LIGHTNING BOLTS

The second theme that shows up in this pairing is when there are two overt controllers, which I call the *lightning bolt pairing*. To outsiders, the lighting bolt couple may look like an engaging, magnetic couple who has it all together.

This couple is an electrically charged pairing, and when things are good and flying high, it is as if sparks are popping off of them. When things are not going well, the lighting bolts attack each other with a vengeance, trying to maintain a feeling of control as they both feel they are losing ground. Their fights can be epic and incredibly destructive. These are also the couples who talk about their great make-up sex. If they are lucky, they get reenergized from their sparring by getting out all of their frustrations, which reinvigorates the pairing and their connection. If they are not so fortunate, their arguments get heated quickly. They use direct insults, threats, and accusations to intimidate and dominate, trying to make the other submissive. It is hard for a lightning bolt to be with anyone other than another lightning bolt. The lightning bolt perceives someone who won't spar with them as weak and doesn't respect them at all.

This pairing sometimes has a truce from their electrically charged battles, but it doesn't last, as they both feel the need for dominance and control. This pairing can survive, but it will be a rocky road.

Two Covert Controllers

The third variation on this theme is where both partners are covert controllers. They are conflict avoiders, so their expression to gain a level of control in the relationship comes across as being passive-aggressive, avoidant, and doing what they want to do anyway. For example, one partner buys an item without asking the other, then asks for forgiveness later—if what they bought is even an issue. They have brought into adulthood the same childhood dynamic of avoidance and quietly going behind the scenes so they don't have to involve anyone else with what they want. They may have learned this behavior to avoid verbal abuse as a child, or they may have grown up in an emotionally unavailable household.

Their avoidance is destructive because they don't talk through any issues in the relationship, they just ignore their reality and hope things get better. They are afraid to bring anything up because it may rock the boat and then uncomfortable things would be out in the open. These are the couples who say they never argue.

Covert controllers live in an illusion of stability
that is enabled by their avoidance.

This couple doesn't always feel close with each other. They just go through the motions, avoiding issues, raising the kids, and living parallel lives. They may feel like they are roommates rather than lovers and companions.

Wounding Origins of the Tug-of-War Controller Archetype

The need for control and safety is hardwired in all of us to some degree. This archetype's childhood family environment was either highly controlling or out of control. No one was guiding the ship, which created a sense of instability and imbalance. The child who felt the need to control, whether overtly or covertly, looked for adults to step in and right the ship.

When the basic need for safety is not met, the child looks for ways to feel safe within themselves. This often comes in the form of what the child has power over, such as their speech, behaviors, and attachments. The child reduces things to a minimum for survival, letting go of play, adventure, and freedom so they can feel safe and get food and shelter. The child becomes highly practical, looking for what needs to be done to help themselves and the family survive.

This wounded child feels overwhelmed, victimized, scared, unsure of themselves, and is afraid to show any signs of weakness lest they be attacked or ridiculed. The child's ability to trust is greatly impacted by such life events. These are the children who appear to be mature for their age, using their mind for a sense of control and not relying on their feelings to guide them.

I believe one of the two strongest indicators for the adult who needs a sense of control is having grown up in a chaotic (emotionally, financially, mentally disorganized, or addicted) household. As a child, they learned to rationalize the need for control over self and others because such control was about competition, survival, or safety. As an adult, they do not want to experience anything that resembles their out-of-control and unsafe childhood.

The second indicator is when a sense of trust was broken in their young life, creating the need for a sense of control. This broken trust or betrayal could have come from something done directly to the child or something traumatic the child witnessed that stood out. For example, the child is caught up in the gears of a divorce and feels out of control because their world is changing so rapidly. The child brings this emotional energy into their core wounding profile. These types of situations create great anxiety in the child, which is then carried into adulthood.

If the child is the oldest in the family, they will take on the role of establishing control and assuming responsibility, especially in alcoholic or drug-addicted households. The other siblings will call this child bossy, or claim that they are trying to be like a parent. (*You're not my mom!*) The eldest child feels justified in this behavior because it is about survival and keeping the family intact, especially if the parents are checked out with addiction or are otherwise emotionally unavailable. This child disregards the siblings' criticisms and will go ahead with their own ideas of how to establish control and stability, because they see it as their job. As the eldest child grows into adulthood, they bring along all of their wounded inner child tools of being in control, being overly responsible, giving orders, and keeping things under control. The eldest child often becomes the overt controller, and younger siblings often become covert controllers.

The opposite plays out if the child grew up in a household where one or both parents were highly controlling. When these children become adults, they either become highly controlling themselves or give free reign to their wounded inner child, relinquishing all sense of control or responsibility as they had to do in their family of origin. They use passive-aggressive covert control to get their needs met, sometimes by sneaky means. This is their inner child's way of rebelling against the dysfunctional pattern from childhood.

Alternatively, they carry the highly controlling patterns they learned in childhood into their adult work and home relationships. This overt control feels natural, and they rationalize this behavior in all situations.

The amount of control we exert over ourselves or others is directly proportional to how much or how little we trust the other person, situation, or outcome.

Wounded Tools of the Tug-of-War Controller Archetype

The wounded tools that the controlling person learned from childhood trauma or wounding include:

- exerting overt and covert control in various forms in all situations
- becoming more controlling when triggered
- being passive-aggressive
- avoiding conflict
- taking power to feel safe

- overusing control instead of understanding the underlying fear
- giving away power and feeling like the victim
- righteously defending oneself, either overtly or covertly
- developing elaborate ways to get needs met indirectly but unable to see oneself as controlling
- becoming defensive when overt or covert behaviors are pointed out

SYNERGISTIC WOUNDED PAIRING—ALEX AND AMANDA

Alex and Amanda are a typical tug-or-war controlling pairing. They have been married for ten years and have two young children. Both want things to go well in their life, and they don't like when things are out of control. Their synergistic wounding is essentially the same, although it comes out in different ways.

Amanda fears that things will spin out of control, so she tries to lock down anything that is unknown. Alex doesn't like conflict, so he fears that he won't be able to get his needs met openly. Both of them developed their wounded fears in childhood. Amanda is highly anxious and the overt controller, and Alex is passively dominant, the covert controller. This synergistic pairing plays out all of the time because one form of control satisfies and directly complements, or meshes with, the other's.

As the overt controller, Amanda is clear about what she wants and is directive with Alex. When she feels particularly anxious, she barks orders, directs Alex and other people, and is not considerate of others' feelings in general. As the covert controller, Alex goes along with this, but he will then use indirect means to try to recover some control. He is a conflict avoider, so trying to regain control indirectly is easier (and safer) for him. He does things behind Amanda's back so as not to upset her, but when she finds out, she gets even angrier and more anxious. Alex calls Amanda controlling, but they both are, in different ways.

Alex and Amanda have learned how to read each other's controlling tactics and switch up their approach if the other changes course. They spend more time dancing around each other than they do dealing with issues respectfully and openly, from a grounded place.

THE STARR RESET FOR THE TUG-OF-WAR CONTROLLER ARCHETYPE

If you recognize your relationship in this archetype, know that there are ways to heal this, but it will take more work than some of the other archetypes.

Stop—The first step is to recognize that you exert some form of controlling behavior, whether overt or covert. Start by observing yourself in your relationships at home and with friends and coworkers to see when and how your need for control gets triggered. See if some of the triggers you identified in chapter 2 apply here. Stop yourself from imposing your control, directly or indirectly, onto someone else.

Be gentle with yourself as you go through this step. Remember that your control issues probably grew out of a need to feel emotionally and physically safe in childhood. Observe yourself to see how and when you try to control the relationship, situation, or outcome. This is your wounded inner child's need to know with a great degree of certainty how something will turn out.

Controllers react impulsively because they have trained themselves to be hypervigilant and the first responders in emotionally chaotic situations.

Think—This step is especially important for the controller, as it is the step in which your responsible adult self has a talk with your wounded inner child to reassure the inner child that not everything is a five alarm fire. Yes, things can be upsetting and unpredictable, and yes, things may not work out, and yes, people may get their feelings hurt. But it is not your job to control every outcome in every situation in the hope that no problems ever happen. That is incredibly unrealistic.

If you are a covert controller, think about the ways in which you get your needs met. Do you talk directly to and negotiate with your partner or others, or do you go behind their backs? You may avoid conversations and situations that you imagine would be bad but in reality wouldn't be. Look at what you avoid because you perceive there will be a conflict, then ask yourself if this is the case or if it is a fear. Use your highly calibrated rational mind to help you look at situations not from the outcome you want but from what is going on, what everyone is saying, and most importantly, whether you should be involved at all.

Act—For either controlling type, the action step involves acknowledging your behavior with your partner. With great courage and humility, admit to your partner your knowledge of your inner child wounded choices. Ask your partner for insight into your behavior. The overt controller might say, *Do you feel I'm controlling or that I tell you what you do right and wrong a lot?* The covert controller might say, *In the past, when I've asked for things I needed or wanted, you shut me down pretty quickly, so I think I make up stories in my head that you're going to* *be mad at me if I ask for what I need. What are your thoughts about that?* Asking these questions with clarity gets to the heart of the conversation. Stay with this conversation; don't lose the opportunity for connection and growth. This will prepare you for your reconciliation.

Reset and Repair—Coming together to a place of repair and restoration is a hard-won honor for the controlling couple. It involves, love, humility, kindness, vulnerability, and patience.

If you are the overt controller, look at how you have been directive with your partner over the years, and see how you can begin to amend your behavior by saying things in a different way. For example, instead of saying *Move that over here now!*, ask yourself how you would say that to a coworker or friend. You would say something like, *Could you please move that over here for me?* You could use your shorthand language with your partner, but that is part of what has gotten you into this dysfunctional situation. Slow down and take your time. Instead of blurting out, try rephrasing what you want to say in a way that you think your partner will hear you. A little honey goes a long way.

The words "I love you" and "I'm sorry" go a long way toward building a bridge of connection.

This new way of talking will feel weird, and you may abandon it soon after you start. All of the couples I work with say how strange it feels at first because they are used to their shorthand, which is usually demeaning, disrespectful, and hurtful. You can also repair the relationship through your heartfelt apology. This goes a long way toward rebuilding the trust, love, and respect within the relationship. An apology shows your strength; it is not a sign of weakness.

Healing the Tug-of-War Controller

The number one thing I want you to know is that this process is not about giving up control. The need to feel in control is not bad; your need to control is your protective nature. You are trying to keep those you love safe from harm, only it is coming out in a way that is not helpful. I want you to learn to discern the level of control you need to exert over yourself and in your relationship. Let this discernment guide you instead of giving your wounded inner child the level of control the inner child wants. These are two very different ways to control.

Setting internal and external boundaries will help you have a sense of safety so that you will not need to manipulate a situation in order to feel in control. You can state your concerns about an outcome and what you need in order to feel safe. Work with the other people in your life; join with them, respect what they say, and ask that they respect your boundaries.

When you feel the urge to control, know that this is your inner child, who is feeling anxious, overwhelmed, and scared. Consider a situation in which you feel your control issues ramping up. You may describe this tension as a worry or fear that something will get messed up or not work out. It may be your intuition, or it may have triggered your broken trust issues. It will take a while for you to be able to determine that, but for now, see if you can slow things down. Take a breath. Stop yourself from immediately going into overdrive control mode, and chill a bit. Listen to what this need is, and feel how it connects to your past.

Follow the exercises in the *Healing Your Lost Inner Child Companion Workbook* to help you better understand this part of you so it can be healed and you can move on.

If you connect to the energy and expression of the tug-of-war controller archetype, say this intention for your wounded inner child:

I know that I have always needed to have a sense of control in my life, especially when things felt out of control when I was younger. I am learning new ways of feeling in control that are healthier and that honor me and those around me. I now know that I don't have to control others or situations, directly or indirectly, in order to feel safe. I now know that my words and boundaries have power, and going forward, this is how I will choose to feel in control.

Healing the Overt Controller

Overt controllers can be loud and defensive in their need to keep themselves and others safe. Your challenge is to discern how you can keep those you love safe without locking everything down and disrespecting them, and then begin listening to them. You probably believe that everything you say to your partner comes from a good place, but do they feel this way? Are you loving and respectful in how you speak to them? Your overt control ultimately hurts the relationship you are fighting so hard to defend. Learning to respect and trust others to find their own answers will take time.

I know how deeply you love, how deeply you care, and how much you would sacrifice for those you love. None of that is in question. This is about dialing back how much and how often you tell others what they should do so that they are allowed dignity, honor, and respect.

Healing the Covert Controller

If you are a covert controller, admit to yourself that you have been avoiding people, situations, and discussions and that this avoidant behavior doesn't help the honest communication within the relationship. Doing things covertly may have let you get things done your way, but it does not help you or your partner grow together. It only plays out the wounded cycle you learned in childhood, when it was easier to hold in your feelings, maneuver, and manipulate so that you didn't bother anyone. Most covert controllers justify their behaviors by thinking they are eliminating problems, but their partner feels manipulated.

Ask yourself how you can more clearly and directly state your feelings and needs, and learn to set boundaries. Boundary setting is first about yourself, then about your partner. Honor how you feel so that you don't have to go behind your partner's back to get your needs met.

Healing the Lightning Bolts

The lighting bolts are a unique synergistic pairing, and they know this. Even though there is often deep resentment and vulnerability below the surface with this couple, there is also an incredible love and respect because they found their match, their mirror. They know that if they were in a relationship with anyone else, they would swallow up the other person, which would be no fun at all—and absolutely no challenge.

The repair work for the lightning bolts couple will take some time. I find that this pairing often loves the intensity of their relationship, as their fighting matches the intensity of their intimacy, so they get a charge out of these interactions.

They are addicted to the adrenaline rush of their arguments, so moving away from these old behaviors is difficult.

Lighting bolts can make tremendous strides if they learn how to use their words positively instead of using them as weapons. Having a momentous crisis may be necessary to get the lighting bolts to pay attention to the fragility of life, and for them to be more humble with each other and respect what they have.

If you are in a lightning bolts relationship, practice saying to each other: *I hear you, and I don't want to hurt you anymore. I love and respect you, and I will work on making sure my actions back up my words. We are in this together, and we will figure this out as a team.* This last sentence can be used for any variation of the tug-of-war controller.

Recommit to your relationship, and let the other know that you will figure this out together the best you know how. This recommitment will help to calm and reassure the wounded inner child so that it doesn't need to act out to be acknowledged.

Can you see how the wounded inner child played out in each controller pairing? Once you are able to look at a situation objectively, you can see how your pain comes forth in adulthood, long after you feel you should be over it. Your inner child will begin to feel validated if you can set strong boundaries instead of using your control tactics to feel safe.

Healthy forms of control have a place in relationships. Evaluate whether you use your control behaviors to manipulate a situation or to respectfully help out your partner. Is this a solitary, one-sided act, or do you feel joined with your partner in sharing the control and the outcome?

The STARR Reset—Alex and Amanda

Alex and Amanda would get into their worst tug-of-war battles when they wanted two different things on important issues. One big fight was about whether they should send their kids to a public school or a private school. Amanda pushed for a private school, but Alex didn't want to spend the money since they were already paying taxes for public schools. Disregarding his feelings, Amanda set up a meeting and tour with the private school to talk about enrollment and cost. She even sent in a deposit to hold a spot at the school without asking Alex. Alex was furious when he found out. He felt that Amanda had crossed a line and was disrespecting him completely. He wondered why she needed him at all if she was just going to make all of the decisions.

Stop—Alex had had enough; he had hit his personal threshold. He told Amanda that she had crossed a line. As much as he didn't like conflict, he knew something had to change. He asked for a reset of the discussion.

Think—Alex saw a different part of himself come forward. He realized that he had always avoided conflict by trying to get his way indirectly, but he couldn't do that this time. He knew he had to put his foot down or Amanda was going to keep on controlling things for the rest of their relationship.

Act—He said to Amanda, "We need to talk about this now, before we go any further. We need to continue this discussion, and I need you to hear me out. I'm tired of my words always being lost. I'm not going to put up with this anymore. I need you to respect my feelings and understand that I'm thinking about what's best for our kids. Just because you feel justified about why a private school is better doesn't mean that that's the better choice. I need you to listen to me, and the two of us need to work on this together."

Amanda rejected his request at first, but she heard something different in Alex's voice this time. There was a sincerity, a confidence, and a resolve that she hadn't heard before. She also heard how angry he was. She said defensively, "I don't want to talk about it. I've already paid, and I can't get the deposit back."

But Alex wasn't going to back down this time. He wasn't going to let her manipulate him with her anger or her bulldozer technique of overriding him. He said, "I don't care that you've put money down. We need to talk about this more before we move forward. I want to make a decision together. I don't want to be told what our decision is!"

Amanda heard him. She agreed that she would cancel the appointment and they would talk about it some more. She added, "It's hard for me to give up control. I hear what you are saying. In the past, I felt you would not say anything and then try go behind my back to get your way. I want to talk with you about these things, but I feel I have to make decisions on my own because you don't like conflict or having hard discussions."

Reset and Repair—Alex said to Amanda, "Thank you for hearing me this time. I love you, and I want the best for our kids, as I know you do. I'm going to try to be more present in our relationship and not avoid difficult discussions."

Amanda said, "Yes, I love you, too, and I'm sorry that I want to have my way all the time, because I know that's not fair to you. I feel passionate about the private school, so let's talk some more about the schools, OK?"

Alex had been the covert controller in the past, but he was pushed to his limit with the school decision and became much more vocal and directive. This situation had pushed him to his personal threshold, and he found strength within himself that he didn't know he had. Amanda is still the overt controller, but now Alex feels empowered to call her out on decisions she makes without his input and when she tells him what to do instead of talking with him about her requests.

Alex and Amanda still struggle with this process. Amanda has a hard time looking at herself, and she gets defensive when her behaviors are pointed out, even when Alex uses his "I feel" language. Her broken trust and anxiety issues go deep, and she may need individual therapy before she and Alex can fundamentally heal their relationship. They are still together, and they both are trying their best, but it is tough. Alex is patient with Amanda, which helps her to know she can trust him, that he is there for her, and that they will get through this together.

Overall, Amanda and Alex's relationship works for them, and they have a good foundation. Alex now asks for what he needs instead of avoiding conflict and trying to get his way through passive-aggressive and covert behavior. They work on their new skills and use the STARR Reset to slow down and be more present with each other, although this doesn't come naturally to either of them.

When couples learn to set boundaries within themselves and each other, their wounded inner child begins to heal, feeling strong, protected, and honored.

Looking Inward

How does this couple remind you of your own wounded struggles within yourself and with your partner? What are some of the inner child woundings that you connect to? How does this match with your own story? What was activated inside of you when you read how this couple worked on their communication using the STARR Reset? Record your impressions in your notebook, as this will help you heal your wounded patterns.

CHAPTER 18

Perspectives

But let there be spaces in your togetherness, and let the winds of the heavens dance between you. Love one another, but make not a bond of love: let it rather be a moving sea between the shores of your souls.
—KHALIL GIBRAN, "ON MARRIAGE"

Archetypes help us to expand our view of the world. They provide perspectives on familiar relationship patterns and the inner child wounding themes that are hidden in plain sight.

The synergistic archetypes presented here are all examples of one or both partners trying hard to compensate for, join with, or ignore their partner's wounding. They show how human nature expresses itself in an attempt to heal. These wounded patterns will continue to happen until either the underlying relationship wounding—the wounded synergy—becomes a healthy synergy or the wounding takes over and the relationship dissolves. The push-and-pull as each partner grows and changes is natural. Over the arc of a relationship, these experiences represent times of great growth.

Now that you have explored the archetypes and read the stories of archetype couples, it is important to step back and get perspective on how they relate to you and your relationship. You probably see your relationship as a combination of some of the archetypes, although yours may not be as severe or dramatic. What insights do you have about these synergistic wounded pairings? Did you recognize yourself, family, or friends? That is normal. We all have aspects of archetypal wounding, and these characteristics will show up at one point or another during our lifetime.

Throughout my three-plus decades of being in a relationship, I have seen various combinations of my healed and wounded parts come forward at different times. You may see the same in your relationship, because we are all changing and growing no matter what age we are or how long we have been in our relationship. Some people tell me they are too old to change, or they have been together too long, or why bother. But I think that is unfair, as each day we have an opportunity to live an authentic life and move away from relationship patterns that no longer suit us.

THEMES ARCHETYPES SHARE

The archetypal examples here share many themes. Some of the stories show how partners adjust, adapt, and try to make their relationship work functionally even when they are codependent. But many couples did not have the necessary tools to heal their wounded parts or make their relationship functional. Codependent behaviors cover up, enable, and perpetuate the wounded cycles couples reenact. Healing these codependent woundings provides a platform and an opportunity for growth and reconnection.

Like all of us, these couples did the best they knew how until they learned better. Most of them had an earnest desire for things to improve, and once they rose above their dysfunctional dance and became more authentic and grounded with the other, their relationship flowed.

Synergistically wounded pairings share one or more of the following themes:

- Both are emotionally wounded and hurting but in different ways.
- When one leans in, the other either supports them or ignores them.
- Fears and unmet emotional needs are usually underneath what they argue about.
- They see their partner as the enemy.
- One partner chases after the other trying to get them to participate.
- They typically respond with inner child yelling and shutting down.
- They can go only as far as they are ready to go in healing their relationship.
- A defensive smokescreen shields underlying insecurities.
- They focus on the gaps, or what is missing, instead of the overlapping strengths.
- They need courageous vulnerability and surrender for healing to happen.
- Successful couples see their challenges as learning experiences and invitations to grow.

It is easy to see how some reactions and behavioral choices that couples make are similar to those they made as children—except now they are in adult bodies and making impulsive decisions that have greater impact and ramifications. Their re-actions are rooted in their unhealed inner child woundings and have a direct impact on the functionality of their relationship.

As you noticed, not all of the relationships worked out happily ever after, because that isn't reality. You may have even wondered why some of the couples stayed together at all. Things weren't perfect for those who did stay together, nor was their wounding completely healed, but they all stated that they felt closer to each other. Most of the couples began to experience a connection to their partner that was similar to what they had at the beginning of their relationship. Once they practiced the STARR Reset, many of the relationships deepened because of their improved communication.

However the relationship turned out, each synergistically wounded partner learned how to express themselves in a new way. How deeply they take in their new communication tools and how consistently they practice is up to them. The difference is that they now have the knowledge—the same knowledge you are gaining. If one or both of you begins to use these tools and speaks with intention and kindness, you can move mountains of hurt. How much you get out of this work is directly related to the amount of effort you put in.

Not everyone is ready for this information. We take in new wisdom when we feel deserving and have healed enough to prepare ourselves for this upgrade. You may find that you and your partner are at different places of growth and change, or that your partner isn't interested in working on your relation-ship and is OK with the status quo. This is normal, as one person in a couple sometimes needs to show the other the way. It is important to realize that not everyone can find the vulnerability and courage to walk toward healing.

More Synergistically Wounded Pairing Archetypes

The following are some common synergistically wounded pairs that I did not write about. You may recognize yourself or someone you know in this list. You can imagine how these synergistically wounded archetype descriptions could be completed:

- The chronic betrayer/cheater and the betrayed
- The ice queen and the man-child
- The narcissist and the codependent
- The "parent" and the "teenage child"
- The sexual explorer and the prude
- The high net worth woman and the emasculated man
- The emotional cheerleader and the grumpy one who doesn't feel worthy
- The chaser and the one who doesn't want to be pinned down
- The misogynist and the "little lady"

Each archetype represents how one partner's synergistic wounding joins with another's. As you have learned, each pairing could use the STARR Reset to develop better communication, heal their wounding, and deepen their connection.

In the archetypes, you read how each partner's codependent wounded responses perpetuated their cycles. Each learned to compensate for the other, bending over backward to make their dysfunctional relationship as functional as they could with limited tools. Any synergistically wounded pairing will continue their codependent dance until one heals enough to see the pattern and wants to change this or move on. What are some other pairings that you can imagine?

All of the synergistically wounded pairings have an opportunity to heal their wounding and become better partners to each other, but whether they take advantage of these windows is up to them. Healing and growing together is the ideal scenario, but in reality it is usually just one partner who is trying to heal themselves (and the relationship) and have better communication. If this is the case for you, know that your efforts are not without notice, that at some level your partner senses a shift and a change within you. You know each other well, so when you start using your new communication tools, they will pick up from you how you wish to talk about your feelings, showing how the relationship can heal. Do this work for yourself first, and hopefully your partner will follow. Either way, you will have a clearer idea of who you are, who you are not, and what you need.

Be the change you want to see in others.

SHOULD I STAY OR SHOULD I GO?

Darlin' you got to let me know, should I stay or should I go?
If you say that you are mine, I'll be here till the end of time.
So you got to let me know, should I stay or should I go?
—THE CLASH

The archetypes are cautionary tales. They show us how relationships can become derailed if the wounded parts are louder than the healed parts, especially if none of this is acknowledged. Now that you have learned about these archetypes and the STARR Reset, you may be looking at your relationship differently and determining your next steps. Any relationship takes some effort, but there should be a flow and reciprocity to it. Maybe you feel you have already put in a lot of effort and your partner isn't participating, or maybe you see some opportunities and want to work on your relationship.

To stay together or not is an agonizing decision for most couples, and the length of time—often years—that some people put into this decision is overwhelming. Maybe you are looking back over your relationship and wondering what you were thinking when you got together with your partner. When you realize that you have to make yourself smaller in some way for the relationship to work, and you have tried everything else, it may be time to look at other options.

If this sounds familiar, take some deep breaths and center yourself. Know that you were making your decision to marry or partner with this person based on where you were emotionally and what you understood about yourself at the time. As you have learned, your inner child wounding and their wounding synergistically matched at the beginning, but then, as time went on, you were not able to come together and heal this between the two of you.

Maybe your partner has no way to keep up with you. They have given what they could up to this point. In other words, they don't have it in them to work any harder at the relationship, they have no desire or interest, or they are preoccupied with some other issue, such as an outside interest, work problem, or health concern. Be honest with yourself, and don't project onto your partner who you need them to be to fit into your narrative. Who and where are they now?

What do you know about your wounded and healed parts and those of your partner? Are you ready to work through some issues with your partner, or do you feel you have tried that, and you are tired of the drama and spinning your wheels? Either way, know that for you to move forward, whether together or separate, you are called to work through your emotional wounding for your benefit, no one else's.

You both co-created the relationship by doing helpful and unhelpful things. Today you may have perspective and a healed luxury because of all the hard work you have done within yourself. But your partner may still be lost in their wounding and that is where they are; you can't will them to be more healed.

Perhaps your partner meets some of your physical needs for shelter and security but not your emotional, sexual, or spiritual needs. It is hard to get the majority of our needs met by one person, but it is not impossible. You may know that you can't carry the load for their emotional needs anymore.

Being honest with yourself today will help you create a clearer vision for your future.

Some people feel a loss if their partner cannot progress with them. They project onto their partner who they need them to be instead of acknowledging who their partner is. They avoid being honest and blame themselves, as if they should have known their partner wasn't going to change or end up who they needed them to be. Regretful hindsight can be a cruel mirror. Don't beat up on yourself, as this will only keep you stuck in a victim space. Own that you would probably do things differently today, and ask yourself what you want to do moving forward.

Now and then I think of all the times you screwed me over,
but had me believin' it was always something that I'd done;
But I don't wanna live that way, reading into every word you say.
You said that you could let it go, and I wouldn't catch you
hung up on somebody that you used to know.
—GOTYE, "SOMEBODY THAT I USED TO KNOW"

Staying for the Right Reasons

Couples often get overwhelmed and exhausted by their relationships, and many stay together out of fear or apathy. When they get to this point, one or both have given up and resigned themselves to the idea that this is how it is to be. I especially see this with couples who have been together twenty years or more. They say they will just live their life out this way, resigning themselves to be in comfortable conformist misery. Their inner child wounding is not being addressed, and in many cases is loud and in charge. They say that what they have is better than what they perceive the alternative to be. The following thoughts go through their mind:

- I'm never going to find someone else.
- I can't imagine dating right now.
- I'm scared to be alone.
- We need to stay together for the kids.
- If I abandon the relationship, I will be leaving my partner just like I was abandoned.
- I won't have anything if I leave; I feel trapped.
- I'm afraid of what they will do if I leave.
- I'm too old to make changes like that.
- My friends and family will be disappointed if we split up.

- I'm miserable, but at least I know what this situation is like.
- I won't be the one to ask for a divorce, so I will wait them out.

You may think such thoughts to justify staying in your relationship. These statements are based in fear and rationalize the choice to stay, but they are not healthy and grounded reasons to do so. Individuals or couples who are at this stage have quit the relationship. They live in a strange comfort of expressing their needs and then slinking back into a dusty corner of conformity when those needs are not met or acknowledged.

If you are tempted to stay in your relationship for logistical or practical reasons, you are staying for the wrong reasons. By remaining in denial and not facing your fears, you will begin to compensate for these issues by overwork, addictions, affairs, or emotionally checking out. If the only way the relationship works is not to speak your truth or cause any problems, then you are just living with denial and avoidance. Your heartache won't go away just because you distract yourself. Living in a married-but-not-together limbo stage is miserable and generally not sustainable. It is familiar and sad at the same time.

Figure yourself out and heal your issues,
because if you don't, you will pick the
same sort of partner the next time.

Sometimes people get to the point where they have done all they can do. They have examined themselves and spoken with their partner, who was unresponsive, slow to change, or unwilling to explore a new direction for the relationship. They enter into a grieving period of profound sadness when they realize they aren't going to get what they want or hope from their spouse or relationship. After all, you can't make someone else into a better version of themselves; all you can do is encourage this.

Sometimes we hold on so tight out of fear;
we need to love ourselves more and let go.

Even though this time is hard, honest reflection is a turning point of recognition and a call to actively work on embracing the healing work within, instead of looking for the answer from your partner.

EXERCISE: GOING DEEP WITHIN

If you are in the same place five or ten years from now, how will you feel? Most people cringe at the thought that they could be in the same place that far into the future. If that is the case for you, then answer the following questions honestly:

Have you done everything you know to do to change and heal the dynamic in your relationship?

If there has been an infidelity, have you and your partner done everything you could to repair this relationship trauma?

Do you feel you have been realistic with your partner about what they could do, or have you placed unachievable expectations on them?

If there was a betrayal of trust, do you feel that you tried to address this within yourself and your relationship, or did you ignore these hurt feelings and wish they would go away?

Have you spoken your truth even when you have wanted to avoid conversations?

Have you tried to heal the hurts, or do you hold on to them or hide behind them as a defense?

Do you have the energy to work through problems, or are you just tired and ready to move on?

Has your partner been working harder at the relationship while you stood back and watched? Or have you been working harder than they have?

Is there anything else you feel you could try?

Have you given couples counseling a try? Was the counselor right for the two of you?

Did you not like counseling and quit because the counselor did not agree with you?

If you honestly answer these questions and from the bottom of your heart say that you can't see any possible way to reconcile, then divorce may be right for you. However, I encourage you to receive professional help so that you can more fully explore these feelings, as this list is not by any means comprehensive. The self-inquiry is only meant for you to do a self-check to see what comes up for you.

You now know a lot about your wounding, but there is more for you to explore before you say to your partner you want a divorce. This whole process is about being gentle and loving with yourself as you embark on a major life decision. This is not easy for anyone, so do not beat up on yourself if this experience feels like an emotional roller coaster. It is natural to be challenged by such a big life choice, as you are being called to step up, be brave, and to love and honor yourself as you never have before. Your healed parts are supporting your wounded parts, giving courage and love.

If you make the decision to walk away from the relationship, summon all the courage, love, vulnerability, grace, and surrender you can.

Speaking Your Truth

If you have given careful thought to separating and say you want to divorce your partner, know that even though it may not be a surprise, the information will still be a shock to them. You have been thinking about this for a long time and are already down the path, but once you announce this, your partner will just be starting on this divorce path. Even though they know there have been issues, they may be in denial. They can't believe this news and will say that it came out of the blue. It will take them a while to get up to speed and adjust. If they have a defensive, confused, or aggressive reaction to your news, you may feel that you are starting back at zero with this whole process. Stay strong. It may help to see a therapist to help manage your frustrations and anger, because the reality is that you are ready to move on. Your partner will have their own experience with this process. Their level of recognition and acceptance of all of this will be completely different from yours.

Someone who is at the point of verbalizing that they may leave has been thinking of and feeling this uneasiness for a long time. Know that you have clarity with how you feel. Just because your partner doesn't feel the same way doesn't mean you are wrong.

Be careful, not careless, with your decisions.

If you or your partner wants to see a couples counselor, do so for the right reasons: either to heal yourself and your partnership, or to determine if the two of you are no longer suited for each other. Many couples come in to counseling with one foot out the door, having a hidden agenda of "checking the box" that they went to counseling. This way they can tell family and friends that they went to counseling and even that didn't work. They have already made up their minds, and a seasoned therapist will see right through this wounded response.

The two of you have come through so much together. Ask yourself how you want to experience this time with someone whom you once loved and with whom you have shared so much. How can you walk through this with integrity and come out as whole as possible? Easing into the idea of breaking up takes a while for many people.

Be brave with your new communication tools, be honest with yourself, and put your truth out there when it is safe for you to do so. Many people are afraid of starting the discussion because they don't know where it will go, but that is precisely the point. If you stay locked in your silent fear, there will be no movement, and you will just go on repeating your wounded dramas.

I need you in a different way now.
I'm asking you to expand, not change.

LOOKING INWARD

As you saw in all of the archetypes, the partners were doing the best they could with the tools they had. As with many of us, not all of the relationships worked out, and many are still playing out their wounded dramas. The difference is that, just like you, these couples now know what they were doing and what they could do. They have a choice to stay and work on their relationship or exit. But even with this knowledge and new tools, sometimes it is easier to go back to old habits and play out this wounding because it feels so familiar and comfortable. You are where you are in your relationship based on the knowledge you have gained and the healing work you have accomplished. You know enough to say to yourself, *I now better understand who I am. Do I want to make this relationship work with what I know, or do I want to move on?*

Look back over the notes you took as you read the archetypes chapters. Which archetype themes did you connect to?

Which couples reminded you of your own struggles?

What were some of the inner child woundings that you connected to?

When you were reading certain stories, what got you stirred up, agitated, or excited?

Which wounded tools do you use that the archetype pairings used?

After seeing how these couples used the STARR Reset, what are some new tools you will begin to use?

Reflect on your answers, and use your new tools to craft some messages you want to give to your partner so that you can move to a more healed place in your relationship. These new insights will help you to feel stronger and to know what you need to do for yourself and your relationship so that you can have a more fulfilling life.

Archetypes help us to see the broader landscape from a higher vantage point so that we are no longer lost in the weeds. By learning of these patterns and themes, you are better equipped to recognize when they show up in your relationship.

MOVING FORWARD

If you decide to divorce, please consider working with a therapist to clean up the emotional trauma from this event and to work through your loss. There are so many things that you will feel on so many levels that it will take a while to work through everything from this experience. It will take time for you to build a new frame for your future, but you can do it. Say this affirmation: *I am working on healing this part of my life now, and I don't know if we fit together in the same way. I'm ready to move on.*

A guide can show us the way, but we still need to walk our path. The walk becomes easier when we have the right tools for the journey.

If you decide to stay with your partner, begin using the STARR Reset and the intentional communication tools you have learned about. Part III will take you deeper into the work of boundary setting and being openhearted. Take this opportunity to make your relationship the best it can be by showing up completely and honestly. Hold out hope for yourself, your partner, and your relationship, knowing that you can heal those hurts and claim a loving connection with each other.

Sweet love and kindness can be found in our relationships if that is the desire of the heart. We just have to reach through the pain to embrace, nurture, and encourage this to grow.

PART III

Restoring a Healthy Relationship

CHAPTER 19

Boundaries—Speaking Your Truth

*What I know for sure is that you feel real joy in direct
proportion to how connected you are to living your truth.*
—OPRAH WINFREY, "WHAT OPRAH KNOWS
FOR SURE ABOUT GROWING UP"

You are well on your way to understanding in a fundamentally
new way how your inner child wounding and that of your
partner brought the two of you together. You have learned that
when your wounded parts are louder, the relationship gets
off balance. You read about the archetypes and learned how
other couples' synergistic wounding brought them together or
tore them apart. You have also learned new ways of speaking
intentionally with your partner using the STARR Reset. You,
right now, are the best representation of yourself. We all can
make better choices and strive to achieve greater heights, but
right now you are the best you that you can be.

In chapter 2 you learned about the red flags you may have overlooked and how you may have codependently compensated to make your relationship work. If you ignored those red flags, then you overrode your boundary system, your intuition, and your gut reaction. This is why paying attention to boundaries is so important, as they create a safety network that helps us navigate our world.

With everything you are learning, you may have decided to work on developing a deeper connection to your partner. If so, it is time to bring all of this new knowledge together and heal your relationship. The way through your wounding and on to a healed place is by having strong boundaries and speaking with intention. Couples can navigate difficult times and have a flow in their relationship when they are in balance, have good boundary systems, and communicate effectively.

BETTER BOUNDARIES, BETTER OUTCOMES

You say boundary statements every day, even when you don't realize that is what you are doing. We all need to use our boundaries every day to see how we feel about a situation, to evaluate a next step, and to say what we want and don't want in our lives.

As you develop better patterns of communication with your partner, you will need a strong boundary sense to protect yourself emotionally, physically, and mentally, and to get your message out so that your partner knows how you feel. This is true even if you already have a good relationship. The STARR Reset and the other information you have learned is teaching you how to be intentional with your language, and a big part of this is speaking up for yourself in what you want and don't want.

Clarity of Thought and Feeling

Boundaries create a sense of personal safety in relationships. When you speak your truth, you are setting a boundary within yourself and with the other person. You don't need to defend or explain your boundaries. If someone does not respect a boundary you stated, they don't respect you. We state boundaries first for ourselves, and secondly for the other person to hear.

Your first gut instinct is essentially your boundary system in action.

For intentional conversations to have meaning and for others to know that you are serious, you first need to know how you feel about a topic, then gain some clarity and put this into feeling words. The clarity of how you think and feel about an issue is the foundation of your boundary statement. You will be able to have a deeper connection and a more openhearted discussion if you put in the time on the front end of a conversation by checking in with yourself and figuring out how you feel instead of rushing in without careful thought.

The more you set healthy boundaries, the more clarity you will have, and the more clarity you have, the more all parts of you will feel connected, safe, and authentic. You will feel free and fully integrated with your true self when you set boundaries.

Check in with yourself before you agree to do what someone else wants. Honor yourself.

The next section focuses on two types of boundaries: internal and external.

CREATING HEALTHY BOUNDARIES

Boundaries mean having the ability to say no to others as a way to protect yourself physically, emotionally, mentally, and sexually, and to know what is good for you and what is not. Whatever boundary system your parents had when you were growing up, chances are that you use similar boundaries now. You watched how your parents responded to situations: whether they gave in and didn't hold their boundaries or put up walls and shut out others—including you—you took in all of these boundary responses and thought that was how you should handle such situations.[1]

Recall that in each of the archetypes, one partner reached their personal threshold. When they got to this point, expressed how they felt, and stated that they needed a reset, they were setting a boundary. You don't need to let unexpressed emotion build up until you reach your personal threshold. Check in with yourself. If you are not comfortable with a situation or have an opinion you want to express, find a way to speak your truth clearly, lovingly, and respectfully.

Your boundary statements will work if you let go of the outcome. For example, if you say, *No, I don't want to go out tonight*, you are not attaching any strings or manipulating the other person; you are simply expressing your feelings out loud. Boundary statements are not about being unfeeling or uncaring, as that would be shutting down your feelings or

---

1. Much of the information in this section is adapted from the author's book *Healing Your Lost Inner Child* (Illinois: Practical Wisdom Press, 2020).

closing yourself off from others in an unhealthy way. They are about being fully connected to all parts of yourself. From this centered place, you can determine how you feel about a situation, event, or comment, and then decide how you want to act based on those feelings. When you say to a friend you don't want to do something, you don't say this to hurt your friend; you say it because this is how you feel, your gut reaction.

Strong boundaries are ways in which we honor ourselves (internal boundaries) and stand up for ourselves (external boundaries).

Internal Boundaries

Internal boundaries are personal statements or agreements that you have with yourself regarding a particular issue. You already make these silent statements regarding multiple issues throughout each day. Internal boundaries are not necessarily discussed with others, as they are internal contracts with yourself. They help you to be responsible to and for yourself.

The following are examples of internal boundary statements:

- I am not going to go to the bar with my friends because I know that environment is not good for me.
- I am not going to yell, scream, demand, deceive, blame, ridicule, or demean others.
- I am not going to take in the criticisms of others.
- I am going to be honest and vulnerable with myself.
- I am going to honor myself today and not beat up on myself if I make a mistake.

- I am going to keep my commitment to myself and go to the gym at least twice a week.
- I am going to find a therapist to help me with my depression and anxiety.
- I am going to maintain strong boundaries with others and say no when I need to.
- I am not going to shut down and avoid difficult conversations.
- I am going to smile more and practice finding the good in myself and others.

These are examples of making commitments to oneself and how to honor and respect those commitments. People who know themselves have a strong internal boundary system. People who look to others to define their world often have fuzzy internal boundaries and are all over the place when it comes to decision-making. They give others the power to define their internal reality and identity.

The word no is a complete sentence.

External Boundaries

External boundaries are statements or positions you establish with another person or situation. They come from a place of internal clarity about what you want or don't want, and then by expressing this clarity to another person in simple, clear, assertive statements.

External boundaries often begin with an "I" statement. For example:

- I feel hurt that you didn't include me.
- I feel disrespected in my personal space when you stand so close to me. Can you step back?
- I feel confused about why you don't ask me for help.
- I feel hurt because of the way you continually talk down to me.
- I feel trusting and safe in our relationship.
- I feel excited that you are taking me on the trip with you.
- I feel great gratitude and joy that you are my friend. Thank you for being in my life.
- I am going to respect you and your personal property by not snooping or listening in, and I ask for the same from you (internal and external boundaries).
- I feel uncomfortable doing what you want me to do sexually.
- I will be respectful of you and will try not to control you.
- I will respect you when you say no, and I ask you to respect me when I say no.

Internal and external boundary statements are not always about saying no. They can also state what you will do or agree to.

A strong boundary sense helps us feel capable and wise.

EXERCISE: BOUNDARY STATEMENTS

What areas in your life do you feel need better internal and external boundaries? Practice writing out your boundary statements to yourself and others in your notebook.

What does stating this boundary statement feel like? Do you feel empowered, or do you feel scared to say this because you don't know how the other person will react? All of these feelings are normal. The more you get used to making boundary statements as a tool to help you live your life in a more functional way, the easier this becomes. Stop living in other people's heads and guessing how they will feel or react if you speak your truth; this is what causes internal distress.

For more exercises on boundary setting, I suggest reading *Healing Your Lost Inner Child* and its companion workbook. You will find many examples and exercises to help you evaluate where your boundary system is today and how to strengthen your boundary muscle.

Boundaries take a while to develop, but remember that your gut reaction is your boundary reaction. When something doesn't feel right, or when you need to stand up for yourself and speak your truth, that is your boundary system in action. When you push down these feelings, you tell the wounded part of you to stay wounded. Pay attention to those red flags, because now you know what they are about and how to respond. When you speak your truth, your inner child rejoices because, finally, you are putting yourself first.

Boundaries will help you move away from feeling like a victim in life to intentionally choosing how you want to experience your reality.

EXERCISE: VISION BOARD

Now that you have a better understanding of yourself and your relationship, what do you want to do with this new wisdom you have acquired? Realistically, you don't have to do anything, but chances are you see some opportunities to improve the quality of your life and your relationship. What are some dreams you have for yourself and your relationship? This exercise will help you bring those dreams to the surface and manifest them.

To help you move forward, define your wants and needs by creating a vision board for where you see yourself in five or ten years. What is the song that your heart wants to sing? A vision board can be made of a large sheet of paper or poster board on which you write out, draw, or paste pictures of your ideal life and, most importantly, what this life *feels* like. Does it feel like travel, love, adventure, solitude, fun, or something else? Once you have made your vision board, look at the themes and patterns you see. What is your subconscious telling you that your heart yearns for?

No one else is living inside of you; what you feel is your own.

Our relationships commingle in union with our healed and wounded parts. Once there are more healed parts than wounded, your relationship will begin to flow and flourish. You are learning so much about yourself, growing and expanding in awareness. You are preparing yourself with many new functional tools that will help you to be fully present in your relationship. The next chapter will bring all of this together and help you to begin to fully embrace a more openhearted love.

CHAPTER 20

Openhearted Love

Just remember I love you, and it'll be all right.
Just remember I love you more than I can say.
—FIREFALL, "JUST REMEMBER I LOVE YOU"

An openhearted relationship is one that feels safe, loving, embracing, trusting, respectful, and free. It is the type of relationship that most people dream about but have no idea how to create. Whether you stay in your relationship or exit, know that becoming openhearted, first within yourself and then toward another, will help your own healing and expansion.

Many people are surprised to learn how freeing it is to be openhearted. It is much simpler to live in a place of trust and ease than it is to be in a place of fear and guardedness. Your boundaries create the guardrails that allow you to enter into this space of being open and free. Trust your boundary system to activate when or if you need these functional skills to protect your heart.

You can create an openhearted connection in your relation-ship when you have healthy boundaries, can align with and give your heart to your partner, and can depend on them to be there for you and to mirror back what you give to them. This reciprocity reassures us and creates a feeling of balance and acknowledgment of the love from the other. Giving of ourselves to someone else is a great act of love, vulnerability, and surrender, all of which helps to create a trusting interde-pendence. Our heart looks for signs from our partner each day, silently checking in that this is the right place to be. By trusting yourself and setting boundaries, you will consistently create relationships in which you feel love, honored, and respected.

Most people don't have trouble giving love. Give yourself permission to receive this love freely from others.

All of the following elements combined will help you to create a full-spectrum loving and committed relationship.

A healthy, loving relationship picks us up when we are down.

A healthy, loving relationship beams with pride at our accomplishments.

A healthy, loving relationship carries a warm heart flame for us, even when we are not around.

A healthy, loving relationship is able to hold an inconve-nient truth when it is said with love.

A healthy, loving relationship walks with us through hap-piness and heartache, through tragedies and triumphs.

A healthy, loving relationship can express anger and fear, knowing this will be respected and heard.

A healthy, loving relationship feels tender and nurtured by the other.

A healthy, loving relationship sees a greater version of us, even when we can't recognize this ourselves.

A healthy, loving relationship feels empathy for the other without doing their work for them.

A healthy, loving relationship establishes trust and worthiness over time.

A healthy, loving relationship has clear boundaries, an interdependence with autonomy, and reliance on the other.

A healthy, loving relationship cherishes love in the moment, not just after it has gone away.

Emotional vulnerability is when you both feel safe to be who you are with no filters, revealing your truth to each other. With this, you will become co-creators of your openhearted relationship.

LOOKING INWARD: SELF-REFLECTION

In the exercise Dream Big—Your Ideal Relationship in chapter 1, you took an inventory of how you saw yourself and some qualities of your ideal relationship. By having done the work throughout this book, you now see the larger landscape through your wise mind and wise heart. Look over what you wrote from this exercise, and think about the ideas you had about yourself and your relationship before reading and working through this material. Now connect to what your idea of relationship was before you read this book and how you feel about it in this present moment.

Now that you understand yourself better and know what it takes to be openhearted, what stands out for you as you reflect on your earlier idea of relationships? Does it represent a smaller version of yourself or what you thought was possible? Do you now see that you can embrace a grander vision for yourself and that you have many more options in how to live your life and express yourself?

Your Ideal Relationship

You probably have some new perspectives about yourself after learning all of the various communication styles and archetypes, and having done the exercises. Look over your answers from before, and then answer the questions that follow to see what insights you have now. Each question requires careful thought, so give yourself some time to answer them, as you will reveal new insights in the process.

What is your reaction to how you previously described yourself and your relationship?

How has your concept of an ideal relationship expanded or changed? What stands out for you?

How are you synergistically wounded with your partner?

Do you see your role and experience in the relationship now as a bystander or an active participant?

What are some wounded parts of yourself that you now realize need more healing work?

How are you living, speaking, and creating with intention? (Or are you on autopilot and just reacting to life?)

If you tried the STARR Reset, what was it like to use this new tool? (Or are you afraid to try it? Why?)

What are some fears you have about speaking your truth? What are these fears connected to?

Are you putting your dream out there? (Or are you allowing yourself to be shaped by your partner's dream of a relationship?)

How are you showing up in your relationship differently after reading this book and practicing the new techniques?

Do you see more clearly how your partner does or does not show up in your relationship?

How are you and your partner working toward becoming more openhearted so that you can feel more closely connected? What are the roadblocks to this becoming a reality?

In what situations would you like to try out some of your new tools to deepen your connection and have more intentional communication?

What are the qualities you appreciate more about yourself and your partner now that you have done this work?

What are three things you would like to continue to work on in your relationship?

How do you demonstrate the loving qualities you desire in your relationship?

What does success in a relationship mean to you at this point?

Your answers to these questions reflect back to you the state of your thinking and feeling. This is just a snapshot of where you are today. If you feel overwhelmed by all of this and feel you should be doing "better," this may mean that you are putting high expectations on yourself or your partner. Scale back and look at what you can heal and what you are in control of. Know that you can heal those wounded parts of yourself that keep showing up. You can start to make small, intentional choices that have a big impact. Be gentle and patient with yourself. You can't do everything at once; you are a work in progress.

There are probably more healed than wounded parts in your relationship, but the wounded parts may be louder, trying to get your attention. We are all pretty good at being self-critical. Just take a deep breath and know that you are where you need to be, and you are doing what you can do and being the best you that you can be.

Relationships can be incredibly rewarding in large and small ways. If they weren't, we wouldn't keep getting into them and trying to make them work.

Your New Skills

Each day you can use your new skills to create demonstrations of a loving relationship that you had only dreamed about. Now you know how to separate out life circumstances and your wounded and healed parts. You are learning to calm and still yourself so that you can be present and available. The insights you are gaining through this work are creating a road map for how you can intentionally live and experience your relationship going forward. This is an unfolding process, so it will need to happen in a gentle and loving way over time for it to be the most successful.

> *You don't have to stay lost in the shadows of your wounding. You can heal your pain.*

You can have deep, heart-centered discussions with your partner instead of giving in to your wounded patterns. A solid foundation can be created between the two of you so that you can face in the same direction by each other's side, feeling loved, supported, and encouraged. Be the change you want to see in the relationship.

KEYS TO OPENHEARTED LOVE

Trust, love, and respect build the foundation that we need to grow into healthy, well-balanced adults, and we need the same for our relationships to flourish. Being openhearted is not being tied to an outcome, it is being open to possibility. Relationships are the adventure, and vulnerable risk and courageous surrender are the keys to open the door to the possibilities within the relationship. The objective, and the challenge, is how to show courage and be humble at the same time.

To create an openhearted relationship, you need to have a level of commitment and intention to bring in most, if not all, of the following key elements consistently:

- humility
- vulnerability
- taking a chance
- kindness
- generosity
- trust
- love
- respect
- surrender
- grace
- gratitude
- patience

These are the commitments we make to each other in ceremony when we marry or join with our partners. They are the gold standard for what we all want to have in our relationships, what we dream about and strive for. We will not have a strong connection to all of them all of the time, but if we have the intention that this is how we want to lead our lives and what we want to attract, then that is what we will experience. Remember to bring in these attributes with your partner on a daily basis—not just at those tender milestone moments, but at those times when you know your partner needs this consistency from you. Your openhearted home is a person you come back to.

Accessing the key elements comes easily at first because we are open to them. Later on, we sometimes have to get out of our way and open our hearts again.

You are learning so much about yourself and your relationship life. See yourself with a loving compassion you wish others could hold for you. A closed heart is one that is hurting. If your heart is still hurting, it means that you still have to some work to do to clear these obstacles so you can get back into the flow of life. Give yourself the gift of loving forgiveness so that you are accepting of your emotional wounds as you work toward healing. Relationships are not about perfection, they are about connection and growth.

Your hard work, your intentional energy to heal yourself and expand your awareness, will come back to you a thousandfold. None of us knows how our relationships or our lives will turn out; all we can do is to try our best with what we know and what we feel we need to do. If it is your intention to be in a loving, trusting, openhearted relationship, then keep this as your goal, and do a little bit each day to create this reality.

EXERCISE: STILLNESS OF THE HEART

This is a healing exercise that not every couple is ready to do, but the healing stillness and contentment it can create within your heart is profound. This entire exercise is about being gentle, so if you get nervous or want to scream and run away, just breathe in through your nose and out through your mouth, as if you were blowing out a candle. The exercise can be hard at first, but stay with it as long as you can.

Our heart wisdom is gently revealed
in the quiet stillness.

Choose an intentional moment without distraction, and play soft background music. Sit opposite each other. Outstretch your arms so that you are holding hands with each other. If you can, sit very close together and find a comfortable position, perhaps with a pillow behind your back so you feel supported.

Look into your love's eyes with a soft gaze, and do not say a word. Hold your gaze and do not look away. As you look into the eyes of your love, relax and unclench all parts of your body.

As you hold the hands of the one you love, remember how you met. Remember the times of joy and connection, the times of sorrow and trauma. You have been through these times together. You are each perfectly imperfect, and you are in the right place at the right time. You are heart survivors in your relationship. Feel the connection. Feel the knowing that you will get through your struggles together with the help of your open hearts.

Try to simply sit in silence. You may want to fill the silence because you are uncomfortable, but when you are still and silent, you can see your love more clearly, without distraction. This is a time of grace and connection.

If you feel tears well up or knots in your stomach, just breathe into it. Let this energy flow out from you. You are ready to release this tension, as it no longer serves you. This release will unlock big parts of your heart that are ready to heal. Your flowing tears are the acknowledgment of the pain you have healed and the love you want to give and receive. Your tears are a message that you are sharing your vulnerability with your partner. You each are holding this loving space for the other by creating this safe container. Your silence speaks volumes, as your heart knows this language.

Sit like this for three to five minutes, or as long as you are able. When you both feel that you have done what you could, embrace each other. Tell each other that you love each other. Rejoin in your commitment to work toward healing your relationship connection as you each say: *I love you, and each day I am committed to you and our relationship.* Embrace, and hold each other in such a way as to hear your heartbeats. BE in this stillness of your heart love.

Create and encourage a deep sense of nonverbal emotional safety between the two of you.

This type of exercise does much more than any words can do because you are tapping into the most tender way of expressing yourself nonverbally, much like when you hold hands and walk quietly. I imagine that just by reading this exercise, your heart center has opened and warmed up. This is the natural calling of your heart yearning to heal. This is what your heart needs, and I imagine this is what your partner needs, as well. The embrace of an openhearted love asks us to be vulnerable to ourselves and another, to surrender to the unfolding process and magic of love and connection.

If you can't imagine doing this exercise with your partner, or if you are thinking of all the ways they would reject this idea, you can do a variation just for yourself. Create a quiet place where you can sit in your stillness with your inner child, holding and loving this part of you that worked so hard to protect you for all of those years. You can look into your own eyes, the window to your soul, or simply close your eyes.

Follow the instructions from the exercise as you give this loving gift to yourself. Know that through your demonstration of your openheartedness, your partner may one day be able to join you in this loving embrace and work toward healing.

Be kinder to yourself. And then let your kindness flood the world.
—PEMA CHÖDRÖN

You Are Magnificent

You will know you are moving in the right direction when you can truly be yourself in your relationship, when you no longer use your wounded codependent tools to help you navigate difficult situations, and when your partner is responsible for their own emotions. You are moving in the right direction when you both have a deep equanimity toward the other and can hold their joy and their pain with love.

Put your highest intention out there for you and your partner. This is what you will be moving toward.

You will know you are moving in the right direction when you only occasionally get into the same dramas, the same arguments as before. At those times, when you use the STARR Reset consistently, you will be retraining yourselves how to speak as functional adults using intentional communication. Look at what you are creating, and see the good in yourself and your life. You will know you are moving in the right direction when you feel more of the openhearted attributes, the key elements, more frequently and without thinking about them. They will just be present, like a warm glow within your heart.

Surround yourself with people who are positive and are doing their work. We energetically align with and model ourselves after those with whom we surround ourselves. Make choices in life and in your relationships that help you grow and expand.

Pay attention to your inner knowing, trust your instincts, and know that you can take deep breaths to regain your grounding, brush off negative energy, and use your healthy boundaries. If you are around someone who is nervous or angry, remember that this is their pain and fear talking. Send this energy back to them with unconditional love. You don't need to carry it for them.

Know that you don't have to impulsively leave your friends or your spouse just because they are not aligned with the same energy you want to bring in to your life. Notice where they are, and have compassion for yourself and them on their journey. You can see where they are more clearly, from further up the mountain of healing, because you have done your work. Give your love a hand and help them up the mountain. See if they like the view as much as you do. Make a commitment to yourself that you will strive to seek out people who will help you achieve the goals you are setting for yourself.

There is a healing power to giving and receiving unconditional love that is beyond words.

Begin to internally promote the idea that you can transform the energy in your relationship through positive intention and purposeful intentional communication. Your unhealed wounded parts will want to go back into their well-worn grooves and act out impulsively. Honor these codependent wounded parts because they have helped and protected you through many situations, but now is the time to begin to heal these cycles. Know that your healed parts can hold the uncertainty of how a relationship is going, and help you to observe this and decide how you want to participate as it unfolds. Trust that you are learning how to express your feelings in a way that you can be heard.

AN OPENHEARTED RELATIONSHIP

Once you have started your journey toward an openhearted relationship, you will know how much progress you have made when you experience some of these feelings and actions:

You are together as a team and working toward a common goal.

You both say to each other in verbal and nonverbal ways, *I have your back. I've got you. I love you.*

You are generous with your forgiveness toward your partner.

Your relationship has more good days than bad.

You feel open and free to show all parts of yourself to your partner.

You know that there are trade-offs in every relationship.

You cherish your partner as you want to be cherished.

You each know at a deep level that the other loves you and accepts you, even with your shortcomings.

You know that your partner isn't perfect, and neither are you.

You can extend a kindness to your partner even when you are cross with them.

You each own your reality and don't push your wounding or agenda onto the other.

Lovers don't finally meet somewhere. They're in each other all along.
—RUMI

You know so much more about yourself now. You have embraced a greater and grander version of yourself, and now it is up to you to honor yourself by using all of the new tools you have learned. The power is in your hands and energized by your open heart. The ripple effects of love will spread out from you. Become conscious of what you carry within your heart and what you send out. Those around you, especially children, feel, sense, and are impacted by your feeling energy. Ask yourself, *What is the energy I want to walk with and create in my life every day?* This energy, whatever it is, will come back to you in many ways well into the future. Sow the seeds of the life you want to manifest in your future by the intentions you set today.

Know that your hard work will come full circle as you work toward a fulfilling, loving connection. You have embraced and healed your pain, and entered into a healed reality. Your healed heart is a beacon to others. You embody a place of greater understanding, greater love, and deeper wisdom.

The power of your intention, the power of your dreams, brings new life and energy force to you. The more you embrace your own power and the capacity to heal that which no longer serves you, the more doors will open within your heart.

Right here, right now, you are creating an openhearted transformation and are on your path of healing.

Stay strong as you create the life you envision for yourself. Trust that you are in the right place and on your path of love, kindness, and compassion. Give the gift of being openhearted to yourself first, so that you can embrace and share this with your love clearly, lovingly, and fully.

It is as simple as
Be Kind.

APPENDIX A

Feelings Chart

This chart lists many words you can use to describe emotional and physical feelings. The words are divided in two categories: feelings we have when our needs are satisfied, and feelings we have when our needs are not met.

Look through the words when you want to express specific feelings so you can be clear when communicating your feelings.[1]

---

1. Feelings Chart reprinted by permission. (c) 2005 by Center for Nonviolent Communication. Website: www.cnvc.org. Email: cnvc@cnvc.org. Phone: +1.505.244.4041.

Feelings when your needs are satisfied

AFFECTIONATE
compassionate
friendly
loving
open hearted
sympathetic
tender
warm

ENGAGED
absorbed
alert
curious
engrossed
enchanted
entranced
fascinated
interested
intrigued
involved
spellbound
stimulated

HOPEFUL
expectant
encouraged
optimistic

CONFIDENT
empowered
open
proud
safe
secure

EXCITED
amazed
animated
ardent
aroused
astonished
dazzled
eager
energetic
enthusiastic
giddy
invigorated
lively
passionate
surprised
vibrant

GRATEFUL
appreciative
moved
thankful
touched

INSPIRED
amazed
awed
wonder

JOYFUL
amused
delighted
glad
happy
jubilant
pleased
tickled

EXHILARATED
blissful
ecstatic
elated
enthralled
exuberant
radiant
rapturous
thrilled

PEACEFUL
calm
clear headed
comfortable
centered
content
equanimous
fulfilled
mellow
quiet
relaxed
relieved
satisfied
serene
still
tranquil
trusting

REFRESHED
enlivened
rejuvenated
renewed
rested
restored
revived

Feelings when your needs are not satisfied

AFRAID	ANGRY	DISCONNECTED	EMBARRASSED
apprehensive	enraged	alienated	ashamed
dread	furious	aloof	chagrined
foreboding	incensed	apathetic	flustered
frightened	indignant	bored	guilty
mistrustful	irate	cold	mortified
panicked	livid	detached	self-conscious
petrified	outraged	distant	
scared	resentful	distracted	FATIGUE
suspicious		indifferent	beat
terrified	AVERSION	numb	burnt out
wary	animosity	removed	depleted
worried	appalled	uninterested	exhausted
	contempt	withdrawn	lethargic
ANNOYED	disgusted		listless
aggravated	dislike	DISQUIET	sleepy
dismayed	hate	agitated	tired
disgruntled	horrified	alarmed	weary
displeased	hostile	discombobulated	worn out
exasperated	repulsed	disconcerted	
frustrated		disturbed	PAIN
impatient	CONFUSED	perturbed	agony
irritated	ambivalent	rattled	anguished
irked	baffled	restless	bereaved
	bewildered	shocked	devastated
	dazed	startled	grief
	hesitant	surprised	heartbroken
	lost	troubled	hurt
	mystified	turbulent	lonely
	perplexed	turmoil	miserable
	puzzled	uncomfortable	regretful
	torn	uneasy	remorseful
		unnerved	
		unsettled	
		upset	

Feelings when your needs are not satisfied, cont.

SAD	TENSE	VULNERABLE	YEARNING
depressed	anxious	fragile	envious
dejected	cranky	guarded	jealous
despair	distressed	helpless	longing
despondent	distraught	insecure	nostalgic
disappointed	edgy	leery	pining
discouraged	fidgety	reserved	wistful
disheartened	frazzled	sensitive	
forlorn	irritable	shaky	
gloomy	jittery		
heavy hearted	nervous		
hopeless	overwhelmed		
melancholy	restless		
unhappy	stressed out		
wretched			

Resources

The following are resources to help you with a variety of needs.

National Domestic Violence Hotline: 1.800.799.7233

Look up your local resource in advance so you understand your rights for establishing a domestic violence restraining order, also known as a temporary protective order in the United States and its territories.

The National Suicide Prevention Lifeline: 1.800.273.8255, www. suicidepreventionlifeline.org

Adult Children of Alcoholics: www.adultchildren.org

Alcoholic Anonymous: www.aa.org

Codependents Anonymous: www.coda.org

Narcotics Anonymous: www.na.org

National Institute for Mental Health: www.nimh.nih.gov

Insight Timer meditation app

For additional material and news about my upcoming works, please visit my website: www.theartofpracticalwisdom.com.

For further reading on inner child work, relationships, and other personal works, the following books may be of interest to you:

Louann Brizendine, MD, *The Female Brain*, Harmony; Illustrated Edition, 2007.

Louann Brizendine, MD, *The Male Brain*, Bantam, 2011.

Brené Brown, *Rising Strong: How the Ability to Reset Transforms the Way We Live, Love, Parent and Lead*, Random House, reprint edition, 2017.

Jeff Brown, *Love It Forward*, Enrealment Press, 2014.

Panache Desai, *You Are Enough: Revealing the Soul to Discover Your Power, Potential and Possibility*, HarperCollins, 2020.

Jessica Fern, *Polysecure: Attachment, Trauma and Consensual Nonmonogomy*, Thorntree Press, 2020.

Matthew Fox, *The Hidden Spirituality of Men: Ten Metaphors to Awaken the Sacred Masculine*, New World Library, 2008.

Lindsey Gibson, *Adult Children of Emotionally Immature Parents: How to Heal from Distant, Rejecting or Self-Involved Parents*, New Harbinger Publications, 1st edition, 2015.

Louise Hay, *You Can Heal Your Life*, Hay House, January, 1984.

Rachel Hollis, *Girl, Wash Your Face: Stop Believing the Lies about Who You Are So You Can become Who You Were Meant to Be*, Thomas Nelson, 2018.

Robert Jackman, *Healing Your Lost Inner Child: How to Stop Impulsive Reactions, Set Healthy Boundaries and Embrace an Authentic Life*, Practical Wisdom Press, 2020.

Noah Levine, *Refuge Recovery: A Buddhist Path to Recovery from Addiction*, HarperOne, 2014.

Jackson MacKenzie, *Whole Again: Healing Your Heart and Rediscovering Your True Self after Toxic Relationships and Emotional Abuse*, Penguin Random House, 2019.

Dr. Karyl McBride, PhD, *Will I Ever Be Good Enough?: Healing the Daughters of Narcissistic Mothers*, Atria Books, 2008.

Resmaa Menakem, *Rock the Boat: How to Use Conflict to Heal and Deepen Your Relationship*, Resmaa Menakem, 2020.

Esther Perel, *Mating in Captivity: Unlocking Erotic Intelligence*, Harper Paperbacks, 2017.

Terrence Real, *I Don't Want to Talk about It: Overcoming the Secret Legacy of Male Depression*, Scribner, 1998.

Ross Rosenberg, *The Human Magnet Syndrome: The Codependent Narcissist Trap*, Morgan James Publishing, 2019.

Babette Rothschild, *The Body Remembers: The Psychophysiology of Trauma and Trauma Treatment*, W.W. Norton & Co., 2000.

Michael Singer, *The Untethered Soul: The Journey beyond Yourself*, New Harbinger Publications and Noetic Books, 2007.

Monica Sweeney: *Let That Sh*t Go: A Journal for Leaving Your Bullsh*t Behind and Creating a Happy Life for Yourself*, Castle Point Books, 2018.

Jonice Webb, *Running on Empty: Overcoming Your Childhood Emotional Neglect*, Morgan James Publishing, 2012.

About the Author

ROBERT JACKMAN is a board certified psychotherapist with the National Board of Certified Counselors who has helped many people and couples on their healing path for more than twenty years. In addition to his private practice, he has taught master's level classes at National Louis University in the Chicago area, led outpatient groups in clinics and hospitals and been a guest speaker on podcasts, panels and telesummits on the topics of codependency, boundary setting, couples communication, inner child, mindfulness and the role of spirituality in healing, and has participated in numerous weekend retreats with Victories for Men.

Robert is also a Reiki master who uses energy psychology in his practice and in his personal development. He considers himself a codependent in recovery and is always working on setting internal and external boundaries, nurturing his relationships and connecting with the authentic self. He and his partner of more than three decades live in the far west suburbs of Chicago and in Oregon. He enjoys photography, kayaking, gardening and spending time with family and friends.

For more information about Robert Jackman, upcoming events, and his published works, including *Healing Your Wounded Relationship* and *Healing Your Lost Inner Child* and its companion workbook, please visit www.theartofpracticalwisdom.com.

Made in the USA
Coppell, TX
12 June 2023

17965398R00203